M000192188

In War's Wake

Oxford Studies in International History
James J. Sheehan, series advisor

The Wilsonian Moment:
Self-Determination and the International
Origins of Anticolonial Nationalism
Erez Manela

In War's Wake:
Europe's Displaced Persons in the Postwar Order
Gerard Daniel Cohen

In War's Wake

Europe's Displaced Persons
in the Postwar Order

GERARD DANIEL COHEN

OXFORD
UNIVERSITY PRESS

OXFORD
UNIVERSITY PRESS

Oxford University Press is a department of the University of Oxford. It furthers
the University's objective of excellence in research, scholarship, and education
by publishing worldwide. Oxford is a registered trade mark of Oxford University
Press in the UK and certain other countries.

Published in the United States of America by Oxford University Press
198 Madison Avenue, New York, NY 10016, United States of America.

© Oxford University Press 2011

First issued as an Oxford University Press paperback, 2017

All rights reserved. No part of this publication may be reproduced, stored in
a retrieval system, or transmitted, in any form or by any means, without the
prior permission in writing of Oxford University Press, or as expressly permitted
by law, by license, or under terms agreed with the appropriate reproduction
rights organization. Inquiries concerning reproduction outside the scope of the
above should be sent to the Rights Department, Oxford University Press, at the
address above.

You must not circulate this work in any other form
and you must impose this same condition on any acquirer.

Library of Congress Cataloging-in-Publication Data
Cohen, Gerard Daniel.
In war's wake : Europe's displaced persons in the postwar order / Gerard Daniel Cohen.
p. cm. — (Oxford studies in international history)
Includes bibliographical references and index.
ISBN 978-0-19-539968-4 (hardcover : alk. paper); 978-0-19-084080-8 (paperback : alk. paper)
1. World War, 1939–1945—Refugees—Europe. 2. World War, 1939–1945—Civilian
relief—Europe. 3. United Nations Relief and Rehabilitation Administration.
4. Refugees—Europe—History—20th century. 5. Refugees—Government
policy—Europe—History—20th century. 6. Jewish refugees—Europe—
History—20th century. 7. Jews—Europe—Migrations—History—20th century.
8. Humanitarianism—History—20th century. 9. Europe—Emigration and
immigration—History—20th century. I. Title.
D809.E85C65 2011
940.53086'914094—dc22
2011005116

In memory of Tony Judt

Acknowledgments

I OWE PRINCIPAL thanks to the colleagues and scholars who graciously offered commentary on all or part of the manuscript: Peter C. Caldwell, Matthew Connelly, Dan Eshet, Julie Fette, Benjamin Frommer, Atina Grossmann, Shirine Hamadeh, William Hitchcock, Anna Holian, Ussama Makdisi, Allen Matusow, Lynne Taylor, Martin Wiener, Patrick Weil, and Lora Wildenthal. I have also benefited from productive conversations with a talented group of scholars specializing in the history of post-1945 refugees: Carl Bon Tempo, Ilana Feldman, Matthew Frank, Peter Gatrell, Anna Holian, Susanne Langlois, Jessica Reinisch, Shira Robinson, Ben Shephard, Sylvia Savatici, and Tara Zahra. I am similarly indebted to Muriel Blaive, Elizabeth Borgwardt, Herrick Chapman, Nicole Dombrowski, Igal Halfin, Linda Kerber, Samuel Moyn, Marci Shore, and Timothy Snyder for sharing their knowledge. I extend my deepest gratitude to my editor, Susan Ferber, for presiding over the publication of this book. This project would not have seen light without her expert guidance.

Parts of the manuscript have been presented at Johns Hopkins University, the University of Vienna, Indiana University, Northwestern University, Temple University, Haifa University, Institut d'Etudes Politiques de Paris, Zentrum für Zeithistorische Forschung in Berlin, Harvard University, and Columbia University. I thank David Bell, Maria Mesner, John Bodnar, Karen Alter, Eran Shalev, Guillaume Piketty, Stefan-Ludwig Hoffmann, Moshik Temkin, and Gregory Mann for organizing these events. Jessica Reinisch invited me to the seminar "Displacement and Replacement in the Aftermath of the War, 1944–1948" and to the conference "Forty Years' Crisis: Refugees in Europe, 1919–1959," both held at Birkbeck College, London. The growing field of "refugee history" owes much to Jessica's initiatives and publications. The workshop "The Refugee in the Postwar World," which I co-organized at Arizona State University with Anna Holian, helped me think about refugees and humanitarianism in a global and interdisciplinary perspective. Hava

Tirosh-Samuelson, director of Jewish Studies at ASU, provided generous support. The thorough editors and peer reviewers of the *Journal of Refugee Studies, Journal of Contemporary History*, and *Immigrants and Minorities* deserve special acknowledgment. So do my undergraduate students at Rice University, who have challenged me to convert tortuous thoughts into intelligible arguments.

Several archivists and librarians have contributed to the making of this book. The former director of the French National Archives, Alain Erlande-Brandenburg, as well as Chantal Bonazzi from the Section Contemporaine granted me special permission to consult unclassified files of the International Refugee Organization. The gracious staff of the Archives des Affaires Etrangères in Nantes made my stay there both fruitful and enjoyable. At the Bibliothèque de Documentation Internationale Contemporaine (Université Paris-X, Nanterre), Sonia Combe introduced me to a wide array of sources relevant to my project. David Clark of the Harry S. Truman Library in Independence, MO, secured rapid access to the George Warren and Harry Rosenfeld Papers. I also thank Rachel Yood, the collection associate at the Tamiment Library and Robert F. Wagner Labor Archives at New York University, for her warm welcome.

My friends Dan Eshet, Graciela and Eric Elghouzzi, Jair and Felix Kessler, Michael Pollack, and Matthieu Varet never ceased to encourage me. Michel Cohen and Jeannie Weissglass hosted me countless times in New York. Alain Cohen helped me format text and illustrations. My parents, Pierre and Marcelle Cohen, thought that this project was interminable and are glad to see it completed. My young daughter, Talia, has watched me write this book with both bewilderment and curiosity. Sadly, *In War's Wake* appears after the tragic passing of Tony Judt, my doctoral adviser at New York University and a long-time friend. Tony was a European displaced person of sorts, although one who naturally embraced the cosmopolitan condition. Like many others touched by his life, I miss his prodigious mind and profound humanity.

Contents

In War's Wake

Introduction

THE LAST MILLION

"WHEN THIS GHASTLY war ends," Franklin D. Roosevelt gloomily predicted in October 1939, "there may be not one million but ten million or twenty million men, women and children belonging to many races...who will enter into the wide picture—the problem of the human refugee."[1] Six and a half years later, Eleanor Roosevelt refined her recently deceased husband's forecast. "A new type of political refugee is appearing," she observed from Europe in January 1946, "people who have been against the present governments and if they stay at home or go home will probably be killed."[2] These statements could also have adequately described earlier instances of forced displacement, not least the refugee exodus from the Third Reich in the late 1930s. Yet although Continental Europe had been awash with stateless people from the end of World War I to the advent of Nazism, the president and his wife envisioned "the problem of the human refugee" as an impending postwar crisis. Two decades of isolationism and restrictive immigration quotas may have blinded Americans to the magnitude of European displacement prior to 1939. The prospect of renewed American engagement with the world, however, revived strong interest in "Europe on the move." Observing this phenomenon at both ends of the conflict, Franklin and Eleanor Roosevelt were undoubtedly right: the scale of the European refugee problem created by World War II exceeded any experienced before.

The Roosevelts were not lone visionaries. As the war progressed, a wide array of British and American politicians, military planners, and social scientists spoke of an incipient disaster. Sir Herbert Emerson, appointed high commissioner for refugees of the moribund League of Nations in January 1939, expected that "when the war ends millions of persons will be scattered over the face of the globe...many of them with no homes to return to and

some of them with no government willing to protect them."[3] Speaking in
Oxford at a gathering of the Fabian Society in December 1942, political scientist Harold Laski anticipated "a movement of people larger than any that history has seen in modern times" after the conflict.[4] The American statesman
Dean Acheson attempted a similar historical comparison: "I believe that not
since the Middle Ages has there been any such movement of population as
this war has brought about."[5] In a report commissioned by the International
Labor Office, the Russian-born population scholar Eugene Kulischer calculated in 1943 that "more than thirty million of the inhabitants of the continent of Europe have been transplanted or torn from their homes since the
beginning of the war."[6] The civilian and military Allied bodies assigned to
cope with the large numbers of uprooted civilians in liberated European territories concurred. The "displaced persons" (DPs), a term coined in the United
States in the midst of preparations for postwar emergencies, were central to
the "relief and rehabilitation" operations in Europe. The United States Army
and the United Nations Relief and Rehabilitation Administration (UNRRA),
created in November 1943, both braced for a daunting logistical challenge:
the millions of DPs expected to be found by advancing Allied troops on their
way to Berlin.[7] A British commentator outlined the task: "The biggest human
problem with which we shall be faced in re-ordering the world after the end
of the war will probably be that of re-establishing the peoples who have been
displaced from their homes or localities for one reason or another. The magnitude of the problem is such as to cause the heart to sink."[8]

Writing on the eve of the Allied victory in Europe, Hannah Arendt also
acknowledged the huge task that lay ahead. "It would be a good thing," she
observed in April 1945, "if it were generally admitted that the end of the war
in Europe will not automatically return thirty to forty million exiles to their
homes." The former refugee from Nazi Germany then revealed one of the
greatest challenges the authorities would face: "A very large proportion," she
warned, "will regard repatriation as deportation and will insist on retaining
their statelessness." Arendt evidently had in mind the Jewish survivors of the
Final Solution, but she also referred to other types of Eastern European displaced persons. Altogether, she presciently pointed out, "The largest group of
potentially stateless people is to be found in Germany itself."[9] In contrast to
the military and humanitarian focus on repatriation and population
management, Arendt believed that the "DP problem" was essentially political.
Throughout the late 1940s, she referred to European refugees as "the most
symptomatic group in contemporary politics."[10] Between 1946 and the end of
the decade, the vocal and conspicuous "last million" displaced persons—a

multinational group of Jewish and non-Jewish asylum seekers unwilling or unable to go home—amply bore out her predictions.

Indeed, the "DP story" comprised two distinct chronological sequences, one logistical and one markedly political. It is generally assumed that at the end of the war there were approximately eight million civilians in Germany who qualified as displaced persons under UNRRA and Allied military directives: foreign workers, slave laborers, prisoners of war, and liberated concentration camp inmates. Between the spring and fall 1945, military and UNRRA officials succeeded in returning six to seven million DPs to their countries of origin—forcibly and often tragically in the case of Soviet nationals reluctant to repatriate to the USSR. After the completion of mass return operations, approximately 1.2 million refugees still remained homeless. The second and longer phase of the DP episode began at the start of 1946. As it became increasingly clear to humanitarian personnel and Allied military commanders, return rates significantly dwindled among the remaining DPs. Their refusal to go home, repeatedly analyzed by various surveys, was motivated by political, economic, and psychological factors. Combined with the fresh arrival of so-called post-hostilities refugees, the diminishing pace of repatriation resulted in the long-term presence of approximately one million DPs in occupied Germany (small numbers of displaced persons also lived in DP camps in Austria and Italy). Like other contemporary statistics documenting the DP world, this figure was not always accurate. The International Refugee Organization (1946–52), the agency created by the United Nations to care for the ever-fluctuating "last million," generally included "free-living" refugees outside of the camps as well as other stateless persons living outside of Germany in order to round up this tally.[11] But without much distortion, the United Nations and the IRO could safely advertise the DPs to the world as the "last million" refugees from World War II desperately searching for asylum countries. Emblematic of the longer political sequence of postwar displacement, this "last million" encompassed Holocaust survivors and non-Jewish anti-Communist refugees, the two distinct components of a wide DP camp system that stretched from northern Germany to Sicily.

Seen through a narrower lens, the "last million" encapsulated a myriad of nationalities. Brought to Germany by the Nazis as foreign workers and slave laborers, 400,000 Poles amounted in March 1946 to nearly 50 percent of the DPs. Roughly 150,000 to 200,000 Estonians, Lithuanians, and Latvians formed a sizeable Baltic group including former Wehrmacht conscripts and volunteers, migrant workers, and slave laborers, as well as civilians who fled the advance of the Red Army. In addition, an important group of 100,000 to

150,000 ethnic Ukrainians was composed of Western Ukrainians who lived until September 1939 under Polish rule and of Eastern Ukrainians who held Soviet citizenship when World War Two broke out. In early 1946 Jewish refugees represented less than 10 percent of the overall DP population. But to the small group of death-camp survivors liberated by the Allies in the spring of 1945 a substantial number of Jewish "infiltrees" of Polish origin was gradually added: during the peak period of 1947–48, approximately 250,000 Jewish refugees dwelled in the American occupation zone of Germany, about 25 percent of them in Berlin and Munich outside the confines of official camps. Alongside such large groups whose size constantly changed due to repatriation, emigration, and new arrivals, small numbers of anticommunist Yugoslavs, Slovaks, Hungarians, and other Eastern Europeans rounded out "the million survivors" mentioned by Harry Truman in a solemn speech to the US Congress.[12] Undoubtedly effective in rallying the American public to the cause of humanitarianism and liberal immigration reform, this label was not equally applicable to all DPs. Poles survived slave labor, Jews survived death camps or narrowly escaped the reach of the Final Solution, and large numbers of Balts and Ukrainians survived the Red Army—or, as numerous critics charged at the time, survived Allied victory. Yet despite this variety of backgrounds, contemporary observers frequently portrayed the DPs as the "human backwash of the war," all similarly victimized by "the inhumane rearrangement of people and the ruthless exploitation of manpower."[13] An outcome of Nazi imperial rule and genocide, the DP crisis was indeed the result of carefully planned state policies. But this volatile mass of refugees had experienced the war in sharply different ways. Rigorously separated by nationality, the "last million" only shared a common opposition to repatriation and a desire to emigrate overseas, preferably to Palestine, North America, or Australia.

Admittedly, the dislocated people placed under Western Allied protection at the end of the war only represented a small percentage of Europe's displaced persons: the nine to twelve million ethnic Germans expelled from East-Central Europe—in the process of which expulsion it is estimated that several hundred thousand died—could have perfectly claimed such a label. As an advocate of German expellees bitterly pointed out, "The displaced persons represented only one-tenth of the total refugee problem in Europe."[14] The postwar settlement similarly forced out of their homes other groups of European refugees. The 250,000 ethnic Italians who left Yugoslav-controlled Istria and Dalmatia; the 520,000 ethnic Ukrainians, Belarusians, and Lithuanians transferred out of Poland by the end of 1946; and the one million and half ethnic Poles repatriated from the Soviet Ukraine, Belarus and

Lithuania between 1944 and 1948 (many of them forcibly resettled in the "recovered territories" of Western Poland) could legitimately be considered "displaced persons."[15] So could the millions of refugees who appeared, between 1947 and 1950, in India and Pakistan, in Israel and its neighboring Arab countries, Hong Kong, Taiwan and Korea. Employed by UNRRA and the IRO in a large DP camp located in Upper Bavaria, the American aid worker Kathryn Hulme vividly recalled this overlap: "It was startling to realize that before our own original mass of displaced had been resolved and resettled, another was forming on another part of the planet as if Displaced... had become the accustomed ailment of the century."[16] Yet the acronym DP exclusively applied to particular victims of Hitler and Stalin, even if "displaced persons" was often used in different contexts. Although generally resented by its unfortunate recipients, the DP label connoted a political and material entitlement limited to non-German European refugees from World War II and its immediate aftermath. Poster children for the unprecedented violence and population movements unleashed by Nazi expansionism, the "last million" constituted the most visible and enduring legacy of the conflict. Like many other military, political, and humanitarian actors of the period, Hulme highlighted the overriding importance of European refugees. From the vantage point of occupied Germany, and despite dire instances of forced displacement elsewhere, the DPs "seemed like the most important show on earth."[17]

For several decades, however, scholars treated this lengthy crisis as a sideshow in the transition from war to peace in Western Europe. The success story of American-backed economic reconstruction and political integration eclipsed darker European undercurrents such as the permanence of an alarming displacement problem in Germany, Austria, and Italy. This approach also failed to recognize that the alleviation of the DP crisis served as a crucial rehearsal stage for European economic reconstruction. Dean Acheson, who helped design and implement the Marshall Plan, revealingly described the American aid package as "an outgrowth of UNRRA."[18] Until the 1980s, the only books dedicated to Europe's displaced persons remained the voluminous official histories of UNRRA and the IRO, as well as surveys penned by American demographers and former military planners.[19] The first postwar cohort of political refugees drew renewed historical attention at the end of the Cold War, driven by new trends in German historiography and mounting numbers of asylum seekers in Western Europe.[20] While "top-down" studies of Allied refugee policies painted the DPs as passive objects of military and humanitarian governance, other works focused on specific national groups such as Polish, Ukrainian, and Baltic DPs, and Jewish refugees and Holocaust survivors.[21] In an effort to give voice to the displaced persons and not just the bureaucracies entrusted with their care, recent authors have addressed the individual and collective experiences of refugees; their struggles toward emotional, physical, and occupational normalcy; their modes of political mobilization; and their tumultuous relationships with occupation authorities, German civilians, and humanitarian personnel.[22] From their chaotic reception in improvised "assembly centers" to their emigration overseas, the "long road home" for Jewish and non-Jewish displaced persons is now solidly documented.[23]

However, the history of DPs cannot be limited to the chronology of Allied humanitarian operations or to the hardships of refugee life. It also involves policy debates that took place far from the camps. "The displaced persons in Germany and Austria are small in number compared to the population as a whole," reported the US Army War Department in 1946, "but they constitute a problem out of proportion of their numerical size."[24] While the intelligence branch of the US military referred to the costly and burdensome upkeep of restive refugees in the American occupation zones of Germany and Austria, this observation may be generalized. More than three years after the collapse of Nazi Germany, the Soviet Union still considered the DP problem "as urgent as ever," while for drastically different reasons the United States treated it as "one of the most unhappy repercussions of the war." For the British government, "the satisfactory disposal of millions of displaced persons involved the wider issues of world peace and stability."[25] Until the end of the 1940s, Europe's displaced persons remained "huddled into camps where they [could not] stay permanently, with no means to go elsewhere and no place open to them if they had means to go," as the chief prosecutor of the Nuremberg Trials, Robert H. Jackson, rightly noted.[26] Yet as a problem of international significance, this acute refugee crisis transcended the boundaries of occupied Germany: its multiple ramifications left a profound mark indeed on the postwar era.

Organized thematically, this book treats the DP episode as a seminal case study in post-1945 international history. It relates the experience of European displacement to the onset of the Cold War, international justice and political retribution, the emergence of the human rights movement, the rise of United Nations humanitarianism, the governance of international migration, and the advent of Jewish statehood. My goal is to shed new light on key features of the postwar period through the prism of displaced persons and political refugees. To capture the importance of DPs in postwar international politics, the book draws on the rich archives of the International Refugee Organization. Never before comprehensively used in the literature, these records offer a different perspective on the DP question than those of the Office of Military Government for Germany or UNRRA. Coinciding with the start of the Cold War, the IRO was created by the United Nations General Assembly in December 1946 to find permanent homes for the "last million." As an American official described it at the time, this body "became by far the most comprehensive agency for refugees that had ever been known."[27] Under the IRO, the so-called care and maintenance of displaced persons—the difficult provision of food, health care, clothes, and housing accommodations in war-torn Germany—remained a high priority. Unlike UNRRA, however, the IRO was not strictly subordinated to Allied military authorities; as such, it belonged to the new constellation of international organizations and protection agencies established between 1945 and 1950.[28] The IRO also exemplified the ambiguities of liberal internationalism in the late 1940s: controlled and predominantly financed by the American government, it helped shape the unbalanced multilateralism peculiar to the postwar years.[29] Through the IRO and subsequent international bodies, the United States assumed unchallenged leadership on the regulation of Cold War migration flows. Above all, the creation of the IRO forced the European refugee problem to the center of the international stage. No longer a temporary humanitarian challenge, this issue was now branded as "one of the gravest cancers gnawing at the peace so dearly won."[30] Speaking at the UN General Assembly in December 1946, Eleanor Roosevelt highlighted the new international significance of the crisis. "As long as a million persons remain with refugee status," she declared, "they delay the restoration of peace and order in the world."[31]

The DP moment, in short, offers an exciting opportunity to revisit the postwar experience from its supposed margins.[32] One million refugees in the heart of Europe do not go unnoticed, as the more recent displacement crisis in the former Yugoslavia confirmed again in the 1990s.[33] Admittedly, the full-page advertisements frequently seen in the 1940s American press lamenting the situation of "one million human beings … condemned to a lingering death in an international twilight zone" and the dispatches penned for the *New Yorker* by the essayist Janet Flanner reached a much smaller audience than the dramatic television reports by CNN's Christiane Amanpour.[34] Except in the United States, where large Polish, Jewish, and other Eastern European immigrant communities remained closely attuned to the plight of their displaced brethren and donated considerable funds, the DP story did not make many headlines. In the midst of economic reconstruction, and already coping with their own war refugees, colonial returnees, or expellees, Western European societies paid scant attention to the DPs. Yet, as this book illuminates, the problems posed by the "last million" encamped in and around the geopolitical center of the period greatly mattered to Western and Soviet policy makers, officials of international organizations, labor experts and reconstruction planners, legal scholars, human rights activists, welfare personnel, Cold War propagandists, and devotees of Zionism.

The first theme addressed in this study is the role played by the DP problem in the outbreak of the Cold War. The subject of tense discussions at the United Nations and other international venues, the fate of the "last million"—in this case, Polish, Yugoslav, Ukrainian, and Baltic anti-Communist refugees—fueled a growing East-West antagonism. As Eleanor Roosevelt wrote from the temporary United Nations headquarters in London, "It was the scene of one of the early clashes between the Soviet Union and the West."[35] Representatives of Communist governments demanded the immediate return of all non-Jewish Eastern European nationals. They also charged that the DP camps sheltered scores of "quislings" and war criminals attempting to evade justice at home. Western governments invoked democratic ideals to oppose compulsory repatriation but agreed to remove from the camps proven collaborators, auxiliaries of the German army, and refugees suspected of being of German descent. The massive "screening" of displaced persons conducted by Allied military and humanitarian personnel mirrored the fault lines of the Cold War. As the 1940s drew to an end, anti-Communism trumped anti-Fascism in the attribution of DP status. With long-term consequences for the governance of political asylum in the West, the political dissident emerged then as the most desirable type of asylum seeker.

The DP episode also affected the ideology and methods of modern humanitarianism. Prior to 1945, the alleviation of human suffering was the responsibility of private charitable organizations committed to war-stricken civilian populations. The "relief and rehabilitation" of Europe's displaced persons, however, was a coordinated international operation: traditional charity gave way to a "machinery of international relief" that for liberal internationalists was to be "vitally related to the kind of world we want to build when peace comes."[36] Religious and philanthropic groups continued to extend badly needed assistance to war refugees but were transformed in the process into nongovernmental organizations integrated into the United Nations system. Although "the idea still prevailed in some quarters that humanitarian work was a matter for private relief agencies," welfare specialists reported in 1947, "this conception has been usefully demolished by UNRRA."[37]

The "last million" left a similar imprint on human rights law. "It is a curious paradox," noted an American official, "that out of a postwar clean up job, out of the wreck of the refugee's fundamental freedoms, there had arisen the first widespread and binding international agreement for the advancement of human rights."[38] This diplomat alluded here to the "Magna Carta for refugees," the still-in-effect 1951 Geneva Convention, but the enduring spectacle of statelessness in postwar Europe impinged upon the international human rights movement as a whole. While the DP problem glaringly exposed the tenuousness of modern human rights, as Hannah Arendt passionately claimed, it also triggered the proclamation of a wide range of international protections. Although the 1948 Universal Declaration of Human Rights only amounted to a "common standard of achievement," the refugee rights adopted in the midst of the DP crisis added enforceable substance to the so-called "human rights revolution."

Finally, the DP experience encroached on international migration. Supervised by the IRO, the "resettlement" of displaced persons around the world was an unprecedented instance of planned population redistribution. Emigration to Israel or New World countries was not simply the final act of a long humanitarian drama; worries about "surplus population" and a desire to disseminate "freedom loving" Europeans in order to countenance the global spread of Communism added demographic and ideological urgency to the departure of refugees from the continent. Nearly 25 percent of all DPs ended their journey in the newly founded state of Israel. In its final section, this book analyzes the nationalizing effect of the Jewish DP experience and the place of Jewish refugees and Holocaust survivors within the postwar refugee regime.

Overall, Europe's displaced persons formed only a small subset of the "problem of the human refugee" foreseen by Franklin D. Roosevelt in 1939. Subsequent waves of Eastern European anti-Communist "escapees" and Hungarian border crossers did not alter this imbalance. Yet from 1945 to the late 1950s, the DPs and their successors epitomized the refugee condition— or "refugeedom"—in the West. Deemed more political than their non-European counterparts, the victims of Nazi and Soviet totalitarianism enjoyed a favorable status in human rights law and a key position in Cold War culture. The World Refugee Year celebrated under the auspices of the United Nations in 1959–60 ultimately challenged this hegemony. This little known fundraising campaign helped resettle most of the displaced persons still languishing in Austria and Germany. Its worldwide scope also acknowledged for the first time the global dimension of the refugee problem.[39]

Initially established to settle the postwar European crisis, the Office of the United Nations High Commissioner for Refugees similarly shifted its attention to forced displacement in the Third World. As a new history of dislocation and misery began on the African continent and in other emerging humanitarian hot spots, another one faded away: at the height of decolonization, the era of European refugees finally came to a halt.

I

The Battle of the Refugees

DISPLACED PERSONS AND THE MAKING
OF THE COLD-WAR WEST

ON FEBRUARY 2, 1946, a *New York Times* editorial urged the world to con-
front the plight of the displaced persons living in occupied Germany. At stake,
the newspaper warned, were "the fate and status of hundreds of thousands of
human beings who are clearly an international responsibility."[1] What had been
a task for the Allies had become a task for the whole world. A month earlier,
the first session of the United Nations General Assembly held in London had
identified "the problem of refugees" as a "matter of urgent importance." The
question was referred to the Third Committee, which addressed social, humanitarian, and cultural affairs. In early 1946 the organization had yet to choose a
permanent location for its headquarters, and the Security Council was preoc-
cupied primarily with a territorial dispute between Iran and the Soviet Union.
The stage was nonetheless set for nearly a year of protracted negotiations.
During its first twelve months of existence, the United Nations would devote
more hours to the refugee problem than to any single question except those
concerning security. "There are few subjects," noted an American diplomat,
"on which more prolonged and exhaustive negotiations have been carried on
between the Soviet Union and the western world than on the subject of refugees and displaced persons."[2] Recognized early on as an "urgent United Nations
problem," asylum seekers and refugees critically shaped the landscape of international politics from the very start of the postwar era.

Conspicuous though it was, the DP question had a limited geographic
scope. The "problem of refugees" pertained first and foremost to the complex
situation of dislocated Eastern Europeans, even if forced displacement
occurred in other parts of the world. Assessing the size of the refugee
population in China in November 1945, a UNRRA official in the Far East

spoke of "twenty-four to forty millions, not counting the approximate
1,400,000 overseas-Chinese who escaped Japanese rule in Burma, Indo-
China and other countries." In addition, Japanese occupation had caused the
internal displacement of some fifty million internally displaced Chinese refugees, allegedly "the greatest mass trek in history."[3] The US Department of
State estimated that twelve million displaced persons lived in Japan at the end
of the war, including returning Japanese nationals from Manchuria, China
and Formosa, as well as two million Korean laborers and their families.[4]
Experts logically assumed that "in addition to the Europeans it is possible that
large numbers of displaced Asiatics also may need international help."[5]
Technically, both European and Asian refugees fell under the auspices of
UNRRA, but in the Far East the agency's resources were severely limited.
Before long the United Nations concerned itself only with the displaced persons in Central Europe. "The persons with whom an international organization for uprooted people must deal," an American expert suggested, "are
almost exclusively the perhaps 2,000,000 European refugees...bristling with
political complications."[6] By drawing the attention of the United Nations to
the crisis in their occupation zones, Britain, France, and the United States
"Europeanized" the focus of postwar global displacement. Each nation nonetheless advocated an international solution to the European DP problem.

   The British government strongly urged the administrative transfer of displaced persons to a new international agency. This possibility was first discussed in November 1945 under the auspices of the Intergovernmental
Committee on Refugees established in July 1938 to assist Jewish refugees from
Nazi Germany.[7] George Rendel, an official of Britain's Foreign Office in
charge of liaison with humanitarian organizations, later wrote in his memoirs
that he was keen "to bring home to everyone concerned the seriousness of the
problem with which we were now being faced."[8] Aware that "the refugee
problem was now becoming a serious political danger," Rendel advocated the
creation of "a new and effective refugee organization on a much larger scale."
He explained that this international body would take on the duties then being
performed by Allied military authorities: "In London, we still believed that
the problem was a political rather than a military one, and that it could not be
solved by short-term military measures."[9] When Philip Noel-Baker, a British
veteran of the League of Nations and future Nobel Peace Prize winner, insisted
on behalf of the United Kingdom that the displaced persons be placed under
the authority of the General Assembly, he was in complete harmony with
Rendel, whose bid opened the way for the internationalization of the DP
question.

As Foreign Office records indicate, the British preference for an international agency was partly motivated by cost-sharing concerns. This solution, intimated Ernest Bevin to the US secretary of state James Byrnes, ensured "that every country realizes its responsibilities and takes its fair share of the burden."[10] This viewpoint, however, was predominantly shaped by the pressing question of Palestine. Alarming reports of Jewish "infiltrees" from Poland into the British occupation zone reached the Foreign Office in the winter of 1945, hinting that large numbers of Zionist sympathizers might be headed for West Germany. The Allies had liberated approximately twenty thousand Holocaust survivors from German concentration camps in the spring of 1945, but since then the steady influx of Jewish migrants rapidly increased the size of the Jewish displaced population. Predominantly of Polish origin, these refugees had survived the war in the Soviet Union and hoped to reach Palestine from safe havens in occupied Germany. In January 1946, Jewish infiltrees already entered the British occupation zone "at the rate of several thousands a day."[11] Since the release in August 1945 of the Harrison Report on the "treatment of displaced Jews"—a turning point in American attitudes toward Holocaust survivors and Zionism—the United States had pressured Great Britain to open the gates of Palestine to 100,000 Jewish immigrants. A temporary compromise was reached when in November 1945 Ernest Bevin and Harry Truman commissioned the Anglo-American Committee of Inquiry into the Problems of European Jewry and Palestine, whose 120-day mandate was "to make estimates of those who wish or will be impelled by their conditions to migrate to Palestine or other countries outside Europe."[12] To deflect attention away from the sensitive Jewish issue, the British government insisted "that the political questions involved were discussed in the widest possible forum."[13] Until the United Nations adopted a plan for the partition of Palestine in November 1947, the Foreign Office worked to dissociate the Jewish refugee problem from the Palestine question so as too weaken Zionist claims against British immigration restrictions. Rendel was well suited to this task. The former head of the Foreign Office's Eastern Department, he was a major architect of British policy toward Jewish refugees and "infiltrees" whom he linked, like Ernest Bevin, to an organized "attempt on the part of the Zionists to force our hand on the issue of immigration into Palestine."[14] For the British, a broadly inclusive discussion was the most preferable course in order to disentangle the Jewish DP question from the uncertain future of Mandatory Palestine.

If the internationalization of refugee governance advanced specific British goals, it also appealed to other Western Allies. In liberated France, immigration experts argued that the recovered French model of republican assimilation could, if applied internationally, lead to the eradication of statelessness in the postwar world. "It will be the honor of France," urged the socialist Marcel Livian, "to take the initiative for this disappearance, not only at the national level but internationally as well."[15] In the same vein, French foreign-policy makers thought of the refugee question as a valuable channel through which French prestige could be reinvigorated. France, after all, had received the bulk of Europe's immigrants and asylum seekers during the interwar era and, despite the taint of the Vichy years, legitimately sought recognition as a generous land of refuge. In July 1945, the Quai d'Orsay (as the French Ministry of Foreign affairs is known) thought that France deserved a leading role in international meetings devoted to refugees: "It is expected that the reorganization of the status of stateless people will soon become an international question. A French thesis must be prepared: France leads the world in the number of stateless people and refugees living on its territory....As such, the French position ought to be given full consideration."[16] This desire was not merely confined to French policy-making circles. The influential intellectual Emmanuel Mounier also referred to the tradition of French political asylum as a palliative to the erosion of French grandeur: "Even if we are unable to build atomic bombs or to bang on tables with an imperial fist like those called the Big Powers, there still remains a way to force ourselves upon History: to be a country where an exiled, desolate, and desperate man will always find a hand stretched out to him with no questions asked."[17] In this regard, the referral of the DP question to the United Nations allowed French officials to claim a dominant role in the emerging politics of international human rights. With less than forty thousand registered DPs in early 1946, the small French zone of occupation in Rhineland-Palatinate and the Saarland was largely depopulated of refugees. It nonetheless seemed "suitable" to the Quai d'Orsay "that a French national be placed at the head of a unified refugee organization mandated by the United Nations."[18] But as French diplomats quickly discovered, leadership of international humanitarian organizations largely remained in American hands.

Within the Truman administration, however, the refugee problem did not initially rank high among immediate postwar priorities. In May 1945, Franklin D. Roosevelt's recently inaugurated successor refused to pay particular attention to the DPs in liberated Germany, despite the prodding of his secretary of the treasury, Henry Morgenthau.[19] The main arbiters of American refugee policy were military commanders in Germany and the State Department in Washington, "whose ideas on the subject," the British

Foreign Office complained in the fall of 1945, "do not yet seem to be very clear."[20] The US Army and the State Department both sought an immediate solution to relieve the US zone from a costly humanitarian commitment shouldered by American taxpayers. Neither conceived of "international organization" as a suitable way to rapidly relieve the American occupation zone of nearly five hundred thousand displaced civilians of multiple nationalities. Faced with this daunting challenge, American authorities initially viewed the British proposal to transfer the question of nonrepatriable refugees to the United Nations as an unnecessary complication.[21] They agreed that existing international organizations such as UNRRA and the near-defunct Intergovernmental Committee on Refugees, were unable "to take effective action," an opinion frequently expressed by General Dwight Eisenhower. But an entirely American civilian agency overseeing the DP question was in their eyes preferable to the creation of yet another international body committed to the long-term upkeep of hundreds of thousands of DPs in Germany.[22] Such a prospect threatened the stabilization of Germany, at a time when American occupation policy gradually shifted from denazification toward helping "the German people to win their way back to an honorable place among the free and peace-loving nations of the world."[23]

Against these misgivings, American internationalists invoked the Charter of the United Nations and its stated goal to "achieve international cooperation in solving international problems of an economic, social, cultural or humanitarian character." Eleanor Roosevelt unexpectedly became one of the leading American voices advocating such a path. Asked in December 1945 by Harry Truman to join the first US delegation at the United Nations General Assembly, the former First Lady would soon publicly declare her support for international action to aid the refugees, who constituted "a source of disturbance in the relationships of nations now affected by it."[24] Her appointment to the US delegation gave her ample opportunity to grapple directly with issues in which she claimed to have taken a keen interest, such as "refugees, relief, and rehabilitation and human rights."[25] Despite such idealist intentions, the stringent immigration quotas based on national origins imposed by the Johnson-Reed Act of 1924 still prevented the entrance to the United States of a large number of displaced persons, just as it had hampered the large-scale rescue of refugees from Nazi Germany on the eve of World War II. Harry Truman's "Statement and Directive on Displaced Persons," issued on September 22, 1945 seemed to indicate a change of course. Drawing attention to the "appalling situation of dislocated people in Europe," Truman asked that "established immigration quotas be used in order to reduce human suffering,"

a timid but not inconsequential liberalization of US refugee policy that soon
enabled the first organized arrival of Holocaust survivors onto American
soil.[26] Yet at the beginning of 1946, the American agreement to refer the DP
question to the United Nations meant that the United States would back,
financially and politically, a multilateral solution not based on large-scale
immigration to its shores. According to George Warren, the main refugee
adviser at the State Department in the 1940s and 1950s, many liberal advocates of international action still opposed the wide scale acceptance of refugees in the land of the free. Their hope was instead "to divert the pressure on
the United States" and to get refugees "off to other countries."[27]

The realization by Allied authorities in Germany that an increasing
number of DPs refused to go home precipitated the search for an international solution under the auspices of the United Nations. Despite intense
efforts by military authorities and UNRRA workers to proceed with the swift
evacuation of DP camps, repatriation rates had slowed to a crawl, particularly
among Polish DPs. Only 13,900 DPs were returned home in January 1946, the
lowest monthly figure to date. UNRRA officials continued to believe that
most of the displaced persons were capable of repatriating, particularly if
enticed by clothing, food, and amenities.[28] Foreign correspondents in Germany
reported a different story: "Everyone connected with the problem wishes this
assumption were correct but knows that it is not."[29] No longer temporary refugees the DPs formed a group of long-term asylum seekers looking to emigrate
to Western European countries, the New World, and, after May 1948, the State
of Israel. The three occupying powers in West Germany consequently pinned
their hopes on a new international body better suited than UNRRA to deal
with the migratory and political dimension of the problem. "By the autumn of
1945," recalled an American planner of DP operations, "it became increasingly
apparent that a new international agency would be needed to resettle those
refugees who, for one reason or another, would not return to their home-
lands."[30] But the establishment of the International Refugee Organization was
not a simple matter: at stake was the "safeguard and sanctuary of people shifted
against their will from one government to another."[31] Recently arrived in
London to attend the first session of the United Nations, Eleanor Roosevelt
felt that the displacement crisis in Germany was rapidly morphing into a
political tug-of-war. "The battle is on about the refugee resolution," she
recorded in her diary on January 9, 1946.[32]

Over the next twelve months, according to an American official, "millions
of words were uttered in prolonged debates," ultimately raising "far-reaching
issues that touched fundamental questions of human liberty."[33] A member of

the US delegation at the Economic and Social Council, Ernest F. Penrose participated in fiery exchanges. His detailed portrayal of the proceedings was infused with unmistakable Cold War rhetoric: "Our negotiators were talking to men whose mercy was not as our mercy, nor their justice as our justice, not their idea of compromise as our idea of compromise." Other contemporary analysts, such as the *New York Times* diplomatic correspondent James Reston, emphasized in similar terms the ideological cleavage revealed by this confrontation: "It began to settle in the minds of the negotiators on both sides that what they were really seeking were two different worlds of the mind and the spirit."[34] Students of Soviet interventions at the United Nations shared the same view: "There has been little evidence that the Soviet Union shares the humanitarian concern for refugees which is so widely felt in the West."[35] Not all commentators framed the East-West divide in clear-cut ideological terms. For a French international jurist, disagreements over the definition and status of displaced persons amounted above all to a "*conflit de qualifications*": potentially reconcilable differences between two juridical approaches more than the collision of two world views.[36] But for the numerous American eyewitnesses to these negotiations, there was little doubt that the issue of displaced persons "shed light on the different conceptions of democracy held in Russia and America."[37] The US secretary of state George Marshall, who claimed he raised this question in "every possible forum," concluded that the DP problem exposed irreconcilable divergences between the "Soviet viewpoint" and the "American tradition."[38]

The "battle of refugees" was indeed the first direct confrontation over political dissidents between the two emerging superpowers: human rights politics did not only hastened the end of the Cold War, as commonly assumed, but also led to its outbreak. In front of the international press corps, Eleanor Roosevelt and Andrey Vyshinsky (who would be replaced as the Soviet delegate later that year by Andrey Gromyko) repeatedly sparred in plenary sessions of the UN General Assembly. The fate of the displaced persons, however, was painstakingly discussed in more specialized commissions reporting to the General Assembly and the Economic and Social Council.[39] This relegation to secondary venues did not however diminish the intensity of the negociations. "The greatest political heat", observed Eleanor Roosevelt, "often came up in the course of grinding committee work."[40] The talks revolved around three core issues: "How were refugees and displaced persons to be defined? Were they to be permitted to choose freely between the alternatives of going back to their countries of origin and remaining outside of them? If so, what international aid should be given to those who choose to remain outside?"[41]

The initial participation of twenty countries, joined by thirty more toward the end of 1946, theoretically secured a broad international setting. In practice, non-Western participants played a secondary role, whether in committees or plenary sessions. Representatives of Middle Eastern countries (Egypt, Iraq, and Lebanon) almost exclusively intervened in the discussions to defend the rights of "indigenous populations" from refugees resettled in other countries, a direct reference to Jewish DPs and their possible emigration to Palestine. "Refugees," a Syrian representative argued in a rare intervention, "should not be forced upon local populations among whom their presence might result in strife."[42] Similarly, Latin American delegations (representing twelve countries by the end of 1946) seldom participated in the debates. Their large number, however, gave them a pivotal role during decisive votes. In one instance, Eleanor Roosevelt skillfully invoked the memory of Simon Bolivar and "his stance for the freedom of the people of Latin America" in order to drum up support for Western proposals.[43] Overall however, non-Western countries remained marginal actors in deliberations entirely focused on refugees in Europe. "Like other immediate issues," the American editorialist Anne O'Hare McCormick summarized, "this is a matter for the Great Powers to deal with."[44]

The main difference of opinion was between the countries of origin of the majority of displaced persons: the Soviet Republics of Russia, Ukraine, and Belarusia, as well as Poland and Yugoslavia; and the three countries administering displaced persons camps in occupied Germany and Austria: the United States, the United Kingdom, and France. The Eastern European bloc argued that only those persons who wanted to return to their countries should be assisted by an international organization. This view was invariably repeated by the Soviets from 1945 onward. After the defeat of the Axis Powers, they contended, "all men of good will" could and should return to their homeland. In the Communist "anti-Fascist" view, repeated throughout the negotiations, Spanish Republicans and Jewish survivors were the only categories of persecuted refugees deserving of international assistance outside their countries of origin. Both types were deemed "unrepatriable" by the Soviet bloc, although for different reasons. In Spain, the persistence of Francoist rule prevented the repatriation of political opponents, and Republicans were seen by the Soviets as freedom fighters temporary unable to return to their homeland. Jews, however, were the only group of permanent refugees accepted as such by the Soviet Union. A particular brand of anti-Fascist philosemitism mixed with more pragmatic considerations accounted for this diplomatic sympathy. This position also reaffirmed on a much larger international stage the rigorous stand previously taken by the Soviets at various UNRRA meetings, namely, that the distribution of postwar aid should be directly tied to anti-Fascist political criteria. As the Soviets contended, "special weight and urgency [should] be given to the needs of those countries in which the extent of devastation...resulted from active resistance in the struggle against the enemy."[45] The USSR held a similar view regarding postwar refugee relief: only true "victims of Fascism" should be entitled to a special international status. The overwhelming majority of DPs did not fall within this category. Whether they were victimized or not during World War II, they remained in Soviet eyes displaced citizens to be repatriated without further ado. For the Communist delegations, according to UNRRA's official historian, "the test of whether an individual was good or bad was whether he wanted, actively and quickly, to return to his area of origin."[46]

In accordance with the Yalta agreement, American, British, and French authorities had lent their hands to the compulsory repatriation of Soviet nationals, most of them prisoners of war and forced laborers found in Western and Central Europe in the months following V-E Day.[47] While still wishing for the rapid closure of DP camps, the Western Allies now argued that the bulk of the displaced persons deserved humanitarian assistance until a solution could be found for them. The role of the international community, declared Eleanor Roosevelt on January 28, 1946, was to find ways "in the interest of humanity and social stability to return...thousands of people who have been uprooted from their homes and their country to a settled way of life."[48] Whether this return to a "settled way of life" should take place in countries of origin or elsewhere in the world she did not specify. Her intentional vagueness on this issue was a first hint to the Soviet side that, alongside repatriation, emigration could legitimately be envisioned as a permanent remedy to the DP problem.

Underlying the East-West controversy, which erupted during the early days of the debates, was therefore a radically different approach toward the various refugee groups in occupied Germany. The USSR and its satellites immediately sought to exclude from the scope of international humanitarian aid their alleged political enemies. While stating in several instances that they did not wish to reject the right of asylum, the Communist bloc found it unacceptable to adhere to an organization providing assistance to "undemocratic" elements. "Has it ever been known in the history of international relations," asked the Yugoslav representative Ales Bebler (a former volunteer in the Spanish Civil War and Titoist partisan), "that a Government contributed to the cost of maintaining its political enemies who have fled abroad or emigrants

who have in fact committed crimes against the people?"[49] To bolster this
position, the Polish delegate Józef Winiewicz recited from the definition of
"refugees" offered by the *Oxford English Dictionary*: "Persons seeking refuge
in a foreign land due to racial or political persecution." This designation, he
maintained, hardly applied to displaced persons who no longer had a compelling reason to abandon their country and who were blatantly shunning the
duty of postwar reconstruction. "We should not let ourselves be hypnotized
by the humanitarian aspect of this question," he concluded, "and allow war
criminals to be taken for irreproachable refugees."[50] His Ukrainian colleague
similarly described the predominantly anti-Communist and nationalist
Ukrainian DPs refusing to repatriate to the USSR: "These so-called refugees…which the Ukrainian people rightly call 'German-Ukrainians,' are not
political refugees but criminals who endanger peace and world security."
Finally, a Soviet representative of Armenian origin summarized this issue in
simple terms: "The only dream of refugees is to go back as soon as possible to
their country of origin," citing as an example the successful return of (a few)
interwar Armenian refugees to the Soviet Socialist Republic of Armenia in
1945. "Our people," he confidently boasted, "reserve the most cordial and dil-
igent welcome to returning displaced persons"—a claim seriously challenged
at the time by anti-Communist advocacy groups and more recently by historians of the Soviet Union.[51] The permanent solution advocated by the USSR
and its followers was the repatriation of all displaced persons (except Jews)
through "bilateral agreements between the countries concerned." This option
amounted to a mere continuation of early Allied repatriation policies
according to which each foreign national found in liberated Europe was
claimed and repatriated by country of origin, with the logistical help of
UNRRA. "My hypothesis," Penrose remembered, "was that the Russians
meant what they said, that they sincerely desired a temporary international
organization with the object of registering refugees and displaced persons
[and] arranging for their repatriation."[52]

For historical and ideological reasons, the Soviet attitude toward DPs
unwilling to repatriate was much less flexible, especially in the case of Balts
and Ukrainians. Like White Russian and anti-Bolshevik émigrés in the 1920s,
"renegades" left beyond the grip of Soviet power raised the specter of counter-
revolution. A frequent Russian accusation, noted the British George Rendel,
was that "our refugee policy was aimed at creating counter-revolutionary
movements like those of Wrangel and Denikin after the First World War."
The dissemination of hundreds of thousands of anti-Communist displaced
persons was also a serious public-relations concern in the midst of the

Communist takeover in Eastern and Central Europe and at a time when accurate descriptions of the forced-labor system in the USSR were starting to surface in the West.[53] In addition, the devastated condition of Eastern European economies created gigantic manpower needs. In the Soviet Union, the Five Year Plan (1946–50) demanded an enormous amount of conscripted labor, and Soviet DPs in occupied Germany were desirable targets of forced-labor policies, alongside the 2.2 million POWs already repatriated and assigned in large numbers to compulsory work. The USSR sought therefore to "deport its own nationals back home," where reintegration often entailed quarantine through forced labor and other forms of political punishment, including summary executions. Historians, indeed, have estimated that one-fifth of the 5.5 million Soviet nationals repatriated by 1946 were either executed or sentenced to twenty-five years of hard labor.[54]

In other postwar instances of European forced displacement, such as the expulsion of ethnic Germans from Czechoslovakia and Poland, exiting refugees were physically and legally barred from returning to their former country of residence. Although the DPs had not technically been evicted but had become refugees by necessity, the Soviets demanded the complete repatriation of exiles whom they otherwise vilified as debased "enemies." It is worth recalling in this respect that in 1921, the government of the Soviet Union massively denaturalized the majority of the 1,500,000 White Russian émigrés who had fled Bolshevism; the formal punishment meted out then to Russian exiles was the coercive dissolution of their citizenship.[55] The Soviet Union took the opposite stance in 1945 when it insisted that displaced persons were not stateless but full nationals required to return to their countries at all cost. In the wake of its Great Patriotic War, the USSR sought to "renationalize" exiting refugees and displaced persons rather than denationalize them. Various retributive goals accounted for this drastic change of approach.

The presumed wartime guilt of certain categories of DPs formed the core of the East-West controversy. On this matter, as in many others, the Communist position left little room for ambiguity: "Those who do not share the dream of returning home are not refugees but quislings," trumpeted a Soviet official.[56] The DP talks allowed Eastern European countries to publicly spell out the numerous political scores they sought to settle with nationals framed as collaborators. The Soviet Union harbored vindictive designs against Balts and Ukrainians who had joined the German army, compulsorily or voluntarily. At least half a million men from the Soviet Union alone, many of them turncoat Soviet POWs who had joined General Vlasov's Russian Liberation Army or other anti-Soviet units, served in German uniform on the

Eastern Front prior to joining other civilians fleeing the advance of the Red Army. Hence the request, for example, of a Soviet Ukrainian delegate to forcibly return DPs who had been members of the Ukrainian Waffen-SS "Galizien" Division, guilty of participating in "annihilating the Polish population and exterminating the Jewish people."[57] Yugoslavia, led by the wartime Partisan leadership, was eager not to let "fascist" Chetniks and former Croatian Ustaše go free. In addition, Yugoslavia presented a particularly detailed laundry list of "criminals" among Yugoslav DPs in Austria and Italy, including pro-German fascist Serbs, Domobrancis (collaborationist members of the Slovenian Home Guard), and "Mahometans from Bosnia" who had enrolled in the SS. The Yugoslav delegation legitimized its demands by reverting to analogy: "There was no special formality followed in the case of Marshall Pétain or M. Laval. Why create difficulties for other countries? Why discriminate?"[58]

Within the emerging Soviet bloc, Poland took the least aggressive position regarding the punishment of expatriate nationals. The vast majority of Polish DPs had been forcibly brought to Germany as slave laborers and subsequently endured extreme hardships; the accusation of "collaboration" hardly applied to their wartime experience. On the question of DPs, Polish diplomats at the United Nations confidently departed from the retributive Soviet line and "had not thrown off the last shreds of independence at that time," as E. F Penrose noted. Yet the emissaries of the Communist-controlled National Unity Government formed in June 1945, still counted various "enemies" among the Polish DP population, such as the members of General Anders's anti-Soviet army and the vocal supporters of the London-based Polish government-in-exile. All in all, Poland shared with its Soviet-bloc partners a common basic position: the ongoing "democratization" of East-Central Europe removed all the obstacles to nationals returning home and participating in reconstruction; their refusal to do so was an irrefutable incriminating sign.

The Communist emphasis on retribution was not dismissed outright by the Western bloc, and not only because 1946 was still a time, according to Penrose, "when the western world had not given hope on reaching an accommodation with the Soviet Union...and was anxious to leave the way open to compromise wherever practicable." The French and Belgian delegations, for instance, included former resisters sensitive to anti-Fascist Soviet claims. Marie-Hélène Lefaucheux, a French diplomat and former member of the Resistance, agreed that proven "war criminals, traitors and quislings" were to be punished and surrendered to their national government. Alexandre Parodi, himself a *grand résistant* and the first permanent representative of his country at the UN security council, wrote in June 1946 to his fellow wartime comrade Georges Bidault (who served as the president of the provisional government as well as foreign minister) that on the refugee question, "France is looking for equitable solutions and seeks to attenuate, for the Russian group, the feeling of isolation resulting from the constant adoption of views inspired by the Anglo-Saxon bloc and shared by the majority."[59] The Belgian representative Fernand Dehousse, a distinguished international jurist and a socialist Resistance member during the German occupation, took his cue from the long lists of collaborators presented by the Soviet side to seek the assistance of the United Nations in securing the extradition from Francoist Spain of the notorious Belgian collaborationist leader Léon Degrelle.

This anti-Fascist kinship between East and West, however, proved limited and qualified. Most Western European countries formerly occupied by the Nazis had by 1946 completed the harsh and violent phase of retribution and purges, and were now focusing instead on the prosecution of high-profile collaborationist leaders and more often than not opted for national unity over the aggressive pursuit of political justice. For their part, Britain and the United States played a dominant role at the Nuremberg Trials and in the process of denazification in occupied Germany, but shied away from vindictive rhetoric during the DP negotiations at the United Nations. The Western side indeed carefully hewed to a moderate position regarding retribution, a stance clearly summarized by Fernand Dehousse. If the search for and prosecution of collaborators among the DPs was legitimate, he argued, "one could also refuse to return to a country of origin and not be a war criminal, a traitor, or even a fascist." In a direct challenge to Soviet criteria, Dehousse added that treason was in itself a very ambivalent and contingent juridical concept: "Should countries of refuge accept the definition of treason prevailing within the jurisdiction of claiming countries"[60]? As it soon became clear, someone labeled a "traitor" in Eastern European anti-Fascist parlance was no longer automatically deemed a collaborator in the West.

Foreboding the lenient admission into their countries of thousands of Ukrainian and Baltic DPs who had fought in German units, British and American delegates particularly opposed the blanket criminalization and punishment of non-Jewish Eastern European refugees.[61] "The United Nations must show a spirit of tolerance and generosity rather than a desire for vengeance. Its task is to bring peace, not the gallows," declared George Rendel.[62] According to the Western majority view, assistance provided to the Nazis during the war did not always amount to collaboration, such as in the case of coerced enrolment in the German army. On behalf of the United

States, George Warren proposed therefore that the new refugee organization should be given a limited retributive mission—the denial of assistance to DPs who voluntarily assisted Nazi Germany and its satellites—without playing the role of a "criminal tribunal."[63] Speaking for France, the French trade-union leader and former Buchenwald internee Léon Jouhaux reinforced the Western position. The nations of the world, claimed the French representative at the Economic and Social Council, "must not make the fate of 1,200,000 displaced persons dependent on that of a few thousand guilty persons."[64]

The landmark resolution submitted to the UN General Assembly on February 12th, 1946, reflected the split between Western and Soviet definitions of wartime treason and collaboration. While the motion required that particular attention be paid to the "surrender and punishment of war criminals, quislings and traitors" and encouraged the voluntary repatriation of DPs "in every way possible," it also constituted the first international recognition of the right of asylum in the postwar era: "No refugees or displaced persons who have finally and definitely, in complete freedom and after receiving full knowledge of the facts,...expressed valid objections to returning to their countries of origin...shall be compelled to return to their countries of origin."[65] Proven traitors should be punished, but other DPs, legitimately opposed to repatriation should be entitled to international aid and authorized to live outside their homeland. Such persons, argued a Dutch representative on behalf of the Western nations, were "entitled to resettlement elsewhere as a basic human right." As such, this resolution went significantly further than Article 55 of the United Nations Charter, which only vaguely called for the "universal respect and observance of human rights and fundamental freedoms" without prohibiting the forcible return of asylum seekers to their country of origin.[66] Andrey Vychinsky, the ill-famed orchestrator of Stalin's Great Purge between 1936 and 1938, vociferously opposed this proposal: "We refuse to accept this tolerance. We paid a high price for it, with too much blood and too many lives. This so-called tolerance is known to history by one name: Munich."[67] *Time* magazine vividly described Eleanor Roosevelt's counterattack: "Her voice shrill with emotion, she urged that UN aid those who refused to go back." While Vyshinsky "preached Soviet doctrine in the form most repulsive to the West, the packed galleries gave her a rousing ovation."[68] Other English-speaking officials used this opportunity to display their own rhetorical skills. To counter the Soviet line, the prime minister of New Zealand, Peter Fraser, read from Ralph Waldo Emerson's poem "Boston": "What avail / The plough or sail / Or land of life / If Freedom fail?" Hector McNeil, a Scottish junior minister at the Foreign Office, reminded the Communist bloc that tolerance could prove beneficial: "We have had a refugee of whom we are very proud: using our libraries and his brains, he laid down a series of principles which were directed dramatically and basically against the kind of society in which he was sheltering."[69] But this sardonic reference to Karl Marx did little to alter the Soviet belief in the collective guilt of DPs who refused to go home.

Despite this acrimonious atmosphere, the UN General Assembly unanimously voted in favor of the resolution with the reserved but decisive support of the five Soviet-backed delegations. "This vote meant that the Western nations would have to worry about the ultimate fate of the refugees for a long, long time," Eleanor Roosevelt conceded, "but it was a victory well worth while." It was a relative success for the Communist side also. Repatriation, even if voluntary, was still being framed in the resolution as the only suitable policy to solve the DP crisis. Moreover, despite stating that the refugee problem was "international in scope and nature," the resolution allayed Communist qualms by avoiding any direct reference to the "resettlement" of DPs outside their homeland. The Communist nations still had a lot to gain by staying the course and blocking Western proposals in backdoor committees. On no issue, Penrose wrote, "did the persistence of the Eastern bloc penetrate further into details than on refugees and displaced persons." Eleanor Roosevelt, for her part, explained this tenacity in more cultural terms. She found that the lengthy DP negotiations revealed the "Russians' oriental streak which comes to the fore in their enjoyment of bargaining day after day."[70]

New controversies inevitably erupted. Eastern European governments asked to be provided with nominal lists of displaced persons and demanded that the personnel administering the DP camps should be mostly composed of representatives of their countries. Against this claim, the British delegation proudly invoked the "Anglo-Saxon conception of law" in which "no one may be both judge and prosecutor in the same case."[71] Another bone of contention was the method of transmitting information to the refugees concerning political and economic conditions in the countries of origin. Soviet-bloc representatives alleged that active coercion against repatriation was carried out in the DP camps, involving "bullets aimed at the chest of those expressing the desire to return to their motherland." In a three-hour-long harangue, Vyshinsky charged that "those bands included among their leaders traitors and quislings who had served in the German Gestapo, who had organized pogroms against the Jews, or who had headed punitive expeditions against Ukrainian and Belarusian partisans."[72] Although regularly debunked by Western counterinvestigations, these accusations were not always unfounded.

The DP camps and other non-Jewish refugee communities in occupied Germany constituted the most vocal centers of anti-Soviet propaganda in postwar Europe. Moreover, many of the antirepatriation agitators, Ukrainian nationalists in particular, had actively collaborated with the Nazis under the banner of anti-Bolshevism.[73] The Western majority acknowledged that "repatriation has been hampered by the dissemination of false rumors," yet they supported freedom of speech and the unrestricted circulation of information in the DP camps. The role of the future refugee organization, the Western nations contended, would be to make sure that "adequate information" on the conditions in countries of origin was supplied to refugees, without granting Eastern European governments any privileges in this process.

These differences of view were not just procedural tactics; the DP talks of 1946 showcased for the first time the blossoming rhetoric of the Cold War West, a geopolitical entity framed in civilizational terms. Three years before NATO founders proclaimed themselves "joined by a common heritage of democracy, individual liberty and the rule of law" and referred to the West as "a cohesive organism, determined to fulfill its great purpose," the United States and its allies seized upon the DP problem to exhibit alleged Western values, such as the right of individuals to be protected from the nefarious acts of states. [74] "Here at the United Nations," proclaimed Eleanor Roosevelt, "we are trying first and foremost to take into account the rights of man, not the rights of governments."[75] Rendel similarly alluded to a definitive chasm between competing ideologies when he ruled out, "at this moment of history," the possibility of reconciliation between two antithetical philosophies.[76] The Belgian jurist Fernand Dehousse clarified the uniqueness of the Western ethos: "We believe in human values that transcend epochs, regimes and governments."[77] That these principles had been blatantly violated by European powers in the colonial world as soon as World War II ended did not hinder this self-celebration. American commentators drew this unambiguous conclusion: "The East wanted a world in which the state was supreme; the West a world in which the individual was above the state."[78] Throughout 1946, negotiations over displaced persons at the United Nations served as the first international stage for a "clash of civilizations" between the coalescing West and the nascent Soviet bloc.

Cold War rhetoric did not however stop European and American representatives from extolling the superior humanitarian achievements of their respective countries. Léon Jouhaux, for instance, reminded the UN General Assembly of France's historic role as a haven for asylum seekers: "France has taken hundreds of thousand of political refugees. What she did, could other countries do it too?" French "traditional hospitality," another official argued, evidently oblivious of the numerous internment camps set up by his country on the eve of World War Two and by the Vichy regime, extended back to "time immemorial."[79] Hector McNeil, the delegate for Britain, declared that the entire English language would disappear "should the words toleration, pity and asylum vanish from its vocabulary" (even if his instructions from the Home Office made clear that the United Kingdom, already burdened with "alien refugees," was not eager to absorb new ones).[80] Delegations from smaller European nations, such as Denmark, also boasted of their contribution to humanitarianism—in Denmark's case on behalf of displaced Germans from Pomerania and Eastern Prussia who escaped the advance of the Red Army on its way to Berlin. The most revealing insight into this humanitarian contest was Eleanor Roosevelt's trumpeting of the American tradition of asylum, couched in the language of American exceptionalism:

> I cannot recall that a political or a religious refugee has ever been sent out of my country since the Civil War. At that time I do remember that one of my own relatives, because he came to this country and built a ship that ran contraband to the South, was not included in the amnesty. But, otherwise, this has not been a question that has entered into my thinking.[81]

Ignored in her statement was the deportation of Chinese laborers in the late nineteenth century and of European left-wing radicals after the First World War, not to mention her late husband's refusal to let into the United States the 973 Jewish refugees on board on *SS Saint Louis* in June 1939.[82] For the first American representative at the United Nations, it was the recent upheavals on the European continent such as "wars, changes in population and ownership of land" that now compelled the United States to tackle the problem of refugees "from a completely different point of view": no longer as an issue external to American experience but as one of the pillars of postwar American internationalism.

These various pronouncements all unequivocally pointed to the West as the historical home of humanitarianism, despite the efforts of other countries to challenge this monopoly. A Lebanese delegate politely reminded his audience that his country took in more than eighty thousand Armenian refugees in the interwar period. His Egyptian colleague added that many Greek, Italian, Yugoslav and Polish soldiers and refugees fleeing Nazi occupation found shelter in Cairo during the war. Yet for Cold War legal scholars and

political scientists, the Western approach to the DP problem undoubtedly
reflected a unique "cult of solidarity with wretched individuals, and in
particular with the victims of tyranny."[83] According to one commentator, "the
Western tradition of freedom of speech and right of asylum was too deeply
entrenched to be lightly dismissed."[84] Not surprisingly, the International
Refugee Organization (IRO), established by the United Nations General
Assembly on December 15th, 1946, was frequently portrayed as "an instrument of the West."[85] The fact that the Soviet-backed side withdrew from this
new "specialized agency" the very day of its creation—leaving the United
States to ultimately supply over half of its funding—certainly gave credence
to this characterization.

After almost a year of tedious negotiations, the constitution of the
International Refugee Organization was adopted by a vote of 30 to 5, with 18
abstentions.[86] It was, however, declared unacceptable by the Eastern European
bloc. By ruling out compulsory repatriation, the Soviet representative Andrey
Gromyko insisted, the West allowed "war criminals" to evade justice instead
of being punished in their own country. Gromyko also reiterated the basic
Soviet opposition to the resettlement of DPs, except in the case of Jewish
"unrepatriables." Emigration, he contended, would condemn the refugees "to
a joyless life far from their homeland, in circumstances of all sorts of
discrimination."[87] This was a new argument in the Soviet repertoire. For several years to come, the USSR would repeatedly accuse Western capitalist
countries of using DPs for cheap labor.

The withdrawal of the Soviet bloc from the IRO also marked the end of
the short-lived era of Grand Alliance humanitarianism inaugurated in
November 1943 with the creation of UNRRA. At that time Soviet representatives had heralded the "mutual understanding" and "the spirit of collaboration" prevailing within the organization.[88] To be sure, the wartime participation
of the Soviet Union in the Relief and Rehabilitation Administration stemmed
from a desire to obtain badly needed material assistance at the end of the war.
Like the Bolshevik regime in 1918, the USSR and its immediate satellites
stood in 1945 at the receiving end of international recovery efforts, a fact later
bemoaned by American critics of UNRRA who realized that "the great bulk
of relief, largely supplied or paid for by the United States, went to Eastern
Europe and was used by governments bitterly hostile to us."[89] Still, the
existence of UNRRA had allowed for a qualified partnership between the
Western Allies and the Soviet Union in the planning of postwar relief operations. The Soviet repudiation of the IRO ended this understanding and pre-
figured the systematic disengagement of the USSR and its satellites from

international organizations.[90] It also widened the gap separating East and West over the meaning and enforcement of human rights. Two years before Communist countries abstained when the 1948 Universal Declaration of Human Rights was put to vote, their withdrawal from the IRO was the first Soviet-bloc denunciation of "bourgeois rights" at the United Nations.

The IRO constitution, however, did not entirely contradict Soviet arguments. A marked anti-Fascist language, derived from classifications established during the Nuremberg Trials, was used by the Western drafters to define persons excluded from the IRO: "No international assistance should be given to traitors, quislings and war criminals, and nothing should be done to prevent in any way their surrender and punishment."[91] The same clause applied to persons "who can be shown to have voluntarily assisted the enemy forces since the outbreak of the Second World War" and who "have assisted the enemy in persecuting civilian populations." Henry Monneray, a French former assistant prosecutor at Nuremberg who analyzed the legal status of refugees in the IRO constitution, clarified the meaning of this exclusionary clause: "Infidelity towards the national state will only be tolerated if justified by fidelity towards the ideals of human rights prevailing within the United Nations community."[92] Interestingly, Soviet legal doctrine later borrowed from IRO language when it exclusively defined refugees as "victims of Fascism." As an American Sovietologist pointed out in 1957, "the USSR seems to have adopted the law of the IRO Charter as the final word on refugees and displaced persons, even though it has opposed its adoption."[93]

Another provision that was quite agreeable to the Soviet side was the exclusion of "persons of ethnic German origin, whether German nationals or members of German minorities in other countries." In conformity with Article 12 of the Potsdam Agreement, the IRO considered the expellees as the exclusive responsibility of the West German government and local welfare organizations. The millions of ethnic German refugees who since 1944 had poured into Germany in fear of the Red Army as well as those forcibly transferred out of Czechoslovakia and Poland immediately after the war were therefore barred from receiving United Nations assistance. "The Organization," wrote the IRO historian neutrally, "was not required to handle the difficulties created by the influx into Western Germany and Austria of German refugees and displaced persons, the so-called Volksdeutsche."[94] Yet by excluding refugees of ethnic German background, the IRO hewed to the retributive principles of "victor's justice." Western refugee advocates eager to extend international help to ethnic German expellees lamented this provision. The IRO constitution, protested the theologian Elfan Rees on behalf of the World

Council of Churches, "was saddled with a definition of a refugee which was narrow, partial and in specific instances discriminatory and unjust."[95]

An additional compromise with Soviet interests was the priority given to refugee repatriation: "The main task to be performed is to encourage and assist in every way possible their early return to their country of origin." Although the IRO, later dubbed "the largest travel agency in the world," was created by the West to facilitate the emigration of displaced persons, its founding charter nonetheless stated that the "re-establishment of refugees should be contemplated only in cases indicated clearly in the Constitution." This cautious language intentionally avoided friction with Soviet-bloc countries demanding the prompt return of their nationals. The constitution also stipulated that "the expenses of repatriation to the extent practicable should be charged to Germany": already intent on exacting enormous material and financial reparations from its own occupation zone, the Soviet Union certainly approved.

Finally, the concern of the IRO to "ensure that its assistance is not exploited by persons...unwilling to return to their countries of origin because they prefer idleness to facing the hardships of helping in the reconstruction of their countries" acknowledged the acute manpower crisis faced by Eastern European countries. During the negotiations, both Western and Eastern European representatives shared the view that the duty of reconstruction was incumbent upon European nationals. Soviet-bloc delegates repeatedly demanded that preferential treatment be given to the courageous repatriates willing to help rebuild their countries, a position strongly supported by France, the United Kingdom, and Belgium. Western European sensitivity to Eastern European reconstruction needs stemmed from a common experience of devastation and rebuilding. In 1946, Continental Europe as a whole was still waging "production battles" involving the recruitment (and in the Soviet Union, coercive enrollment) of citizens into the drive toward economic recovery. Stipulated in the IRO constitution, the exclusion of displaced persons who intended to escape "hardships" at home in favor of the "idleness" of refugee life did not only reflect the productivist climate of the period: it also initiated the formal separation of political and economic migrants in postwar asylum policies.

The multiple references to retribution, repatriation, and reconstruction in the IRO constitution led American anti-Communist commentators to lament the overly compromising tone of the text. James Reston believed that, in spite of the Soviet withdrawal, "there is now in operation an organization that not only does not have the membership of the Soviet Union, but is much weaker than it would have been but for Moscow's amendments."[96] Supporters of the IRO invoked the urgency of the crisis to justify these concessions. "A sore on the body of mankind which is not safe to ignore," as Eleanor Roosevelt described it, the DP problem required a prompt solution. They also dispelled the charge of exaggerated Western overtures. Cooperation with the Soviet Union, Penrose retorted, never "encroached on the liberties of the refugees and their right to choose freely between repatriation and resettlement."[97] If the exclusionary clauses of the IRO constitution were inspired by anti-Fascist language and principles, its more inclusive aspects ran indeed counter to Communist demands.

Contrary to Soviet expectations, the IRO expanded the notion of displaced persons and brought it closer to the concept of political refugees. In deference to the Soviet position, the drafters of the IRO constitution initially separated the two categories. Displaced persons were defined as civilians forcibly uprooted by the war outside of their country of origin and soon to be returned to their proper national environment. If the reasons for their displacement "have ceased to exist," the constitution stipulated, "they should be repatriated as soon as possible." The much narrower category of refugee only encompassed the victims of Nazi or Fascist regimes, mainly Jews and Spanish Republicans who were "unable or unwilling" to avail themselves of the protection of their country of nationality. Yet the possibility offered to all DPs to express "valid objections" against returning to their countries eventually blurred the distinction drawn between displaced persons and refugees. When the IRO formally replaced UNRRA in June 1947, the overwhelming majority of DPs were treated as permanent asylum seekers. "Once repatriation ceased," its historian Louise Holborn acknowledged, "the Organization had under its mandate only refugees."

The list of "valid objections" in the IRO constitution included "persecution, or fear based on reasonable grounds of persecution because of race, religion, nationality or political opinion." This explicit mention of "persecution" was a radical innovation in the history of political asylum. It was undoubtedly assumed throughout the interwar period that refugees were indeed persecuted people. But the term "persecution" never appeared in international conventions, which, like the landmark 1933 Geneva Convention, primarily defined refugees as stateless persons. Subsequent arrangements secured in 1936 and 1938 under the League of Nations on behalf of German émigrés similarly identified statelessness, and not victimization, as the salient feature of refugees.[98] The Evian Conference, convened in July 1938 by Franklin D. Roosevelt to find safe havens for Germans and Austrians "who must emigrate on account of their political opinions, religious beliefs or racial origin," seemed to change course. But, drafted during the heyday of appeasement, the founding resolution of the Intergovernmental Committee on Refugees created by the Evian Conference on July 14, 1938, cautiously refrained from referring to "persecution." Eight years later, the 1946 IRO constitution finally offered a bolder terminology. Persecuting countries were not directly named, yet "persecution," as well as "political objection," became the main factors warranting the protection of displaced persons.

The introduction of these new concepts was to significantly alter the attribution of refugee status in the decades following World War Two. Prior to the creation of the IRO, one legal scholar noted, "an individual applying for refugee status did not have to justify his claim in the light of the specific circumstances which obliged him to leave his former home country."[99] But as the Cold War intensified, access to the DP world became increasingly dependent on a decipherable and convincing narrative of persecution. Elaborate "screening" procedures, first carried out by Allied armies under UNRRA and more systematically by the civilian "eligibility officers" trained by the IRO, sought to purge refugee camps from unworthy types and to ascertain the "democratic" identity of the DPs. As the next chapter describes, the rigorous separation of the wheat from the chaff attempted by Allied humanitarianism in occupied Germany shaped new legal and political definitions of asylum seekers in the postwar era.

2

"Who is a Refugee?"

FROM "VICTORS' JUSTICE" TO ANTI-COMMUNISM

"WHO IS A genuine, bona fide and deserving refugee?": this question in a handbook for IRO field personnel summarized one of the most daunting challenges faced by the soldiers and civilians in charge of the DPs.[1] Throughout the crisis, the detection of "true" and "false" refugees in occupied Germany and Austria remained a permanent concern for Western occupation authorities. Compared by a contemporary jurist to a "net cast by the Allies to fish a chosen few among stateless people, displaced persons and refugees," the so-called screening of the DP population amounted to a massive enterprise of individual scrutiny.[2] This policy started in earnest in March 1946 after UNRRA resolution 92 called for the "complete registration of all displaced persons in assembly centers" and the compilation of "occupational data," particularly within the large group of Polish DPs. A conciliatory gesture toward Eastern European governments, this move encouraged "prompt repatriation" by offering to countries of origin accurate information on displaced nationals willing to return to their homeland.[3] When repatriation slowed to a standstill, however, screening procedures became harsher. By mid-1946, the avowed goal of Allied counterintelligence and UNRRA personnel was the expulsion of suspicious "war criminals, collaborators, quislings or traitors of whatever race, nationality, or religion" from the DP camps.[4] After July 1947, the civilian staff of the International Refugee Organization followed a similar course of action but also faced the arrival of new "infiltrees" and "escapees" who had crossed the Iron Curtain. From 1946 to 1951, the identification of "genuine" refugees among Europe's displaced persons served as a testing ground for the granting of political asylum in the Cold War era.

The vetting of the DP population was, however, motivated by more pragmatic concerns. Chief among them was the desire of Allied authorities to drastically reduce the number of camp inhabitants by denying them benefits or forcing them on the German labor market. In early 1946, General Joseph McNarney and Field Marshal Bernard Montgomery, the American and British commanders in occupied Germany, respectively, requested the imposition of strict cut-off dates after which a "displaced person would be set to work as a civilian in Germany living on German rations and under conditions parallel to Germans."[5] In April 1946, the US Departments of State and War recommended the closure of all DP centers in the US zone, making an exception for Jewish camps. But six months before the midterm elections of November 1946, Harry Truman ruled out this risky option. "The Poles in this country and the Catholic Church are simply going to have a spam if we close out these camps," Truman replied to his secretary of state, James Byrnes.[6] Yet the American commitment to the DP camp system did not halt efforts to bring down the number of refugees under Allied care. In instructions issued in April 1946, the US army was ordered to immediately remove or arrest any DP not entitled to "United Nations care." Within a few weeks, British and French occupation authorities adopted a similar policy.[7]

In addition, the screening of displaced persons limited access to the precious resources provided by Allied armies, international agencies, and the charitable organizations working under their umbrella. In contrast with the rudimentary aid and diplomatic protection afforded to stateless persons by the League of Nations during the interwar period, the DPs gradually received a wide range of material, medical, legal, and educational services. Among the millions of homeless persons in Central Europe, observed a New York Times correspondent, "the best cared for at the moment are the approximately 1, 000, 000 persons in displaced persons camps in Germany."[8] Largely funded by American subsidies, this new humanitarian largesse employed selection methods resembling those used by New Deal agencies or emerging European welfare states. "Eligibility to receive services," the IRO historian Louise Holborn explained, "would require quite as much investigation as would the recipients of any social benefits." Although the process "took into account certain political aspects," its purpose was to determine who among the refugees was entitled to international humanitarian assistance.[9]

Holborn largely understated the significance of these "political aspects": the screening of displaced persons crucially imported the "politics of retribution" into the extraterritorial refugee enclaves of Germany and Austria. Across Europe, the aftermath of the war saw a general sorting out of good and bad, victim and victimizer, hero and villain, and the DPs were categorized according to similar binaries. This retributive dimension was not lost on contemporary observers. The French international jurist Henry Monneray drew a revealing parallel between the punishment of traitors and collaborators in a national context and the banishment of suspicious refugees by Allied powers. For the former assistant prosecutor at the Nuremberg Trials, the exclusion of specific categories of DPs was grounded in the premise of "international indignity," an expanded version of the charge of "national indignity" leveled against collaborators in various parts of liberated Europe.[10] In the historical scholarship on postwar retribution and trials, the prosecution of Nazi criminals at Nuremberg is commonly described as the only international exception to the policies of "national cleansing" carried out by postwar regimes in Western and Eastern Europe alike.[11] Yet as a supranational instance of *épuration*, Allied screenings were similarly intended to sanitize the DP community by expunging unworthy types from its midst. Tellingly, this process borrowed from denazification proceedings. Just as German citizens filled out much-despised questionnaires designed by Allied occupiers to uncover active supporters of Nazism, their DP neighbors were handed "eligibility questionnaires" issued by UNRRA to verify nationalities, dates of displacement, and wartime personal histories. Strong connections existed therefore between denazification, retribution, and the detection of illegitimate refugees. If the granting of DP status was an international recognition of victimization, its denial was tantamount to a guilty verdict.

To be sure, not all the components of the "last million" faced the prospect of exclusion. Singled out early on as "persecutees," Holocaust survivors found in liberated Germany, as well as subsequent Jewish border crossers from Eastern Europe, were spared the travails of eligibility review. The 320,000 non-Jewish Polish DPs still present in Germany in March 1946 were similarly granted DP status once they expressed "valid objections" to returning to Communist Poland. Nonetheless, Allied repatriation efforts and the presence within this group of ethnic Ukrainians who lived under Polish rule until 1939 imposed on them stringent registration and sifting procedures.[12] Baltic nationals and Soviet Ukrainians who had at various points during the war served in the German army formed two categories particularly targeted by military and counterintelligence investigations. Under the IRO, new categories of self-declared political dissidents were scrupulously vetted. Not limited to the "relief and rehabilitation" of postwar refugees, the international response to the DP crisis also generated a systematic monitoring of identities, wartime credentials, and persecution narratives. A baffled IRO official outlined the complexity of the task: "How to discover, within this enormous flux of uprooted beings, the authentic refugees and displaced persons?"[13]

The confounding presence of illegitimate refugees among the millions of displaced civilians in liberated Germany did not, however, come as a surprise. During the war, American planners expected that "the leading collaborators will probably be disposed of by the United Nations or their own irate nationals, but the rank and file of local fascists—the little Lavals and Quislings who are known only in their own communities—may be punished by being rendered homeless."[14] Yet Allied forces only paid limited attention to the purge of collaborators prior to the liberation of Europe. They simply decided that "ex-enemy nationals" encountered by advancing armies would not receive international help, except those, like Jews, who were the victims of Nazi persecution. Only in August 1945 was a distinction between eligible and ineligible displaced civilians explicitly drawn. UNRRA resolution 71 stipulated that the "Administration will not assist displaced persons who may be detained...on charges of having collaborated with the enemy." The Western Allies proceeded then to divide the DPs in three types: "good who accepted repatriation, good who did not want to return for legitimate reasons, and bad (collaborators, criminals, etc.)."[15] The overall assumption was that the DP population undoubtedly included a collaborationist component: a vast number of "unrepatriables," according to the Soviets, or a smaller group hidden among legitimate DPs in the eyes of the Western Allies.

The unchecked entrance of displaced civilians into Allied "assembly centers" during the chaotic first months of occupation reinforced this belief. "In the pandemonium that followed the war," Allied officials worried, "how many slipped into the camps without the right to do so? How many sought a shelter simply to evade justice at home?"[16] The American relief worker A.J. Gould offered a gloomy answer: "All of these people, the voluntary workers for the Greater Reich, the SS, the evacuees, the Nazis as well as the anti-Nazis, the people who came to help Germany as well as the slave laborers, flocked to the camps and were admitted."[17] Ira Hirschmann, the American business executive who toured Germany in 1946 on behalf of UNRRA's director, Fiorello La Guardia, claimed that great numbers of non-Jewish refugees had in fact been "displaced of their own volition," an accusation also made at the time by American Jewish organizations.[18] By the end of 1945, however, the completion of the DP camp network enabled a better tracking of potential suspects. In the three Western occupation zones, UNRRA administered 227 assembly centers in which the identification of intruders was easier to perform. "Interviewing people on the spot had many advantages," a participant in such interrogations acknowledged later, "the main one being that witnesses could be produced...people who knew the DP and could give information as to his activities before the war."[19]

A first round of systematic screening was carried out between June 1946 and July 1947, the last twelve months of UNRRA operations. In the American occupation zone alone, thirty-eight vetting teams, working six days a week, reviewed the eligibility of 330,000 DPs at the pace of forty interrogations a day.[20] While UNRRA workers tried to ascertain the identity of refugees, the investigation and eviction of suspected "security threats" remained the prerogative of military personnel. Yet young American soldiers on the verge of demobilization, poorly trained and seldom able to understand Slavic languages, struggled to grasp Eastern European complexities. Adding to this disorganization was the existence of three separate DP policies in the American, British and French zones. These differences pertained in particular to "cut-off dates" after which entering refugees could not obtain DP status. Moreover, the widespread forgery of personal documents by refugees trying to avoid repatriation severely hindered their identification. "By 1945 the production of false identity papers in Europe had become almost a major industry," Sir Frederick Morgan, the British senior officer who served as chief of UNRRA Operations for Germany, pointed out in his memoirs.[21]

Despite these chaotic conditions, some semblance of a process was put in place. Informed by the practices of the International Military Tribunal at Nuremberg, the purge of unlawful DPs relied on various lists of collaborationist and military organizations compiled since 1945 by Allied bodies such as the Berlin Document Center. Whereas the detection of wanted war criminals was left to intelligence units such as the Counter Intelligence Corps in the US zone, military and UNRRA screeners sought out "impostors" who lied about their wartime experiences. Evidence of active duty in German military formations was easily uncovered when SS tattoos were spotted on the arm of interviewees. Yet the exact status of Estonians, Latvians, Lithuanians, and Ukrainians who had joined the German army was often impossible to determine. Proven members of the murderous Baltic paramilitary Selbstchutz ("self-defense") units or the Ukrainian SS "Galizien" division were successfully screened out. In the absence of conclusive evidence, however, a clear distinction between volunteers and draftees was difficult to establish. Veterans of German units, such as the former soldiers of the Latvian Legion, invariably charged that compulsory mobilization was inescapable and that their struggle was above all directed against Soviet occupation. When they did not pass themselves off as Polish citizens in order to avoid repatriation to the USSR, Ukrainians similarly claimed that enrollment in the Wehrmacht helped them avoid compulsory labor in Germany and that they were equally motivated by anti-Soviet nationalist sentiment.[22]

Prior to the start of IRO operations, however, anti-Communist credentials did not easily earn claimants the benefit of the doubt. The whole
screening process, complained a Lithuanian DP publication, was an
"American-Gestapo farce" marred by blatant arbitrariness: "a changed
answer, a forgotten date, a charge of collaboration, any fact that nameless
and faceless officials might seize on becomes a nightmare for the DPs."[23]
A French visitor of DP camps was puzzled by the "striking mistrust of
DPs in the controlling authorities. In their mind, the purpose of screening
was to make them plead guilty for acts that they did not commit. Every
question sets a trap."[24] In the United States, advocates of Soviet DPs
charged that screening officers were under explicit orders "to expel a fixed
percentage" by imposing "real terror" on displaced persons.[25] The presence
of a "few collaborators, disguised Germans and even war criminals" was
undeniable, a British UNRRA official admitted for his part, sympathizing
with Soviet DPs, but a pervasive atmosphere of fear forced many innocents
back to the USSR: "One day perhaps, returnees will finally reveal how the
infamous 'screenings' conducted by UNRRA actually worked."[26]

Yet despite being denounced by targeted refugees as a "time of terror" and
"mental suffering," the first round of screening did not yield a high number of
exclusions. Out of 320,000 DPs screened by the US army and UNRRA by
July 1947, 12.3 percent were declared ineligible. During the same period,
178,000 DPs were screened in the British zone, out of which 10.4 percent
were rejected. French authorities checked the eligibility of 36,000 refugees in
their zone but only disqualified 2.8 percent.[27] Most of the refugees expelled
from the DP camps were simply handed over to German authorities or left to
fend for themselves without further prosecution. Others moved to different
camps with the hope of being found eligible under new circumstances. And
for all their efforts to sift refugees, military interrogators and UNRRA
workers only reduced the DP population by about 3 percent.

When in July 1947 the IRO took over UNRRA operations, the fear that
poor vetting had excluded many uncertain cases prompted the organization
to launch a retroactive review of more than 700,000 cases.[28] The scope of this
second round extended beyond occupied Germany, since the IRO was also
mandated to care for the smaller DP populations in Austria and Italy. In
addition, the IRO faced a sudden surge in the number of applicants for the
coveted DP status. As the American welfare worker Eileen Egan noted, refugees who had until then been fearful of entrusting themselves to UNRRA
now "came out of the cellars of the bombed-out streets of German towns to
ask for help in settling overseas."[29] Created with this goal in mind, the IRO

viewed screening operations "of first importance in its work": the detection of "war criminals" not only helped cleanse the DP camps of illegitimate DPs but also ensured the emigration of "clean refugees" to reception countries in Europe and overseas.[30]

The search for unlawful refugees, which had been slapdash and chaotic under UNRRA, turned into a complex bureaucratic venture when conducted by the civilian personnel of the IRO. "It is a formidable fact that the Refugees have filled in more forms and documents concerning their past history than we in 'form satiated England' could ever imagine!" protested the Refugee Defence Committee, a British advocacy group supported by Lord Beveridge, the Nobel Prize winner Norman Angell, and the journalist-politician Harold Nicolson. "It does not need a complicated system of legal jurisdiction, such as that set up by the IRO to discover the fact that a person is a Refugee."[31] This labyrinth of forms and questionnaires was not the only innovation introduced by the IRO. The organization also required from its eligibility personnel "high moral standards" as well as extensive knowledge of European history, politics, and law. A clear illustration of this new professional ethos was the *Manual for Eligibility Officers*, reprinted and amended three times during the existence of the IRO. From the first 1948 edition, a short interpretative guide, the manual expanded into a 160-page volume issued for the last time in 1950.[32] This growth reflected the constant addition of historical information pertaining to various categories of refugees as well as a multitude of sample cases designed to guide eligibility officers in their decision process.[33] Juggling a combination of historical facts, refugee testimonies, and their own personal intuition, IRO officers were asked to carefully consider each individual case on the merits: "A heavy responsibility weighs upon those entrusted with the fate of a man or a family. According to the decision reached, a petitioner and his relatives will either be assisted or sent back to the misery from which he hoped to be rescued."[34]

A Review Board for Eligibility Appeals, created in November 1947, similarly bolstered professionalism and due process. Dubbed "semi-judicial machinery" in administrative language, this internal institution served as an appeal tribunal for refugees turned down by IRO screeners. Its chairman was Marcel de Baer, a Belgian lawyer and judge who had served during the war as a member of the United Nations War Crimes Commission and drafted the plans for the Nuremberg International Tribunal.[35] The board's seat was at the IRO headquarters in Geneva, but a team of five experienced international jurists traveled to DP camps in Germany, Austria, and Italy to directly hear appellants. "From a juridical standpoint," observed a scholar of international law in 1948, "here is the most interesting institution created for the displaced persons."[36]

Contrary to the methods employed by military personnel and UNRRA, the IRO eligibility process therefore relied on clear juridical guidelines. It was "incumbent upon claimants" (*actori incumbat probatio*) to prove the facts presented in support of their arguments, but "if there was no apparent reason to exclude a candidate, it was not his duty to furnish proof of his right to be included."[37] The burden of proof was only on refugees unable to correct an "unfavorable impression," who were then pressed to turn in personal documents, family pictures, sworn statements, and testimonials. IRO officers then compared this information with the sources already at their disposal, such as intelligence information on particular individuals or detailed historical reports documenting the events relevant to the petition. The process of discovering whether a refugee was entitled to receive DP status, the eligibility staff was told, "is a cooperative venture between him and the organization."[38] In practice, however, this idealistic partnership between claimants and screeners was hampered by deceitful testimonies and fraudulent declarations. As an IRO official reported, "many know that they only have to destroy their identity papers to force eligibility officers in a position of having to accept a 'plausible story'...and they also know what will be accepted as a plausible story."[39] To visitors to DP camps, it was clear that "the displaced persons committees are clandestinely circulating the right answers to the questionnaires used by the IRO to determine eligibility."[40] Within the organization, it was widely believed that "after many months of observation and listening, the DPs are told what to say and know how to craft an acceptable story leading to eligibility."[41]

To counteract the propensity of interviewees to lie, IRO screeners where taught how to recognize untruthful statements. The *Manual for Eligibility Officers* included samples of "false pretenses," a collection of claims made by those who wished to hide their true identity or past actions. Because of their importance in the determination of DP status, dates of displacement were falsified frequently in the course of interrogations. Baltic refugees, for instance, knew that forced laborers sent to Germany following the invasion of the USSR in June 1941 were generally accepted as DPs by both UNRRA and the IRO. Those who had fled the advance of the Red Army in 1944, however, looked more suspicious due to the presence among them of German army volunteers and conscripts. A date of displacement prior to 1941 was also likely to raise concerns, since many Baltic nationals (including those of ethnic German descent) voluntarily resettled in the Reich to flee Soviet annexation or to earn better wages in Germany. Some of them had in the process received German citizenship and faced disqualification for IRO protection.[42]

Yet even when exposed, such falsifications did not necessarily bar refugees from receiving DP status. The IRO recognized that "many applicants, even bona fide refugees, are under various pressures to make false statements; it is important to regard refugees as ordinary human beings with ordinary faults and failings." IRO officers were therefore advised to concentrate on facts and to disregard previous false statements "except when there is a doubt about a refugee." Some Review Board members opposed this leniency, particularly so in the case of DPs unable to present identification papers. After "individually examining thousands of refugees," Marcel de Baer concluded that DPs without documents had "something to hide from the IRO."[43] His French colleague Henri Trémeaud proposed a more benevolent approach: "Let us take people at their word, even if they do not have papers or have destroyed them out of fear of forcible repatriation."[44] Throughout its existence, the IRO pledged to guarantee "justice and equity in all areas." Precise guidelines and uniform jurisprudence were supposed to shield its staff from improvisation and arbitrariness.

The complexity of the cases encountered made this lofty goal often unachievable. A Review Board report issued in 1948 regretted that "there is still much uncertainty in the application of the IRO definitions and a large number of eligibles should never really have been considered to be the concern of the organization."[45] These shortcomings were at times justified by the extraordinary workload imposed upon IRO agents who in some cases interviewed more than one thousand refugees per month. More frustrating was the realization that screening operations unavoidably extended well beyond the realm of law. "From a body established to apply the Constitution of the IRO," conceded Marcel de Baer, "the Review Board had developed into an organ having the characters of an investigator, psychologist, and judge."[46] Henri Trémeaud similarly recognized the importance of personal intuition in the determination of DP status: "The only way to sort out the truth from falsehoods is to hear a claimant and sometimes a few witnesses. Even patient interrogations do not always ascertain their sincerity. In this case, decisions are based on plausibility and the benefit of the doubt."[47] The records of hearings conducted by the Review Board indeed show that both judicial and extrajudicial factors were taken into consideration in order to ascertain "who is a refugee."[48] They also shed light on the main types of refugees targeted by the IRO between 1947 and 1951: ethnic Germans, high profile collaborators,

Baltic and Ukrainian veterans of the German army, and those in the growing category of "economic refugees."

The constitution of the IRO stipulated that the approximately twelve million ethnic German expellees from East-Central Europe who flooded the occupation zones of Germany at the end of the war were not entitled to international care. As a result, displaced persons and expellees formed two distinct categories of refugees simultaneously living on German soil, with rare points of contacts between them. Only in exceptional cases did the IRO assist German expellees "by harboring fresh arrivals for one or two nights until other provisions could be made."[49] Otherwise, sharp physical and institutional boundaries separated the DPs from their ethnic German counterparts. Yet for various reasons, numerous expellees sought admission in the DP world. Living conditions in IRO camps were far superior to those prevailing in reception centers administered by local German authorities. Moreover, DP status enabled emigration to a Western European country or the New World. To that end, ethnic Germans seeking IRO assistance registered themselves as Czechs, Slovaks, Poles, Romanians, or Hungarians; whether as a strategy or out of national sentiments, they paradoxically claimed the citizenship of countries committed to their full removal and dispossession. In accordance with IRO policies, expellees where routinely turned down by eligibility officers but often appealed their rejection. Asked to weigh in, the Review Board investigated the ancestry of appellants suspected of being of German descent. "In order to ascertain the ethnic origin of an individual," explained IRO officials, "it is not enough to examine his name, religion, language or the school he attended. It is also necessary to scrutinize his past."[50]

To reverse an initial negative decision, ethnic German appellants were indeed required to provide extensive documentation on their genealogy. In the case of a petitioner initially rejected as an ethnic German from Hungary, the Review Board stated his appeal "produced conclusive evidence in the form of at least 20 original birth and marriage certificates proving that his parents, grandparents and their forefathers were of non-Germanic origin. He himself speaks little German. Found within the mandate."[51] Native fluency in a non-German language also helped suspected expellees to win a case. In one instance, a Yugoslav appellant became a DP thanks to impeccable linguistic skills: "His name sounds German, but his mother's maiden name is typically Hungarian. He has a perfect command of Serbo-Croat without the slightest accent. Benefit of the doubt."[52] In general, however, the Review Board easily unmasked the German descent of such applicants. Titus Hoffman, a Polish citizen born in Lemberg under the Austro-Hungarian Empire, was mobilized into the Polish armed forces in 1939 before being captured by the Wehrmacht.[53] He then escaped to Soviet-annexed Eastern Poland, which was overrun by the Germans in June 1941, and lived there until the end of the war: "Name Hoffman, as well as mother's maiden name Lehner, suggests German origin; signed a *volksliste* [i.e., registered in the German People's List which classified inhabitants of German descent in Nazi-occupied territories] in 1943, but claims it was done under duress. Does not furnish evidence that it was so in his case. Petitioner is a volksdeutscher from Poland, residing in Germany."[54] Similar arguments were advanced in the case of Robert Reisenbuchler, a refugee from Transylvania: "The names of his antecedents create a strong presumption of German ethnic origin. Mother born Mueller. Claims his mother tongue is Hungarian, but according to interpreter, speaks poor Hungarian."[55]

Evidence of formal expulsion from East-Central Europe on the basis of German ethnicity was another incriminating factor. Janos Riegler was a petitioner whose descent proved difficult to ascertain, despite his German-sounding family name. Yet despite being unable to precisely establish Riegler's origin, the Review Board rejected his petition on behalf of the fact that "there is no doubt that his wife, who is unquestionably of German ethnic origin, was expelled as such from Hungary."[56] In another case, a refugee named Josef Tetz admitted having worked as a journalist for a Sudeten German newspaper owned by the pro-Nazi Sudeten German Party led by Konrad Henlein. He nonetheless described himself as a Slovak displaced from his homeland, but his acknowledgment "that he was thrown out of the Czechoslovak Republic in April 1945 and not allowed to return by virtue of President Beneš' decree of August 2, 1945" offered indisputable ground for exclusion.[57] In this case, as in several others, evidence of forcible eviction outweighed all other attenuating circumstances. Even a strong anti-Nazi record did not enable refugees of German origin to be recognized as DPs:

> Petitioner, an exceptionally deserving case, was an anti-Nazi who had tried to escape from the German army to join the Allies in 1942. Sentenced to death by a German martial court, and pardoned. Helped prisoners of war, passed over to the Allied lines and cooperated with US troops in psychological warfare against Germany. Nevertheless, he is a German national in Austria who might be transferred to Germany and as such excluded from IRO assistance.[58]

Similarly, the Review Board rejected the petition of Wilhelm Gernert, a deserter from the German army defined by the IRO as "a Czech from the Sudetenland of German ethnic origin."[59]

To clear these hurdles, numerous ethnic German appellants portrayed themselves as victims of Communist oppression in order to increase their chance of admission. Although the IRO considered punishment for ideological dissent a legitimate form of persecution, this strategy generally failed. The Hungarian Lorenz Ruff, for instance, "alleged he had ridiculed the three years plan on the platform of the tramcar in Budapest. Spent 8 days in prison." Against his claim, the Review Board discovered that "his mother's name was Schutzmanhoffer" and found him a mere "economic emigrant who used the event described above as a pretext to leave his country."[60] Friedrich Enz, a twenty-five-year-old Pole from Kraków, told the following story: sent by the Germans to slave labor in Silesia, he was later captured by the advancing Red Army and forced to dig trenches. He returned to Poland after the war but his "refusal to join the communists" eventually forced him to flee to Austria via Czechoslovakia. As in similar cases, the Review Board argued that "the natural supposition is that he was expelled as a Volksdeutscher, despite poor spoken German." Benefit of the doubt could not be granted since "it was impossible to establish with certainty wartime and post-war activities."[61] In her official history of the IRO, Louise Holborn wrote that the agency "made it a rule to make individual decisions and...not to eliminate a candidate merely because he belonged to a certain group."[62] Yet, as seen above, a notion of collective guilt undoubtedly prevailed in the case of German expellees. Whereas anti-Communist credentials soon helped other questionable candidates to obtain DP status, the screening of ethnic Germans under the IRO remained unaffected by the evolving Cold War.

The Prague Coup of February 25, 1948, nonetheless marked a turning point in the governance of Europe's displaced persons. Interpreted by the United States and its European Allies as a signal of alarming Soviet expansion, the Communist putsch in Czechoslovakia also influenced the policies of the IRO. "As a result of the changes in the political scene after 1948," explained the IRO general director Donald Kingsley, "the organization liberalized the interpretation of its own definitions in order to fall into line with a wider conception of a refugee."[63] The IRO jurist Henri Trémeaud similarly commented that "as the general situation of the world evolved, so did the policies of the Organization."[64] Louise Holborn succinctly described the main effect of this policy shift: "As the Cold War developed, there was growing appreciation of the fact that many persons might technically have collaborated with the Germans and yet were in refugee status."[65] Anti-Communist criteria, in short, played an increasing role in the screening operations conducted in the wake of the Communist takeover in East-Central Europe.

High-ranking officials from "ex-enemy countries" did not benefit from this new climate, however. Having escaped retribution at home, several collaborationist leaders and civil servants appealed to the IRO for legal and material protection. The most prominent among them was Admiral Miklós Horthy, the ex-regent of Hungary who after the war spent the rest of his life in exile in Portugal. Submitted in December 1948, Horthy's petition exemplified the arguments of political collaborators and public figures seeking refuge in the West through the IRO: as shields against Bolshevism, leaders and officials of puppet regimes depicted themselves as authentic defenders of their homeland. Unfortunately for his cause, Horthy found in Marcel de Baer a thorough prosecutor with solid footing in the history of World War II: "The futility of the argument that Hungary's policy has never been directed against the western powers but only against Soviet Russia immediately appears: at the time when Hungary joined the Axis, Germany was at war with Poland and the Western Powers only, and not with Russia." Moreover, added de Baer, "if there had been a real discrepancy between the policy of his government and his own views, it would have been possible for him, by resigning from his post, to show the world his disagreement." Admittedly, "Horthy did not see eye to eye with Hitler on every subject." He remained, however, "the first and foremost member of the clique which put Hungary into the war on the side of the Germans and it is impossible to accept that his role in this connection was other than one of first importance." As a result, the IRO concluded that Horthy had provided "voluntary assistance to enemy forces" and denied him recognition.[66] Other upper-echelon collaborators were subjected to the same severity. László Nagy, for instance, was a Hungarian barrister who served as secretary of state for justice in the Government of National Unity led in the last months of the war by the fascist Arrow Cross party leader Ferenc Szálasi. In his appeal, submitted in 1949, Nagy challenged his categorization as war criminal, "since anti-bolshevism and love for one's country do not constitute war crimes."[67] The Review Board's uniform policy, however, was to reject appeals presented by collaborationist civil servants.

Only in rare instances did political collaborators receive IRO status. The petition presented to the Review Board by the Slovak refugee Belo Martinovic is a case in point. A former leader of the Hlinka Youth Organization in Bratislava (the youth division of the main collaborationist party in wartime Slovakia), he was declared ineligible by the IRO in 1947. At the end of 1949, the Review Board reversed this negative decision on the grounds of "additional information substantiating that his reluctance to repatriate is based on fear of persecution for his political and religious opinions."[68] According to

Marcel de Baer, "an unexpected amount of information on events during the war" could now justify reversals of judgments. Advised by American specialists in Eastern European politics and history, the IRO eligibility personnel acquired accurate knowledge on wartime governments, collaborationist groups, and resistance organizations: "It is only through the precise examination of these tangled facts," stated de Baer, "that the behavior of an applicant can be ascertained."[69] Theoretically only concerned with historical evidence, constitutionality, and due process, the Review Board was supposed to refrain from passing political judgments. For particularly vociferous American anti-Communists, this commitment to neutrality masked blatant political bias: "Four years after the war ended, IRO still speaks of Nazi persecution but never a word about Soviet tyranny." The rejection of genuine freedom fighters from the Eastern Bloc, they charged, amounted to "crimes against humanity."[70]

The aftermath of the Prague Coup, however, led to a new understanding of wartime events, particularly so in the case of Baltic and Ukrainian refugees who had served in German uniform or helped the German army as "Hiwis" (voluntary assistants). Simon Wiesenthal, who shortly after his liberation from the Mauthausen concentration camp assisted American counterintelligence in the tracking of Nazi criminals hiding in Upper Austria, took notice of this evolution. The IRO, the Nazi-hunter charged in October 1948, was outrageously lenient toward suspected war criminals: "Where are all those thousands of ex-enemy Lithuanians, Latvians from the American Zone? Where are the thousands members of the Ukrainian division Galizien infiltrated in 1947?... You have to know that all these peoples are now United Nations DPs; many of them live in IRO camps or have emigrated with the help of IRO."[71] As a founder of the Jewish Historical Documentation Center created in Linz in February 1947, Wiesenthal collected information on Nazi criminals and provided the IRO with lists of former German army conscripts believed to be responsible for the murder of Jews.[72] Despite his allegations, the IRO reversed several ineligibility decisions. The Lithuanian Juozas Zubrickas, for example, was initially denied DP status following Wiesenthal's claim that he was responsible for the killing of ten Jews. On appeal, the Review Board found the charge unsubstantiated and declared him a DP.[73]

While there is no evidence that the IRO engaged in blanket pardoning of war criminals, the charge of "voluntary assistance to enemy forces" undeniably lost much of its incriminating potential as the Cold War unfolded. In 1949, the IRO considered that due to a Nazi decree of forcible mobilization in April 1943, all Baltic refugees who had been coercively drafted into the

German army after this date could technically be declared eligible. In addition, the Review Board decided to take into account not only the wartime actions of appellants but also their "moral intention." This emphasis on ideological motives paved the way for the clearance of "volunteers" who had enlisted in German units prior to 1943. If their "moral intention" was to oppose the Soviet regime without manifest hostility toward the Western powers, members of this category were no longer automatically barred from DP status.[74] The successful appeal presented by Juris Krauls, a Latvian who voluntarily joined the Waffen-SS prior to April 1943, is revealing of this new trend. In his petition, Krauls skillfully described the anti-Soviet motivations of his fellow Baltic soldiers, whether volunteers or conscripts: "We started to defend ourselves against the Soviet peril and bloodshed after NKVD killed many thousands...Somebody may think, we had only the right to die or to go to Siberia and not defend ourselves, only because USSR was a member of UN, though the worst member." To increase his chances of admission, Krauls attached to his file American newspaper clippings from July 1950 in which Senator Harley M. Kilgore, a Democrat from West Virginia, and Representative Paul W. Shafer, a Republican from Michigan, called for Communists to be "put behind a high fence in a concentration camp."[75] This softening of eligibility criteria was indeed in line with the evolution of American refugee policies. In an amendment to the Displaced Persons Act of 1948 passed in June 1950, the US Congress liberalized the admission of Jewish DPs in the United States but also considered Baltic Waffen-SS units "as separate and distinct in purpose, ideology, activities and qualifications for membership from the German SS." Their members, the amended DP Act stipulated, no longer belonged to "a movement hostile to the Government of the United States."[76] The IRO implemented this provision by dismissing the charge of "voluntary assistance to enemy forces" in the case of Baltic nationals. The new policy also affected the former soldiers of the Ukrainian Waffen-SS "Galizien" division who sought DP status. After consultation with the Ukrainian Central Relief Committee, it was also decided that the unit was recruited by force and not composed of voluntary collaborators.[77] The official IRO historian, Louise Holborn, openly admitted that such a measure likely helped several war criminals and Holocaust perpetrators to unduly pass themselves off as political refugees: "A certain number of persons who have effectively and voluntarily helped enemy forces have succeeded, by concealing their actions, to be recognized within our mandate."[78] By 1950, refugees deemed "impostors" and "security threats" in the days of UNRRA were now offered the chance to emigrate to Australia or the North American continent.

Another effect of the Cold War on DP policies was the predominance of "fear of persecution" in the evaluation of refugee claims. The IRO Constitution of December 1946 already listed "fear based on reasonable grounds of persecution because of race, nationality or political opinions" among the main objections to repatriation. In the course of their encounters with appellants, Review Board jurists further elaborated on the meaning of "fear of persecution." To retain its effectiveness, they argued, this notion had to be dissociated from "fear of punishment" irrespective of the grave consequences faced by persons rejected on this ground. This reasoning is apparent in appeals brought by Yugoslav refugees who claimed that their refusal to join the partisans during the war exposed them to persecution if they returned home. They were told in response that "fear of punishment for not having joined the Partisans is not a valid objection, whereas if it is allied with clear political objection, it may well be."[79] When three Serbian brothers who had deserted from the partisans in 1944 sought IRO protection out of fear of political retribution, they were tersely notified that "nothing in the file indicates persecution on account of political beliefs."[80] This attitude stemmed in part from the high regard for Yugoslavia among international civil servants since the days of UNRRA operations. British and American welfare officers posted in liberated Yugoslavia often ignored the retributive violence perpetrated by victorious Titoist forces and instead openly professed their admiration for the "fiery zeal" and "revolutionary enthusiasm" of heroic Partisans.[81] IRO staff members later reported that the Yugoslav government was genuinely committed to the "good reception" of its returning nationals.[82] "Fear of punishment" alone was therefore not sufficient for IRO eligibility. A Slovene refugee fully understood the importance of this nuance. A non-Communist Chetnik resister during the war, he too feared harsh treatment at the hands of the Yugoslav government. The "clarity and sincerity" of his political arguments, however, persuaded the Review Board that he also feared persecution.

These examples reveal the high stakes involved in the evaluation of dissent when DPs claimed, in conformity with the IRO constitution, to have "a genuine political conviction contrary to that of their government."[83] To be credible, the *Manual for Eligibility Officers* stipulated, political opposition had to be expressed assertively: "The absence of agreement with a regime is not sufficient. For example, the mere fact of not being communist is not adequate for valid political objections to a country with a communist government." Objection to a regime had to be evidenced by religious or political grounds, or by "proven membership to a political party…known to be subject of persecution." Applicants to DP status were therefore required to clearly articulate the reasons for political dissent or show proof of political involvement. Passivity was frowned upon: "The Organization is not obligated to prove that an applicant falls within its mandate if this person remains silent."[84] As such, the IRO offered asylum seekers strong incentives to overemphasize the political nature of their flight. The stage was set for the dramatization of persecution narratives, a key rhetorical feature of postwar refugee hearings.[85]

The entrance of Czechoslovak border crossers into the US occupation zones of Austria and Germany following the Communist seizure of power in Prague offered a unique opportunity to test the criterion of fear of persecution on a sizeable group of "political infiltrees." From 1948 to 1951, approximately twenty-five thousand Czechoslovak nationals fled to the West by taking advantage of openings in the borders with Austria and Germany.[86] Because of a "freeze order" issued in June 1947 to spare the agency additional expenditures, refugees from Communist Czechoslovakia were not initially placed under the mandate of the cash-strapped IRO. Until the summer of 1948, they were sent to rudimentary camps administered by German authorities. At times, Czechoslovak émigrés and Sudetenland ethnic Germans evicted from their homes at the end of the war inhabited the same camp, an unexpected coexistence deeply resented by the post-1948 refugees.[87] Their lot nonetheless began to improve in June 1948 after US secretary of state George Marshall called for a forceful humanitarian response.[88] The IRO promptly lifted its "freeze order" and instructed its screening personnel to evaluate the eligibility of Czechoslovaks who sought DP status. Writing in the fall of 1948 from a German village near the Czechoslovak border, the American journalist Janet Flanner reported that the IRO "at last knows what to do with a Czech when it sees one." After a long period of hesitation, the refugee agency was now prepared "for a steady, heavy stream of what are technically called political persecutees."[89]

The IRO, however, doubted that all of these refugees were political exiles fearing persecution in their martyred homeland. Many of them, the agency suspected, were more "adventurers" with transatlantic aims than political dissidents fleeing the new Communist regime. Young people who asked to "emigrate with the sole purpose of improving their material existence" were seen as especially suspicious: "Refugees with economic motives more than political claims, they are not of interest to the Organization."[90] The fact that Czechoslovak escapees routinely showed up without identification documents reinforced this assumption. "The refugees," observed Janet Flanner, "often dress like hikers and, to heighten the illusion, carry tourist-club cards, but never passports. The current refugees arrive carrying for identification only an old school certificate or a receipted bill."[91] Fearing a ploy by illegitimate intruders to seek unwarranted privileges, the IRO turned the distinction between economic migrants and political refugees into a central feature of the screening process.

The sharp distinction drawn by the IRO between economic refugees and victims of persecution marked a decisive moment in the history of political asylum in twentieth-century Europe. During the interwar period, the High Commission for Refugees (1921–30) and the Nansen International Office for Refugees (1930–38) did not differentiate between the two categories. Whether "economic" or "political," asylum seekers denaturalized by their government were collectively recognized as stateless refugees based on the determination of the League of Nations that certain groups automatically deserved this status, Armenians and Russians in particular. The first calls for the exclusion of labor migrants from international asylum programs coincided with the spread of economic depression and the refugee exodus from Nazi Germany. Called together in 1936 by the League of Nations to discuss the status of German refugees, the representatives of France, Belgium, the Netherlands, and Czechoslovakia requested maximal latitude for neighboring host countries to restrict the number of "persons who had left for economic reasons."[92] The last-ditch effort by the League of Nations to alleviate the plight of refugees from the Reich reflected their concerns: the Refugee Convention of February 10, 1938 barred "persons who leave Germany for reasons of purely personal convenience" from international protection. This new hierarchy of refugees did not appeal exclusively to proponents of restrictive immigration and asylum policies. In his landmark report on European forced population movements published on the eve of World War II, the British Liberal politician and humanitarian John Hope Simpson singled out the uniqueness of political migration. A refugee, he wrote, distinguished himself from ordinary aliens "in that he has left...not because of economic conditions or because of the economic attractions of another territory."[93]

In the immediate aftermath of the war, however, the potential presence of economic migrants among the displaced persons in Germany did not raise major concerns. To be sure, UNRRA relief workers and officials were convinced that within the predominant group of Polish DPs, few refugees qualified as political migrants. As the American welfare officer Marvin Klemme observed, "It was not the fear of political reprisals that kept most peasants and workers from returning to Poland, but rather it was the fear of conditions they would find when they got there."[94] During his visit to Germany in 1946, Ira Hirschmann similarly noticed that Polish DPs were not "politically aware of the issues and were simply taking the easiest way out through UNRRA."[95] Surveys carried out in May 1946 among Polish DPs living in UNRRA camps confirmed this assumption.[96] Yet, being exclusively committed to the return of DPs to their home countries, UNRRA disregarded the economic motivations of its refugee population. The IRO, however, had solid reasons for tracking down "adventurers": since it was in charge of the costly redistribution of displaced persons throughout the world, the agency reserved the privilege of transatlantic migration for individuals formally recognized as "persecutees."

Wary of claims of political fears disguising economic woes, IRO officers devised various strategies in order to separate proven dissidents from regular migrants. A useful method of detection was the examination of a crucial piece of identification, the so-called *Arbeitsbuch* used in postwar Czechoslovakia to document employment histories. This information enabled the Review Board to determine whether an appellant had fled for economic reasons: "It often reveals that a petitioner who claims to have been dismissed from his job for political reasons (or for refusing to join the communist party) has in fact had employment to the last day." Details gleaned from the *Arbeitsbuch* indeed helped expose deceitful refugees: "They have been forced to admit that they had told lies and that the real purpose of their flight was love of adventure, economic reasons, etc." Marcel de Baer valued this investigation method: "The benefit of this experience should not be wasted, and refugees should not be accepted unless they can produce their Arbeitsbuch."[97] When refugees claimed to have lost their identification papers, Review Board jurists required from them precise information on their employment background.

The case of Jan Izolt reveals how seemingly innocent answers quickly resulted in self-incrimination. In the course of his interview, the twenty-eight-year-old refugee singled out "his refusal to join a Work Brigade" as the main reason for his flight. After further investigation, IRO eligibility officers countered that such groups were not instruments of political coercion. Instead, they alleged, the brigades were civilian bodies created by the Czech Communist Party to enroll young workers in the hard labor necessitated by postwar reconstruction. For the IRO, refusal to enlist merely meant that Izolt preferred to flee to Germany to improve his material situation. "It was undoubtedly felt," they concluded, "that he left for economic reasons."[98] Similarly, a young Czech waiter stated that he escaped to Germany "because his father, during a birthday celebration, expressed anticommunist sentiments and was denounced. Two days later, he was informed that the police had sought him and fled to Germany." The IRO did not believe this statement since this refugee also

added that "his salary of 600 Kcs was insufficient for his needs."[99] The young
student Alois Janak was rejected on comparable grounds. Enrolled in a college
in Prague, he failed his "political examination" and consequently feared
employment discrimination. He then alluded to his scarce career options:
"A political ignorant," his petition asserted, "can expect work only in mines or
in the forest." The IRO disagreed: "Dismissal for failure to pass an examination in a subject, however tendentious, cannot be considered political persecution."[100] Overall, Czechoslovak DPs suspected of having come to Germany
to better their condition were subjected to particularly high eligibility standards. The case of Frantisek Zalesak illustrates this severity. On appeal, this
refugee told the Review Board that he feared imprisonment "because of his
democratic convictions." He nonetheless failed to impress upon his interviewers "that his anti-communist convictions were such as to make his arrest
imminent."[101]

Greater leniency toward suspected economic migrants was noticeable in
1949, however, when the IRO, pressured by the Truman administration to
accept large numbers of Iron Curtain refugees, rejected only "the few who are
naive enough to admit that they are economic emigrants."[102] This liberalization also resulted from a sharp decrease in the number of Czechoslovaks seeking DP status. The crossing of the border into the US occupation zone in
Germany had become increasingly difficult and the cost of exit permits too
exorbitant to have been used "as a method of escape by any other than the
genuine political refugees whose situation is desperate."[103] IRO screening officers were now receptive to political arguments worded in seemingly economic
terms. Tales of victimization by Communist strongmen leading to loss of
employment or the breakup of properties were considered acts of persecution. A Czechoslovak refugee claimed to have obtained after the war the
trusteeship of a butcher shop previously owned by an evicted ethnic German.
Following the Prague Coup, the Communist regime seized his newly acquired
business because of his "Western orientation." Although his argument was
entirely framed in economic terms, the IRO found him "within the mandate."[104] Benefit of the doubt was also accorded to appellants who offered
verbal guarantees that material considerations did not play a role in their
escape. Joseph Svetko, a young man born in 1925, had initially stated that his
refusal to join the Czech Communist Party "had made his position untenable
and prevented him to obtain other work."[105] His deposition convinced the
IRO that he was an economic emigrant. Yet when his case was heard on
appeal, Svetko declared that "he preferred exile to subscribing to views with
which he was not in sympathy," leading the Review Board to consider him

"a political dissident."[106] Jan Houska, a Czech miner born in 1927, was among the last petitioners who failed to provide similar assurances. Instead, he mentioned that he was given the most hazardous work in the mines after refusing to join the party. The Review Board found his "indications insufficient."[107]

The laborious identification of political dissidents and economic migrants was not exclusively carried out in Germany and Austria. In the late 1940s, other types of European asylum seekers were screened along similar lines. Stretching from the Pyrenees to the Basque Country, the French-Spanish border was another site of rigorous selection. Following worsening relations with the Francoist regime (a Spanish Republican and former resistance leader in southern France had just been executed in Madrid), the French government closed its border with Spain in March 1946. This measure triggered a wave of clandestine immigrants composed of leftists militants on the run mixed with grape pickers and beet harvesters in search of seasonal employment in France: overall, there were 40,000 entrants between 1946 and 1952.[108] Faced with such an influx, local French authorities distinguished between political refugees and "economically weak" immigrants. They also complained that manual workers in search of employment overwhelmingly outnumbered genuine victims of Francoist persecution. Since Spanish Republicans fell under the mandate of the IRO, the French government entrusted the international agency with the screening of refugees entering the country. In January 1948, the IRO deployed eligibility personnel in southwest France to single out authentic political refugees among the estimated ten thousand Spaniards who illegally crossed the border each year. "Our local delegates," explained the IRO, "operate as auxiliaries of the French authorities and sort the refugees admissible in France from those to be sent back to Spain."[109] The methods employed to unmask Spanish economic intruders bore a strong resemblance with the detection of "adventurers" in Germany and Austria. A twenty-seven-year-old refugee, for instance, was denied IRO status after telling his interviewers that he had deserted the army and "could not live under the Franco regime." He then made a costly mistake: "He also stated that life was too difficult and expensive in Spain."[110]

Like their colleagues in central Europe, IRO officers in southwest France often found the difference between political and economic refugees difficult to ascertain. The specificity of the Spanish case added to the complexity of the task. As a postwar refugee expert pointed out, "the difficult economic conditions in Spain, which can always be laid at the door of the regime, are often a cause of embarrassment when it comes to sorting out the political refugees from the economic immigrants."[111] Intricate procedures were therefore devised to ease the screening process. Gustav Kuhlman, a Swiss jurist and a legal adviser for the IRO, proposed the following course of action: "Eligibility officers could obtain their C.V. since 1936 and put on the applicant the burden of showing that they belonged to some Republican Army or Republican government service. The allegations of applicants could easily be checked from lists owned by the Spanish Government in Exile."[112] Kuhlman also warned against fraudulent claims. He knew for instance that trade unionism was compulsory under the Second Spanish Republic (1931–39). For this reason, he argued, membership in a trade union prior to the defeat of the Republicans did not offer sufficient evidence of persecution; only proven members of underground organizations banned after 1939 by Franco's Phalangist regime were to be considered political refugees.[113] These detailed guidelines hardly achieved the desired results, in part because Spanish refugee organizations assisting the IRO at border checkpoints discretely tipped off fellow nationals to the answers expected by eligibility officers. The IRO representative in France, Maurice Grimaud, acknowledged in 1949 that "in spite of the tightest discrimination, the number of Spanish refugees looked after by the IRO remains high."[114]

The separation of dissidents from alleged economic migrants was also carried out in the nascent Federal Republic of Germany. From its birth in 1949 to the completion of the Berlin Wall in 1961, West Germany faced an exodus of East German citizens who could still cross the border with relative ease. Already in charge of millions of expellees, the West German state sought to only grant refugee status (and the right to welfare and housing benefits that came with it) to individuals proven to have left the German Democratic Republic for political reasons, as opposed to others lured by the "German economic miracle" in the making. This preference for East German "persecutees" over economic newcomers castigated as "illegal" or "asocial" led to screening practices reminiscent of the DP system. In order to be recognized as genuine asylum seekers, escapees from East Germany were required to present credible claims of political dissent or persecution in front of a civil servant or a vetting committee. An important semantic shift ensued: initially encompassing the masses of expellees resettled after 1945, the term "refugee" (*Flüchtling*) now officially connoted a restricted group of politically conscious "freedom fighters" from East Germany.[115]

These intense efforts to distinguish legitimate refugees from among the muddled masses of European displaced persons ultimately produced limited results. Czechoslovak DPs, irrespective of their political or economic background, eventually found their way to the United States even when denied status by the IRO. At the height of the Cold War, the initially restrictive "escapee programs" crafted by the US administration in the early 1950s ultimately afforded American visas to most Eastern European refugees able to exit the Soviet bloc.[116] For their part, Spanish refugees found by the IRO to be economic migrants were only rarely sent back and blended without difficulties with the large contingent of Spanish immigrants already established in France.[117] In this regard, the liberal migratory context characteristic of "thirty glorious years" of reconstruction and economic growth (1945–75) greatly softened the dichotomy between political and economic refugees, in France as in the rest of Western Europe: during this period, both types of refugees routinely obtained the right to stay and settle down in the country of their choice. Finally, the sharp distinction between heroic and materialist refugees from East Germany lost much of its salience in 1961 when the new policy adopted by the Federal Republic stated that the desire for improved material conditions did not necessarily preclude political motivations.

Artificial as they may have been, these new categorizations first tested under the IRO had a long-lasting effect on the postwar era. Intertwined for most of the interwar period, "refugees" and "migrants" became strictly separated in the governance of international population movements. Specific institutions, such as the United Nations High Commissioner for Refugees and the Intergovernmental Committee for European Migration, both created in the early 1950s, solidified these distinct typologies.[118] Whether the hyperpoliticization of refugee status guarantees the human rights of genuinely persecuted people or unfairly excludes from protection a large number of other types of migrants is a question still fiercely debated in academic and policy circles, particularly so when the contemporary relevance of the 1951 Geneva Convention on Refugees is being seriously questioned.[119] Undeniably, however, the European past still shapes current perceptions: the "bogus refugees" generally suspected of abusing the right of asylum in contemporary Europe are a late incarnation of the "adventurers" excluded from DP status in the years following World War II. The emergence of the "dissident" as the most desirable type of refugee in the West was not the only innovation brought forth by the DP experience, however. As the following chapter describes, the assistance provided to the "last million" of European refugees also drastically transformed the practice of international humanitarianism in the postwar era.

3

Care and Maintenance

THE NEW FACE OF INTERNATIONAL
HUMANITARIANISM

COMMONLY PORTRAYED AS a dark era of total war and genocide, the first half of the twentieth century in Europe also witnessed the formidable expansion of civilian humanitarianism: the bloodiness of warfare not only caused massive loss of human lives but also spawned professional actions and vocabularies intended to alleviate the suffering of mankind. Inspired by the ideas of the Swiss philanthropist Henry Dunant, the Geneva Conventions of 1864 and 1906 opened a new era of collective efforts on behalf of victims of war. The conventions enshrined the protection of noncombatant populations in international law and recognized the International Red Cross and its national branches as legitimate auxiliaries to military forces. Millions of European civilians were thus able to receive assistance in or around the battlefields of World War I.[1] In 1918, hostilities gave way, for the first time in the history of modern humanitarianism, to extensive postconflict interventions. The large deployment of Protestant evangelical philanthropy in the Near East; the Rescue Movement, launched on behalf of Armenian victims under the aegis of the League of Nations; and the creation in 1921 of the Office of the High Commissioner for Refugees announced the rise of permanent and transnational humanitarian organizations. Charitable societies were affected by a similar transformation; created in 1919 by the British social reformer Eglantyne Jebb, Save the Children Fund was conceived as "a powerful international organization, which would extend its ramifications to the remotest corner of the globe."[2] This trend continued during World War II with the creation of prominent Anglo-American aid organizations such as the Oxford Committee for Famine Relief (Oxfam), the International Rescue Committee, the Catholic Relief Services, and the Cooperative for American Remittances to Europe

(CARE). In 1945, the "relief and rehabilitation" of Europe's displaced persons could therefore rely on a vast experience of assistance programs and expertise. Yet Allied operations in postwar Germany significantly departed, in philosophy, scope, and methods, from earlier interventions. Indeed, the DP camp system provided a unique terrain for the rise of new humanitarian practices and ideologies.

The career of the British welfare worker Francesca Wilson exemplifies this discontinuity. Born in 1889 to a Quaker family and trained in history at Cambridge, Wilson began her long humanitarian journey during World War I working with French, Belgian, Serbian, and Montenegrin uprooted civilians. In the early 1920s, she was involved in famine relief in Russia and oversaw British Friends operations in refugee-flooded Vienna. Between 1936 and 1939, she dedicated herself to the plight of Spanish Republicans in Spain and later in French camps. Following the German invasion of Poland in September 1939, she coordinated assistance operations for Polish refugees in Hungary and Rumania. In 1945, her activities in Dachau and Feldafing among liberated Jewish concentration camp inmates capped off several decades of fieldwork on behalf of war victims and refugees. The long-time humanitarian noticed a fundamental change at that time in the organization and delivery of emergency relief: as she wrote shortly before the liberation of Europe, "We have at last become planning-minded." In November 1943, the creation by forty-four nations of the United Nations Relief and Rehabilitation Administration had indeed profoundly transformed the nature of refugee aid: "a super-State body in charge of relief," UNRRA represented "an advance of incalculable importance on last time when no prior survey of needs was made and nation was allowed to compete with nation for food and necessities."[3]

A leading proponent of internationalism and collective security, the Canadian-American scholar and policy adviser James T. Shotwell also acknowledged the end of the charitable phase of modern humanitarianism. Before UNRRA, the Columbia University scholar wrote in 1944, "the American organizations for relief . . . were never officially coordinated and the organizations of other nations ran independent courses. This was inevitable so long as governments, as well as private organizations, still thought in terms of charity."[4] The British political scientist Harold Laski held a similar view. In his mind, post-1918 humanitarian aid and reconstruction assistance merely amounted to "a kind of International Red Cross, which moves in to do ambulance work after a flood or an earthquake." Laski advocated instead "a machinery of international relief" as part of a system of institutions "vitally related to the kind of world we want to build when peace comes."[5] In the same vein, Herbert K. Lehman, the former governor of New York who was appointed director

general of UNRRA in 1943, told a skeptical US Congress that the new institution was "the first bold attempt of the free peoples to develop efficient habits
of working together." With nations acting for the common good, he added,
"peace will have her victory no less than war."[6] Seen as a unique platform for
the internationalist age to come, postwar humanitarian assistance was confidently heralded by Anglo-American liberals as a "sample for world organization" and "the first blueprint of the postwar order."[7]

In this respect, the odd-sounding acronym "UNRRA" reflected the new
trend set into motion during World War II. Undoubtedly, the words "relief
and rehabilitation administration" recalled the language of New Deal recovery
programs and the myriad of "alphabet agencies" created by the Roosevelt
administration after 1933. As Elizabeth Borgwardt has argued, UNRRA projected onto the international stage some of the core principles and methods of
New Deal liberalism: "The transition from the private to the public realm in
relief and rehabilitation marked a further internationalization of New Deal–
style problem solving."[8] Also significant were the letters UN: created at the
midpoint between the Declaration by United Nations of January 1942 and the
United Nations Charter of June 1945, UNRRA shaped the future world organization into a central humanitarian actor. This alone distinguished the United
Nations from its predecessor: throughout the interwar period, the League of
Nations functioned merely as the coordinator of relief operations independently carried out by private philanthropic organizations. In order to mitigate
"suffering around the world," the League's covenant simply encouraged member
states to cooperate with Red Cross committees or similar charitable bodies.[9]
Post-1945 intergovernmental cooperation markedly reversed this pattern:
"UNRRA will operate through governments," one of its American proponents
promised, "and not by distributing alms to individuals."[10] Writing in the last
weeks of the conflict, Francesca Wilson rightly predicted that "voluntary societies will have less scope this time than after the last war."[11]

To be sure, the assistance provided to postwar displaced persons by dozens
of predominantly American welfare organizations was a much-needed
addition to what UNRRA and its successor the International Refugee
Organization could ever provide. Between 1945 and 1948, the amount of
private contributions sent to Jewish, Protestant, and Catholic philanthropic
groups in the United States reached an unprecedented level.[12] Although a
historian of American philanthropy overstated this phenomenon when he
described the refugee camps of Europe and the Far East as the "crucible for
America's postwar conscience," private aid societies nonetheless played a
crucial part in international refugee relief.[13] "Voluntary agencies," the United

Nations acknowledged in 1948, "have provided supplies worth many millions of dollars. With years of experience in refugee work and international relief programs, they have sent scores of specialists to assist the refugees in solving their problems."[14]

Yet placed under the supervision of UNRRA and occupying armies, philanthropic societies were barred from operating in Germany without proper authorization. They were also deterred from favoring a particular national or religious group, although the American Joint Distribution Committee was allowed to operate exclusively in Jewish DP camps.[15] One consequence of this subordinated status was the increased secularization of relief work: as Francesca Wilson pointed out in 1945, one of the peculiar features of the new humanitarianism was its "non-proselytising impulse." Above all, the subservience of aid societies to Allied armies and UNRRA meant that the Good Samaritans of the first half of the twentieth century, such as the Red Cross and private philanthropy, no longer led the international humanitarian movement. Although after the war "the idea still prevailed in some quarters that refugee work was first and foremost a matter for relief agencies," as welfare professionals stated in 1947, "this conception has been usefully demolished by UNRRA."[16]

The so-called care and maintenance policies enforced between 1945 and 1951 under UNRRA and the IRO in the displaced persons camps of central Europe illustrate this evolution. Throughout this period, securing the welfare of displaced persons amidst the acute food, health care, and housing scarcity of postwar Germany and Austria remained the main goal of Allied armies and international agencies alike. Yet the "care and maintenance" program was only one component of a far-reaching and unprecedented enterprise in humanitarian management. "Surely in recorded history," observed the head of UNRRA Displaced Persons division in 1947, "there has been no group of unwilling migrants that has posed such complex problems."[17] Spanning the second half of the 1940s, the UNRRA-IRO experiment transformed international humanitarianism in several respects. First, the DP crisis attracted a new generation of aid workers dedicated to liberal internationalism and modern welfare techniques. In addition, the "relief and rehabilitation" of Europe's displaced persons standardized the use of refugee camps as humanitarian enclaves and sites of stabilization, with important consequences for the functioning of humanitarian agencies such as the United Nations Relief and Works Agency (UNWRA) and the Office of the United Nations High Commissioner for Refugees (UNHCR).[18] Finally, the welfare policies carried out under UNRRA and the IRO inaugurated the era of humanitarian "governmentality": an abundance of statistics, reports, and censuses, as well as the enforcement of uniform nutritional, medical, and housing standards sought to shape the heterogeneous "last million" into a cohesive "refugee nation."

Although UNRRA was a near-global reconstruction agency with offices in China, the Philippines, Korea, the Middle East, Ethiopia, and the Balkans, it is mostly remembered today for its work on behalf of Europe's displaced persons. "No operations of the Administration were to get so much publicity," UNRRA's official historian explained, "and no other field operations were to require the employment of so many people."[19] Indeed, more than 5,000 "Class I" internationally hired relief workers (including doctors, nurses, social workers, dietitians, and professionals of various kind) were assigned to the Displaced Persons Operations in Germany, by far the highest amount of nonlocal personnel deployed by the administration anywhere in the world.[20] Predominantly British, American, and French, UNRRA relief workers also came from other European countries, the Dominions, and India. A handful of Burmese, Egyptian, Iranian, Indo-Chinese, and other non-Western nationals also took part in the DP operations. The international outlook of UNRRA staff struck many contemporaries as a remarkable novelty. "Like the displaced persons assigned to their care, the relief teams were themselves a new phenomenon," the American social worker Kathryn Hulme observed in her recollections. These "small wandering tribes from Babel" had been "thrown off into the wilderness of World War II's destruction . . . to do a work that had never been done." The thousands of idealists who joined UNRRA at the end of the war, Hulme added, encapsulated "the United Nations in a test tube."[21]

Other fieldworkers emphasized the unique "one-worldist" mindset characteristic of their colleagues. Susan Thames Pettiss, who for three years assisted displaced persons in various part of Germany on behalf of UNRRA, recalled an atmosphere of "pervasive idealism" among her peers: "All hoped to see established a true world community with new social systems and international relations."[22] Such ideals were also embraced by the Quaker nurse Isabel Needham, the Wellesley College graduate Gene Delano, or the future bestselling British writer Iris Murdoch: like many of their peers, they had volunteered for UNRRA work out of pacifism and strong faith in international cooperation. In particular, child welfare specialists dealing with traumatized orphans and so-called "unaccompanied children" liberated from concentration camps viewed themselves as agents of postwar democratization and enforcers of human rights.[23]

The liberal internationalist fervor noticeable among this new cohort of relief workers should not, however, be overstated. A former park ranger from the American heartland, the UNRRA officer Marvin Klemme despised the "indoctrination in idealism" at the hands of "instructors belonging to the extreme left wing of economic and political thought."[24] In a passage that is emblematic of the widespread criticism leveled at UNRRA throughout its existence, another American writer mocked the alleged virtues of international cooperation: "Working among fifty-odd nations is like working in the midst of fifty loaded rifles held by fifty trigger happy marksmen."[25] In the United States, UNRRA's efficiency as an international institution was repeatedly called into question. A common line of attack was that the agency "doubtless attracted a number of workers whose days of top efficiency are past."[26] For her part, Francesca Wilson was wary of "drug addicts, alcoholics, criminals fleeing from the law, worming their way into relief work, especially if they have good qualifications."[27] She also resented the presence among her colleagues of day-dreamers, "tired of the sameness and restricted opportunities of life at home." Yet despite her qualms about "ill-organized, badly-recruited and overstaffed UNRRA," she believed that international relief work stood at the core of the postwar order: "If the international bodies that the United Nations is setting up fail to remember its lessons and to carry on its more constructive activities, it will be a bitter indictment of our age."[28]

Judging from the praise lavished upon its cosmopolitan staff, the International Refugee Organization fulfilled this vision. With a "truly international staff representing forty-one different nationalities and speaking nearly all the languages of the world," the IRO represented a remarkable example of efficient international cooperation. "Around the dinner table," noted René Ristelhueber during a visit of an IRO center in Germany, "sat a former colonel of the British Indian Army, his American deputy, their Danish secretary, a French doctor, a Belgian student on leave from her studies, an Australian social worker and a Dutch information officer. Their national origin had faded away, overshadowed by the *esprit de corps* animating those devoted to a common task."[29] A former IRO staff member himself, the American political scientist John Stoessinger marveled at the "submerging of national differences" achieved under the organization: "In extending to the unfortunate people the protection of the international community, the men and women working under the emblem of the symbolic life buoy did full justice to the humanitarian task for which they had been recruited."[30]

Although indicative of a new pattern of civilian humanitarianism, these admiring descriptions of cosmopolitanism warrant several qualifications. Most of the 1,450 fieldworkers employed by the IRO were Anglo-Americans previously employed by UNRRA. The San Francisco native Kathryn Hulme is a good representative of this continuity: recruited by UNRRA in the spring of 1945, she worked from 1947 to 1951 as an IRO welfare officer in the large camp of Wildflecken located in northwest Bavaria. There she rapidly found many of the "same old stagehands left around, willing to go on with the show and use their sad know-how of caring for homeless masses."[31] Among UNRRA veterans employed by the IRO, British welfare specialists outnumbered Americans. Already organized since 1942 within the Council of British Societies for Relief Abroad (COBSRA), well-trained British professionals were more easily transportable to the DP camps of Germany and Austria. By April 1945, COBSRA had already deployed 455 staff members to northwestern Europe.[32] This British predominance was nonetheless counterbalanced by the extensive collaboration between the IRO and American aid societies. Indeed, the majority of the thirty-six charity groups contracted by the organization to perform "care and maintenance" operations originated from the United States. In dire need of "supplementary services," the IRO joined forces with the Catholic War Relief Services, the Protestant affiliates of the Church World Service, and Jewish relief organizations such as the American Jewish Joint Distribution Committee and the Hebrew Immigrant Aid Society. As a result, 1,250 Americans, half of them members of Jewish organizations, were added to its welfare staff. Even though they were limited to auxiliary activities, philanthropic organizations gained much from this cooperation. As Louise Holborn noted, "The IRO bestowed upon them its own international status. If left to their own devices the societies would in many cases have been unable to expand their activity beyond the limits of emergency aid."[33] Relief work in the DP camps enabled therefore the transformation of traditional charity groups into "nongovernmental organizations" (NGOs), with long-lasting consequences for the role played today by nonstate actors in global governance. The critical presence of American philanthropic institutions within the galaxy of NGOs operating in postwar Europe also gave humanitarianism a distinct transatlantic sheen. The "breath of American fresh air" that greeted a French visitor to the IRO headquarters in Geneva bears ample testimony to this influence. Struck by the "democratic uniformity" of the compound, René Ristelhueber compared the IRO operational center to an "island of youth and dynamism magically transplanted from the Hudson River to the ancient and blissful banks of Lake Geneva."[34] This universe similarly puzzled Maurice Grimaud, a French civil servant assigned to the IRO: "The simplicity of work relations, the sharing of information, the distaste for political and intellectual speculations and the marked preference for concrete solutions priced in dollars sharply contrasted with French habits."[35]

More importantly, the Americanization of humanitarianism deeply affected the conduct of relief work. Within UNRRA, American social workers trained in the Depression era championed a dynamic form of welfare aimed at encouraging self-help among recipients of care. This ambitious goal reflected a recent evolution: under the successive Roosevelt administrations, American social work had evolved into a "well-integrated technique of modern public welfare," expertise skill now ready for export.[36] Indeed, the DP crisis enabled the deployment of American social work principles and methods. As the president of the National Conference of Social Work and Associate Groups proclaimed in May 1946, "This the opportunity we have dreamed and longed for; it is also a crucial test of our vision, our courage and our competency."[37] Mary McGeachy, the Canadian head of UNRRA's Welfare Division, was puzzled by the determination of her American colleagues "to convey American experience and standards abroad." Accused of personifying the "English approach to the old-fashioned kind of relief," McGeachy faced the constant criticism of American welfare professionals dismayed by her simplistic "charitable" worldview.[38] Yet British relief workers themselves challenged the tenets of old-style Victorian charity. UNRRA specifically appealed to Francesca Wilson because its stated goal was "not only to relieve, but to revivify."[39] Issued in 1942, the Beveridge Report had already placed reinvigoration and "rehabilitation services" at the core of liberal social policies: like Depression-era Americans or postwar Britons, the displaced persons were to benefit from a radically modernized approach to welfare.

According to UNRRA's official history, it is indeed in the "field of human rehabilitation that the Administration made its contribution to the care of the displaced persons."[40] The term "rehabilitation" was hazy enough to perplex even some of the founding fathers of UNRRA such as Dean Acheson, for whom "the word had no definition: rather it was a propitiation by the unknown."[41] This concept was nonetheless clear enough to Eleanor Roosevelt who explained after visiting DP camps in Germany that "charity is a wonderful thing, but it does not give one that sense of security. What is important is rehabilitation [of the person]....The sooner those people can be taken where they can become citizens and feel that they are actually building a new life, the better it will be for the whole world."[42] UNRRA's official historian was later able to provide a more precise and noticeably gendered description of the rehabilitation process: "Any mother who has tried knows that when she first teaches her children how to perform simple household tasks..., it requires far more time to teach the children to do such work and to supervise their doing than to do such work herself." As opposed to Allied military commanders "who thought that if you made things hard enough in the camps, the DPs would go home," the predominantly female UNRRA relief workers were committed to the "development of free, independent and self-sufficient human beings." In particular, they fostered self-government, the cornerstone of human rehabilitation and "the goal toward which all activities were pointed." This technique allegedly yielded impressive results: by the time the IRO took over UNRRA activities in June 1947, "most displaced persons in most camps and assembly centers were capable of governing themselves with little or no outside supervision."[43] The subsequent "DP municipalities" organized by the IRO further allowed elected leaders to represent the DPs in their dealings with civilian and military authorities and made the administration of refugee camps similar to that "of any modern town."

The "care and maintenance" of displaced persons democratized the organization of refugee welfare but also widened the scope of humanitarian aid. Under both UNRRA and the IRO, assistance covered not only food, clothes, and housing, but also child welfare, healthcare, recreational and artistic activities, sport, education, language, and vocational training, as well as employment counseling. In a DP camp located near Brunswick in northern Germany, the British Quaker Margaret McNeill "found the magic word 'welfare' could be expanded to take in practically everything."[44] Indeed, DP humanitarianism bore little resemblance to the assistance provided after 1918 to the European civilians battered by World War I. Led by Herbert Hoover, the American Relief Administration (1919–23) counted as its main achievement the delivery of six billion tons of food to twenty-three European nations, including Bolshevik Russia.[45] That the aging Hoover was summoned in 1946 by Harry Truman to help coordinate operations in occupied Germany indicated that food relief still ranked high in "relief and rehabilitation" efforts.[46] Yet the satisfaction of basic material needs was not the only goal. "After having fed, healed and assisted the refugee," boasted René Ristelhueber, "the IRO restores his conscience and human dignity. This is the crowning achievement of its work."[47] Even if not intended to last from cradle to grave, DP humanitarianism functioned as an alternative welfare state for the stateless. Its citizens were the "last million" refugees from World War II awaiting a solution to their predicament. Its territory was the refugee camp, the emblematic and conspicuous site of displacement in postwar Europe.

"Camps spread like a cancerous growth all over Central Europe," United Nations envoys reported in May 1948. The growing number of refugee installations, they warned, "obstruct the work of peace-making, aggravate the congestion of population of Germany and Austria and sap the feeble forces of those countries so sorely needed for the work of reconstruction."[48] While Nazi concentration camps encapsulated the uniqueness of World War II in European memories of the conflict, the large number of DP camps stretching from northern Germany to southern Italy epitomized the harsh realities of the post-1945 period. When UNRRA terminated its operations in June 1947, the agency supervised 688 camps in the American and British occupation zones in Germany, as well as twenty-one in Austria and eight in Italy. Its successor the IRO took over approximately seven hundred camps, 75 percent of them still located in western Germany.[49] Freshly arrived from the United States, Kathryn Hulme was mesmerized by the universe of the DP camp: "Closed away from that outside world as effectively as if you inhabited a small planet adrift from earth like a raft in space, you knew only the queer inverted life of the DP camps, which had to be learned step by step because never before had anything quite like it been even imagined."[50] Eleanor Roosevelt experienced similar numbness when she toured DP camps in February 1946: "I felt all the time...a kind of spiritual uprooting, a kind of being lost."[51]

Yet refugee camps were by no means a postwar novelty. The avalanche of displaced individuals triggered by the end of World War I had already led to the widespread use of such institutions. The Russian refugees who massively fled the Soviet Union after 1921 did not for the most part experience camp conditions in the countries neighboring the USSR, even if, according to Fridtjof Nansen's deputy, there was hardly a "frontier town or village the whole length of the Russian border...which did not witness the exodus of those unhappy people."[52] But in the Caucasus, Syria, and Lebanon, Armenian refugees from Turkey flocked into rudimentary camps in which American Protestant missionaries provided basic services. A refugee camp in Beirut, visited by an international delegation in 1926, was described as "a town of cards or at best of match boxes. The streets, or rather alleys, are so narrow as to make it difficult for two persons to pass each other."[53] In Greece, too, refugee camps sprang up in the early interwar period. Overburdened by refugees from Turkey and Bulgaria following the population exchanges of 1923, the Greek territory remained cluttered with a multitude of desolate encampments until a special body of the League of Nations secured the necessary funds for the permanent settlement of newcomers. Henry Morgenthau, Sr., the head of the Greek Refugee Resettlement Commission, discovered in Athens a "refugee horde... huddled in tents pieced out of burlap bags, or in huts extemporized out of the ubiquitous five-gallon Standard Oil cans."[54] Well before the postwar era, the

Balkans, Asia Minor, and the Near East had already experienced their fair share of DP camps.

The dramatic exodus into France of refugees from the Spanish Civil War brought large refugee camps to Western Europe. Following the fall of Barcelona on January 26th, 1939, nearly 500,000 Spanish Republican soldiers accompanied by wounded and destitute civilians crossed the Pyrenees under particularly dire conditions. They were then directed to emergency reception centers hastily built by the French authorities in the southwest of the country. Yet Argelès, Saint-Cyprien, and Gurs, the largest centers created in February and March 1939, had only dismal medical and sanitary amenities to offer. "There has never been anything as horrible as this since the Middle Ages," Francesca Wilson was told at the time by a doctor sent to France by the British Quakers.[55] These deplorable conditions reflected the extraordinary extent of the Spanish humanitarian crisis as well as the dire lack of suitable infrastructure on the French side. Yet the reception centers for Spanish refugees were innovative in one important respect: initially designed as humanitarian shelters, they rapidly blurred the distinction between assistance and incarceration. In most cases surrounded by barbed wire and placed under strict military control, the camps paved the way for a larger network of internment centers used by the late Third Republic and the Vichy regime. After the return within a year of most Spaniards to their country, the next inhabitants of these quasi concentration camps were central European Jews deemed "undesirable aliens" amidst mounting tensions with Nazi Germany.[56] Although similar but smaller internment camps were opened in 1939–40 in Britain and the Netherlands to isolate "enemy nationals," the French camps demonstrated the possibility of a narrower distance between humanitarian aid and political quarantine. Hannah Arendt, interned for a few weeks at Gurs in 1940 prior to her timely emigration to the United States, garnered there solid empirical evidence for her later depiction of refugee and DP camps as "holes of oblivions" for modern pariahs. But long before the publication of *The Origins of Totalitarianism* in 1951, the image of refugee camps as "states of exception" was already firmly entrenched, in large part thanks to the French precedent. Writing in 1943 in a special issue of the *Journal of Abnormal and Social Psychology* in which Bruno Bettelheim presented his pioneering analysis of internment-related trauma, a German émigré stressed the unique place of refugee camps within the constellation of similar modern institutions: "Legally the refugee camps must be listed between the war-prisoner and the concentration camps."[57]

From this point of view, the DP camps differed markedly from their predecessors. "What child's play it will be this time!" rejoiced a seasoned British relief worker in 1945; "we were groping in the dark then. Now we know what vitamins are needed for every type of malnutrition."[58] This forecast did not immediately come true. In the first months of Allied occupation, an American welfare worker recalled, "life in the DP camps did not present a really substantial change, at least physically, from life in slave labor camps in Germany and Austria."[59] Yet even during the initial phase of DP operations, refugees received army rations supplemented by requisitioned German supplies. Despite their perpetual quest for better and more fulfilling food, Margaret McNeill realized that "the DPs were not starving. Had they been starving, we would not have been running English classes."[60] The Allied medical response was equally effective. As opposed to the devastating influenza plague of 1918–19, the threat of postwar epidemic was successfully contained due to aggressive vaccination and delousing campaigns: "Displaced persons by the millions were dusted with DDT powder, thousands were given medical treatment and epidemic diseases were kept in check."[61] In 1946, refugee onlookers could legitimately wonder whether "any other population in the world is receiving a similar amount of health services."[62] Malcolm Proudfoot, who oversaw refugee relief operations on behalf of the US Army, espoused a similar opinion. "Compared with the general conditions prevailing throughout the remainder of Germany and in certain countries of Eastern Europe," he wrote in 1946, "the lot of the displaced person was an easy one."[63]

The DP camps also distinguished themselves from prewar installations in that they were not built with the detention of refugees in mind. During the war, American and British planners advocated the creation of temporary camps in order to channel the uncontrolled flow of civilian displacement and its potentially dangerous consequences. "If panic, chaos and raging epidemics are to be prevented," the first director general of UNRRA, Herbert K. Lehman, declared in 1943, "there must be orderly movement and the essence of orderly movement is that some people should stand still." The creation of "assembly centers" in occupied Germany was also prompted by the main goal of Allied refugee policies: the return of DPs to their respective countries from organized staging areas. "Where large groups await repatriation it will be necessary to fix areas of assembly where the work of rehabilitation can begin," advised a British expert in 1942. The establishment of camps was essential, "as it may be some months, or even years, before it is possible to complete the repatriation of the ordinary civilians."[64] For Hannah Arendt, however, the idea of transitory centers was strikingly reminiscent of the 1930s: "The internment camp is the only thing that again and again comes out of all suggestions, plans and memoranda."[65] In 1949, she still denounced the fact that the "internment camp...has become the chief resort in solving the problem of domicile for displaced persons."[66] In *The Origins of Totalitarianism*, she again referred to DP camps as a type of concentration camps, "the only 'country' the world had to offer to the stateless."[67] Yet, contrary to her belief, the vast camp system put into place by Allied armies and UNRRA was mainly the product of logistical preparations designed to facilitate a speedy transition from war to peace.

The variety of DP camps also set these new structures apart from those in existence during the interwar period. After 1945, an "assembly center" could be alternatively defined "as a camp or a group of camps or a community of detached dwellings."[68] A British relief team arriving in Germany in the summer of 1945 was thus able to drive into a DP camp "without recognizing it to be one."[69] The official histories of UNRRA and the IRO provide detailed descriptions of these heterogeneous settings. Occupied Germany featured a multitude of "refugee camps" ranging from requisitioned hotels, sanatoria, and schoolhouses to former Wehrmacht barracks and SS caserns winterized for civilian use. These former garrisons, Janet Flanner reported for the *New Yorker*, were now "ironically housing what is left from the expatriate nationals whom the Nazis maneuvered around Europe as doomed inferiors."[70] German military installations, despite visible signs of Allied bombings and DP repairs, generally offered decent forms of accommodation: "The German Army and SS Units," quipped UNRRA's historian, "had not lived too badly." UNRRA also took over German public buildings, tenement houses, and sections of villages from which Germans were deliberately expelled by occupying armies. In other cases, UNRRA also built new camps consisting of temporary wooden barracks. In addition, slave labor camps left over from the Third Reich were turned into DP centers. "The fact that an essentially adequate number of such installations was found," admitted Malcom Proudfoot in 1946, "was a fortunate but unanticipated by-product of Nazi militarism and totalitarian planning."[71] The number of inhabitants in DP camps generally ranged from two to three thousand, but Wildflecken, with its 18,000 Polish-national inhabitants, was even more densely populated. While overcrowding worried relief workers, psychiatrists, and foreign observers, living conditions were significantly better than in the past. "The displaced persons had some sort of roof over their heads," observed George Woodbridge, "and reasonably adequate washing and sanitary facilities." Speaking at the United Nations General Assembly in February 1946, Eleanor Roosevelt was not mistaken when she simply described the DP camps as "places of refuge for people belonging to different nationalities."[72]

According to these accounts, therefore, the DP camps humanized the refugee condition. This process was nonetheless painstakingly slow. Earl Harrison, Harry Truman's personal envoy in Germany and Austria, was appalled by the situation of liberated Jews. As he reported in August 1945, "Many Jewish displaced persons are living under guard behind barbed-wire fences."[73] Indeed, tens of thousands of recently freed Jewish inmates of Dachau, Belsen, or Buchenwald in Germany and Ebensee, Gusen, and Mauthausen in Austria remained confined for several months within these infamous camps.[74] For this reason, the fund-raising campaigns launched by American philanthropic groups pictured the DPs "in rags behind barbed wire with begging hands extended toward the reader."[75] Along with military watchtowers, these fences, vivid reminders of Nazism, were ultimately removed by the US and British army: "A symbol of the difference between liberty and freedom," proudly proclaimed René Ristelhueber in 1951.[76] Yet historians still argue that as late as 1947, high walls or rolls of barbed wire encircled some DP camps.[77] Overall, however, the vast majority of camps administered by UNRRA and later by the IRO did not feature clear boundary markers. Wildflecken, the large Bavarian DP camp famously compared by Kathryn Hulme to a "magic mountain of sugar and Spam" rising up before hungry German eyes, "did not even have a fence around it."[78] In her detailed study of displaced persons in Munich, Anna Holian found that for the refugee population "the camp and the city were not fundamentally different kinds of places."[79] Of course, occasional army curfews or required travel authorizations curtailed the free circulation of DPs outside their camps. As a French doctor sardonically wrote, "the DPs enjoy full freedom of movement within a five miles radius."[80] Yet the DPs remained free to come and go at will or simply disregarded travel regulations, in particular in the vicinity of urban centers. As such, DP life was not exclusively defined by spatial confinement. Even if the camp system drove a wedge between the displaced persons and German society, multiple types of encounters between Germans and their former victims ensued from this flexibility. At Wildflecken, noted Kathryn Hulme, Poles "paid off ancient grudges" by luring German civilians from the town and into the camp where the DP police promptly arrested them for black marketing. Similarly, unexpected interactions between Jews and Germans were made possible by the absence of physical borders between DP camps and their surroundings,[81]

Despite its openness, the DP camp system came under sever criticism. H. B. M. Murphy, a British psychiatrist employed by the IRO until his resignation in 1950, charged that the governing principle of humanitarian aid was not "rehabilitation" but strict surveillance: "It is usually regarded as useful or necessary that refugees, as aggrieved and rootless people, should be kept under a centralized and mobile control, and should not be allowed to forget their special status until those in control decide that it is advisable."[82] Other opponents of DP camps argued that Allied humanitarianism was disturbingly reminiscent of Nazi methods. Unsettled like many of her colleagues by the camp environment, the American Catholic welfare worker Eileen Egan feared that "the moral trap of using human beings as things awaited both sides in a total war. The DP camps were a sign that our side had succumbed to that moral trap."[83] In neighboring France, DP camps were commonly portrayed as incarnations of the "concentrationary universe," the powerful concept developed by the former Buchenwald internee David Rousset in his penetrating account of Nazi camps.[84] Claude Bourdet, a wartime resistance leader and a dedicated advocate of refugees, considered the "displaced persons vegetating in camps similar to those built by Mr. Himmler" as the "great scandal" of the postliberation period. With their myriad of "double entries index cards, forms and occasional barbed wire," UNRRA and IRO camps continued "the work of their genius precursor, Adolph Hitler." Their external appearance was reminiscent of "Argelès and Barcarès," the camps for Spanish Republicans created in 1939, and of "Buchenwald and Oranienburg," two powerful symbols of political deportation and Nazi violence in postwar France.[85] The DPs were perhaps "free, protected and guarded," wrote the young French novelist and pro-refugee activist François Nourissier in the same vein, "but the poison distilled by this form of internment is particularly subtle."[86]

The multiple detractors of Allied refugee camps were nonetheless forced to reckon with the surprising willingness of displaced persons to live in such installations "The camps," H. B. M Murphy admitted, "have been desired as much by these peoples' own leaders as by the supervising authority."[87] Jewish DPs used camps as self-ruled territories, enabling the shaping of a Zionist political consciousness, the thriving of a pioneer youth culture, and the physical and emotional regeneration of Holocaust survivors.[88] After years of intense suffering, the Jewish DP camps of the American zone functioned as humanitarian shelters eagerly appropriated by their inhabitants. A Polish Holocaust survivor summarized the benefits of this separation. In the Jewish camp of Feldafing, he felt "free, without fear, freed from Poland, and from the concentration camp."[89] For Ukrainian or Baltic DPs, camps constituted protected enclaves enabling the expression of a national identity distinct from Soviet citizenship. Hosting the largest component of the DP population, camps for ethnic Poles fostered the birth of a political diaspora supported from afar by Polish American organizations.[90] Whether Jewish or Slavic, the "nation-in-exile" blossomed within the loose and ambivalent boundaries of DP camps.

The transformation of postwar European camps into sites of active political mobilization challenges the disenchanted vision of humanitarianism evident today, among others, in the influential writings of the philosopher Giorgio Agamben. This post-Arendtian approach postulates that displaced persons and refugees secluded in humanitarian camps are reduced, like concentration camp inmates, to a "bare life" devoid of political voice and expunged from the boundaries of the state.[91] Echoing the postwar critics who drew parallels between Nazi and DP camps, Agamben identifies a mimetic relationship between rescuers and victimizers: "Humanitarian organizations... can only grasp human life in the figure of bare or sacred life, and therefore, despite themselves, maintain a secret solidarity with the very powers they ought to fight."[92] Despite their good intentions, international bodies such as the IRO were therefore "absolutely incapable" of solving the postwar refugee problem.[93] Expanding upon Agamben's analysis of the camp as a metaphor of modernity and a "pure, absolute, and impassable biopolitical space insofar as it is founded solely on the state of exception," scholars in the field of refugee and migration studies have applied this notion to the predicament of endangered populations targeted by contemporary humanitarian interventions: "Like the concentration camps, the famine or refugee camp set up during a state of emergency after a disaster or drought also rapidly becomes a permanent space of exception."[94] Yet heuristic as it may be, the concept of "humanitarian violence" hardly reflects the DP experience. Despite regulated camp conditions, the humanitarian assistance provided to the refugees of World War II symbolized the demise of Nazi inhumanity while sheltering many endangered individuals from the reach of the Soviet state.

If theory needs to be invoked, postwar humanitarianism is better explicated by Michel Foucault's concept of governmentality: "the institutions, procedures, analyses and reflections, the calculations and tactics that allow the exercise of this very specific albeit complex form of power, which has as its target population."[95] Although Foucault never included the refugee camp in his investigation of multifarious forms of power, few institutions lend themselves so well to such an analysis.[96] With their regulatory practices specifically designed for displaced people, the DP camps enabled a new art of government independent from the nation-state. The anthropologist Liisa H. Malkki rightly identified in the DP experience the moment when "the refugee camp became emplaced as a standardized, generalizable technology of power in the management of mass displacement."[97] Arranged into "disciplinary and

supervisable places," the administration of displaced persons introduced techniques of population management later reproduced in other humanitarian
theaters.[98] The "care and maintenance" of Europe's displaced persons indeed
elicited new perceptions of uprooted and exiled people. From then on, the
idea of the refugee did not just imply statelessness and the quest for asylum
but also critical dependency upon humanitarian expertise. In particular, the
"refugee nation" fashioned between 1947 and 1951 by IRO welfare policies
facilitated the transformation of war-displaced civilians into targets of humanitarian management. In his survey of displaced persons prepared for UNHCR
in 1951, the refugee expert Jacques Vernant took notice of this innovation:
"The great majority of refugees lived for years in camps, where a paternal
administration drew up the menu, fixed meals and curfew times, allocated
accommodation, repaired footwear, washed linen and provided cigarettes,
chocolate, etc., according to carefully worked out scales."[99] From the point of
view of the administrations in charge of their upkeep, the DPs were indeed
"objects of policy rather than subjects of history."[100]

Issued in 1950, an IRO pamphlet urged countries to open their doors to
"100,000 human beings in distress" desperately lingering in camps. For
dramatic effect, the advertisement featured anonymous and decontextual-
ized faces of DPs looking forward to a new life. "These photographs," read a
caption, "are a representation of the refugee nation."[101] This newborn national
community was also recorded on film. In keeping with a new humanitarian
documentary genre initiated under UNRRA, the IRO commissioned a
series of short films focused on the DP population.[102] *Home for the Homeless*,
a ten-minute movie narrated by Henry Fonda, followed the daily routine of
the "refugee people" in an unspecified DP camp from dawn to dusk.[103]
Another IRO production entitled *The Hard Core* featured refugees physically or mentally unable to find resettlement destinations in the West.[104]
Equally silent on the ethnic or national origins of DPs, *Passport to Nowhere*
(1948) showed "the encamped professionals, the skilled craftsmen, the cheer-
less and the orphaned." Coproduced in the United States by the IRO and
the Citizens Committee on Displaced Persons, *The Time Is Now* documented
"the plight of displaced persons, their unwillingness to return to eastern
Europe, and what we can do for their liberation."[105] In photographs and on
screen, the "refugee nation" was showcased as an authentic supranational
collectivity.

This harmonious "refugee nation" was, however, highly fictional. The soci-
ologist Edward Shils, the author of a landmark study on the social and

psychological consequences of internment, emphasized the complete absence of international solidarity among refugees in Germany: "There was no community among the displaced persons such as ultimately developed among prisoners of war."[106] The organisation of DP camps along ethno-national lines particularly hindered the rise of a "DP identity." Drawn up in the middle of the war, Allied military plans for the repatriation of displaced persons in Germany stipulated that "national groups should be maintained in separate centers." This policy did not initially include Jewish refugees, but the "Harrison Report," issued in August 1945, called for the rapid establishment of separate Jewish camps in the American zone in order to alleviate the suffering of Holocaust survivors. Whether Jewish, Polish, Baltic, or Ukrainian, the DPs ultimately lived among their own kind. "In order to maintain peace and cut down the number of fist fights," reported Janet Flanner, "the IRO tries to arrange matters so that each camp houses only one religion or nationality."[107] When multiple ethnicities remained mixed up, noted an IRO official, "invisible boundaries" still kept one group from the other.[108]

Although camps were divided along national and ethnic lines, the IRO nonetheless tried to offer their inhabitants standardized living conditions. Initiated in July 1947, the consolidation of seven hundred UNRRA "assembly centers" into newly created "static centers" was designed to turn refugee camps into uniform spaces. According to IRO rules, buildings were to house a minimum of three hundred people. Thirty-five square feet of living accommodation were initially granted to each resident, a figured later increased to fifty square feet. Similar guidelines regulated communal areas. "Where there are more than three lanes of beds in any room," the IRO stipulated, "ten percent of the floor should be calculated as corridor space." Cubicles had to be at least nine feet high, and each room had to "have window space not less than one sixteenth of the floor area." To provide the DPs with some degree of privacy, family groups were accommodated in separate rooms. This thorough reordering of refugee space was also intended to secure a minimum level of hygiene. One bathroom with showers was assigned to every group of twenty-five persons, and DPs were required to take one weekly bath.[109]

Alongside the regulation of living space and cleanliness, nutritional standards were another important component of "care and maintenance" policies. At the start of its operations, the IRO found dietary standards that were unbalanced and insufficient, too high in carbohydrates, and ranging from 1,500 to 1,900 calories a day. Due to scarcity, the agency could only offer "as low a ration as is possible without damaging health or leading to disturbances in the camps."[110] To that end, nutritionists devised a temporary solution whereby protein intake could be raised without increase in calories. Yet thanks to American food imports, unpalatable military rations, local German products, and supplemental packages from charity organizations, including the well-stocked parcels delivered to Jewish DPs by the American Jewish Joint Distribution Committee, the food crisis gradually dissipated. The standard of 1,900 calories a day set in the United States by the National Research Council was surpassed: by the end of 1948, average diets had risen to 2,230 calories per day. As the number of DPs started to dwindle, more food became available to a smaller number of refugees. This remarkable focus on calories over quantity (let alone taste) did not stem only from nutritional concerns. It also tied refugee humanitarianism to the "foreign policy of the calorie" conducted by the United States since the Progressive Era. In the early part of the twentieth century, argued Nick Cullather, "food lost its subjective, cultural character and evolved into a material instrument of statecraft." The calorie now represented food as fungible, "composed of interchangeable parts, and comparable across time and between nations and races." First used as a tool of American benevolence and power during the days of the American Relief Administration (1919–23), the "foreign policy of the calorie" entered its second and long-lasting phase at the onset of the European refugee crisis: "The current world pattern of humanitarianism, exchange, and subsidized dumping began to emerge only after the Anglo-American allies recaptured the calorie among the spoils of World War II."[111]

In addition to calorific measurements, the compilation of statistical data stood at the core of IRO governance. As a field welfare officer, Kathryn Hulme took special pride in working "not with charts and statistics but with the living material in the mill." Yet at the IRO headquarters in Geneva, the impression of the French delegate Maurice Grimaud was drastically different: "I found that we spent too much time in conferences, statistics and in calculation and recalculation of the net cost of a refugee." After touring numerous DP camps, Janet Flanner arrived to a similar conclusion: "The displaced persons are willing to go anywhere on earth except home. In the course of this suspended period of time, these people have turned into statistics and initials."[112] Indeed, the construction of the "refugee nation" hinged on relentless efforts to collect information on various aspects of DP life. Each IRO field office in Germany had to submit a monthly narrative report on up to "twenty-two functional subjects." One of them, the narrative report on health, "was itself divided into nineteen subheadings." Detailed information on nationality, age, sex, family status, and occupation were systematically passed on to headquarters for collation. "I am morally and physically extremely tired as a consequence of a long, exhausting and unequal race with statistics," wrote one IRO agent in his letter of resignation. "For more than one year the field welfare officers have been harassed with continuous new programs, with deadlines and with such urgent statistical tasks that the care work became a luxury. Reports, nominal rolls, surveys, etc., filled the major part of the working days." Numerous reasons were advanced by the IRO to justify extensive data gathering: "The material assistance of a population on the move…, the planning of definitive emigration and the monitoring of new arrivals necessitate the meticulous compilation of statistics."[113]

It is therefore in the postwar European context that refugees became objects of precise social-scientific knowledge. Less than ten years after the end of the DP crisis, a British journalist visiting the UNHCR headquarters was startled by this evolution: "You can learn at Geneva… about the theory of the refugee world almost as if it were an academic subject, like metaphysics or the natural sciences. But to the refugee himself all this bears little relation to the reality he knows."[114] Originating in the refugee governmentality characteristic of the IRO, this quasi-scientific management of displaced populations had a profound effect on what Jacques Vernant generically called, in 1953, "the refugee in the postwar world." Blurred into a single humanitarian category, refugee experiences lost their historical specificity. In the 1950s, popular expressions such as the "refugee world" and the "refugee family" connoted, like the "refugee people" or the "refugee nation" under the IRO, an abstract group of dispossessed people united by a need for special care: Europe's displaced persons were the first postwar refugees to experience such disempowerment. The verses of a "DP's Song of the Song" written by one refugee-poet in response to a questionnaire suggest that "relief and rehabilitation," far from instilling vigor and energy, could also result in denial of historical agency: "Would you please excuse me / That I nothing know / I am a number / In the long IRO row."[115] Responding to a similar survey, the Holocaust survivor and Czech-Jewish writer H. G. Adler derisively reported "how happy, oh so happy" he was, "like a cuckoo in the woods."[116] Yet against these disgruntled testimonies stand the numerous thankful letters and postcards sent by grateful DPs to the IRO.[117] Bureaucratic, regimented, and inspired by military planning, postwar refugee humanitarianism nonetheless rescued the "last million" of Jewish and non-Jewish displaced persons from unbearable living conditions. Midway between old forms of charity and the current role played by the United Nations as the "West's mercy mission," the international assistance provided to DPs after 1945 marked the transition, under heavy American influence, between two dramatically different types of humanitarian regimes. As the following chapter discusses, the problem posed by Europe's displaced persons also deeply affected the emergence of international human rights in the second half of the 1940s.

4

Displaced Persons in the "Human Rights Revolution"

ALTHOUGH SELDOM USED by the activists and political actors of the 1940s, the expression "human rights revolution" is today commonly employed to describe the advent of the human rights era in the aftermath of World War II. According to this popular view, it was during this pivotal decade that a handful of dedicated visionaries, not all of them of Western origin, mounted a successful attack against the old concept of state sovereignty: following the "gathering storm" of the interwar years and the ideological "crusade" of the wartime period, the "revolution" launched in 1945 challenged the Leviathan state to curtail some of its traditional prerogatives in favor of the rights of individual citizens.[1] In this evolutionary narrative, the predominantly "juridical revolution" of the postwar years allegedly laid the groundwork for subsequent "advocacy" and "enforcement" revolutions in the last decades of the twentieth century.[2] The idealist celebration of human rights as the "idea of our time,"[3] particularly prevalent in the West since the end of the Cold War, hinges therefore on a revolutionary reading of the 1940s: against overwhelming odds and despite many contradictions (such as the persistence of racial segregation in the United States and of European rule in the colonial world), human rights became a matter of international responsibility, challenging the nation-state's monopoly on the conduct of international affairs. "For the first time," wrote Michael Ignatieff optimistically, "individuals—regardless of race, creed, gender, age, or any other status—were granted rights that they could use to challenge unjust state law or customary state practice."[4] In the same vein, Samantha Power sees in the second half of the twentieth century "a true revolution in the development of norms and the enshrinement of those norms in international law."[5]

This approach undeniably stands on firm empirical ground. From the Atlantic Charter of 1941 to the 1951 Geneva Convention relating to the Status of Refugees, the burgeoning Euro-Atlantic "human rights talk" of the wartime period solidified into a wide array of landmark declarations and agreements. During this decisive decade, the Charter of the United Nations (1945), the Universal Declaration of Human Rights (1948), the Convention on the Prevention and Punishment of the Crime of Genocide (1948), the Fourth Geneva Convention Relative to the Protection of Civilian Persons in Time of War (1949), and the European Convention on Human Rights (1950) shaped the basic architecture of the postwar human rights regime. "What the United Nations is trying to do," explained the Canadian lawyer and first Director of the UN Division of Human Rights John Humphrey in 1949, "is revolutionary in character."[6] To be sure, this project was met with widespread suspicion from its inception. As opposed to René Cassin or Eleanor Roosevelt, skeptical jurists, anticolonial resisters, and Communist opponents of "bourgeois rights" did not see the Universal Declaration as a "beacon of hope for humanity" or a "Magna Carta for all men everywhere." Yet despite their contested meaning and numerous critics, human rights gained unprecedented visibility in postwar international politics.

The revolutionary dimension of this moment remains, however, subject to historical debate. Realist-minded writers have cautioned against idealization and attractive morality tales; the emergence of international human rights derived neither from a "war-weary generation's reflection on European nihilism and its consequences" nor from tenacious visionaries eager to erect "fire-walls against barbarism." Since there was no Holocaust consciousness in the immediate postwar era, Samuel Moyn argued, human rights could not have been a response to the Nazi genocide.[7] According to Brian Simpson, interest in human rights resulted instead from "complicated interrelationships between individuals, institutions, and governments, with their varied ideological commitments and perceptions of reality, history, and self interest."[8] In addition, the dawn of the human rights age stemmed from the desire of Great Powers and small nations alike to finish off the moribund interwar system of minority rights in favor of more expedient individual rights, abstract enough to be safely embraced. As Mark Mazower pointed out, staunch advocates of mass expulsions of ethnic minorities, such as the Czechoslovak leader Edvard Beneš, could at the same time ardently champion "a Charter of Human Rights throughout the world" for the postwar era. A "strange triumph" more than a smiling revolution, the politics of human rights paradoxically reinforced the supremacy of state sovereignty.[9]

Nonetheless, one common feature unites these diverging lines of interpretation: whether critical or apologetic, assessments of the "revolution" primarily focus on the motivations of activists and drafters rather than on the

actual enforcers of human rights in the late 1940s. This imbalance is easily jus-
tifiable: as decried by numerous international jurists at the time, the noble
proclamation of human rights at the United Nations was noticeably devoid of
enforcement mechanisms. For the famed legal theorist Hans Kelsen, the occasional references to human rights traceable in the 1945 Charter of the United
Nations were nullified by the absence of formal implementation devices.[10]
Although himself a firm believer in the human rights project, the eminent
Cambridge lawyer Hersch Lauterpacht lamented the absence of a right of
individual petition to back up abstract proclamations. Like the "vacuous gen-
eralities" of the 1948 Universal Declaration, the impossibility for citizens to
appeal to the United Nations against abuses perpetrated by their governments
left intact the almighty power of the state.[11] René Cassin, one of the main
architects of the Universal Declaration, fiercely opposed this pessimism.
"From one side of the world to the other and from the bottom to the top of
the social ladder," the French jurist countered in 1950, "workers on strike, victims of racial and religious discrimination, persecuted intellectuals…all
invoke with great hope this Universal Declaration." Yet like his colleague
Eleanor Roosevelt, Cassin readily admitted that the covenant, as its preamble
stated, only set "a common standard of achievement for all people and all
nations" to be attained in the future. Cassin was indeed well aware of the
limited enforceability of the declaration, a necessary concession in order to
win the support of American policy-makers wary of international account-
ability, among others. For the time being, he recognized, the declaration only
served as "a magnet and a goal for the aspirations of mankind."[12] In the words
of the émigré jurist Josef Kunz, it was "a maximum program of a legally nonbinding character."[13] Despite the efforts of the United Nations to advertise the
impact of the Universal Declaration on jurisdictions worldwide, sympathizers
of the "revolution" conceded that it was more suggestive than legislative, more
declarative than binding.[14]

The limited number of nongovernmental organizations specifically
concerned with human rights further prevented the principles of the "revolution" from being put into force. As opposed to the thousands of human rights
NGOs operating in the world today, only a handful of such organizations
were in existence in the mid- to late 1940s. The most prominent among them,
the New York–based International League for the Rights of Man and the
Paris-based International Federation for the Rights of Man, epitomized the
historical and geographical continuity uniting the "human rights revolution"
of the 1940s with the "Atlantic revolutions" of the late eighteenth century.
But like the more numerous and predominantly American civic, religious,

labor, educational, or women's organizations enlisted by the United Nations to participate in the drafting process, their role remained essentially consultative. Indeed, postwar NGOs were primarily committed to the establishment of international norms by which the conduct of states could be measured. As such, they may well have "revolutionized the language of international relations, which statesmen of an earlier era and even some of the recent period would have found strange and unacceptable."[15] But until the later appearance of more militant watchdogs committed to fact finding and implementation, the "enforcement revolution" made possible by the unraveling of the Cold War still remained a distant prospect.

The history of displaced persons in postwar Europe, however, complicates this chronology: the DP experience immediately put to test the language of human rights hammered out by Western powers in the 1940s. Despite the fact that, from the Middle East to India/Pakistan and China, mass displacement occurred across a large part of the globe between 1945 and 1950, the "last million" of Europe's displaced persons constituted a field of experimentation for postwar human rights principles. In February 1946, the first human rights resolutions ever adopted by the United Nations General Assembly prohibited, against the opposition of the nascent Soviet bloc, the forcible return of DPs to their countries of origins.[16] In addition, key articles of the Universal Declaration such as "the right of everyone to leave any country" (Article 13), "the right to seek and enjoy in other countries asylum from persecution" (Article 14), and "the right to a nationality" (Article 15) found concrete instantiation within the extraterritorial DP universe of occupied Germany. So did the list of guarantees against state interference with freedom of movement: the propaganda activities of "repatriation missions" dispatched to the DP camps by the governments of Poland, Yugoslavia, and the Soviet Union to coerce refugees into returning home were strictly limited, under the IRO constitution, to the distribution of "adequate information" on the situation in home countries.[17] As the first UN high commissioner for refugees, G. J. van Heuven Goedhart, stated in 1951, Europe's refugees were people "for whom, not less than for you and me, the noble preamble to the Declaration of Human Rights was written three years after the Second World War."[18]

The problem posed by the DPs in Germany indeed loomed in the background of the "human rights revolution." Their legal position raised the vital question of the place of individuals in international law. "Behind the affairs of people deported and exiled from their homes," noted the former refugee and legal scholar Eduard Reut-Nicolussi, "there is the chief question of the relation of the individuals towards the international community."[19] To be sure, the treatment of other types of European refugees could be similarly branded as archetypal cases of human rights violations. In the thought of West German jurists such as Rudolf Laun, the millions of ethnic German expellees evicted from East-Central Europe were the victims of abuses unfairly ignored by the international community. Their dire situation elicited an alternative vision of human rights founded on "the right to one's homeland" (*das Recht auf die Heimat*), a doctrine grounded on the prohibition of mass deportations and deeply resentful of "victors' justice."[20] But outside the German juridical community, Western legal internationalists concerned with the place of refugees in international law saw in the DPs, more than in any other type of forcibly displaced populations, a potent justification of effective international rights. For the French jurist Roger Nathan-Chapotot, the international protection of displaced persons tested the world's commitment to "the exercise of man's free will." That in the postwar era refugees could be protected from the reach of abusive governments announced the demise of "Hegel's apotheosis, the state as God on earth."[21]

The important place occupied by refugees in the "human rights talk" of the late 1940s indicates therefore that the legal and political consequences of the DP crisis weighed in various ways on the postwar human rights project. This argument naturally challenges Hannah Arendt's somber pronouncements on powerless refugees and the disintegration of human rights spelled out in *The Origins of Totalitarianism* (1951). An important shift, ignored by Arendt, occurred in legal framings of statelessness after 1945: no longer perceived as a juridical pathology menacing the international order, the loss of citizenship was treated after World War II as a direct consequence of political or racial persecution. Whereas the prewar "stateless" was negatively defined as an individual deprived of citizenship, the postwar "political refugee" was positively branded as a victim of human rights violations entitled to international protection. In a second section, this chapter describes how the management of displacement in Europe exemplified the individualization process set in motion after 1945: the decisive abandonment of interwar "minority rights" in favor of "individual rights" found a concrete illustration in the individual definitions of refugees produced by the DP crisis. Finally, a third section examines how representatives of the International Refugee Organization contributed, through their advocacy for refugees and displaced persons at the United Nations, to the design of human rights law.

In several articles published between 1944 and 1949 introducing the main themes developed in *The Origins of Totalitarianism*, Hannah Arendt linked the situation of Europe's displaced persons to the "pariah condition" of stateless people during the interwar period: as "superfluous" creatures placed outside the nation-state, individuals in both categories were dramatically stripped of "the right to have rights."[22] A few weeks before VE-day, Arendt predicted that the imminent refugee crisis was likely to generate widespread "rightlessness," defined in her thought as the legal and physical removal from a rights-based polity.[23] "The many millions who today mill around in Europe in compact if unorganized herds," she warned in April 1945, "are the surest and most frightening sign of the disintegration of the national state."[24] Like the stateless persons of the interwar period, the DPs heralded a momentous political crisis but also provoked unprecedented interest in human rights. "Today," Arendt observed in 1949, "the whole question of the Rights of Man has taken a new life and pertinence." This new concern was due to the interwar "emergence of an entirely new category of human beings...who do not possess citizenship," and also to the "new millions of displaced persons" added by "the events of the forties." The DPs, she implied, propelled human rights to the center of international politics: "The problem of statelessness on so large a scale had the effect of confronting the nations of the world with an inescapable and perplexing question: whether or not there really exist such 'human rights' independent of all specific political status and deriving solely from the fact of being human?"[25]

In various instances, however, Arendt's description of the DP problem is factually questionable. When she argued that "the postwar term 'displaced persons' was invented expressly to liquidate this troublesome 'statelessness' once and for all by not recognizing it," she ignored the fact that the vast majority of DPs, including Polish Jews who infiltrated the American occupation zone of Germany soon after the war ended, were not technically stateless. In their case, loss of citizenship no longer derived from systematic denationalization policies such as those enforced by the Soviet Union and Turkey between 1921 and 1927 or by Nazi Germany between 1933 and 1941. When Arendt also claimed that "non-recognition of statelessness always means repatriation," she did not accurately describe the evolution of Western refugee policies with regard to forcible return. Although occupying armies and UNRRA hoped for the mass return of refugees to their countries, repatriation policies came to a grinding halt in the first half of 1946. Stateless or not, the "last million" was allowed to remain in the Western zones of Germany before permanent solutions could be found. Oblivious of these facts, Arendt merged prewar and postwar refugees into a single continuum of rightlessness: both are portrayed as identical groups of "stateless people" similarly deprived of a political existence in the world. Yet by framing European refugees as "the most symptomatic group in contemporary politics," Arendt nonetheless offered a unique explanation for the exponential interest in human rights after 1945: as the epitome of modern vulnerability, the "calamity of the right-less" strongly weighed upon the new international protections declared in the second half of the 1940s.

While she acknowledged the importance of the refugee problem in their emergence, Arendt did not place much faith in the politics of human rights. In her eyes, international jurists and activists were inexperienced "professional idealists which no statesman, no political figure of any importance could pos-sibly take seriously."[26] As a result, statelessness remained as in the past "the most vexatious and insoluble point on the agendas of all international confer-ences."[27] But Arendt also blamed stateless persons for stalling the emergence of effective human rights: "Neither before nor after the Second World War have the victims themselves ever invoked these fundamental rights." Although banished by nation-states, refugees only sought national solutions for their plight: "The more they were excluded from right in any form, the more they tended to look for a reintegration into a national, into their own national community." Thus, by breaking down human rights into mere national rights, "the victims shared the disdain and indifference of the powers that be for any attempt of the marginal societies to enforce human rights in any elementary or general sense."[28] As such, the DP crisis only confirmed the "end of the Rights of Man" traceable since 1919 in the appearance modern refugees. Against Arendt's skepticism, however, a more optimistic account of postwar human rights can be drawn from the legal trajectory of statelessness before and after 1945: an abhorred juridical pathology for most of the interwar era, the absence of bonds uniting an individual to a state reached the status of par-adigmatic human rights abuse warranting international redress.

The rise of modern statelessness before the eyes of the international community is commonly associated with the end of World War I. Seldom noticed prior to 1919, stateless persons formed an imposing mass of "international tramps" in the wake of the Versailles Treaty. Indeed, the collapse of the Russian, Austro-Hungarian, and Ottoman empires left an estimated three million people outside the legal and political categories created after the war.[29] A product of the post–World War I settlement, the conspicuous *Heimatlos* or *apatride* was suddenly deprived of citizenship or, as in the case of Jews, not afforded the minority protection to which successor states in eastern Europe and the Balkans were theoretically committed.[30] To these categories were soon added one and half million Russian émigrés and 300,000 Armenians collectively denationalized by the Soviet Union and Turkey. Remembered today as the iconic identity document of the interwar years, the "Nansen Passport" encapsulated the League of Nation's understanding of the mass refugee phenomenon: a problem of statelessness more than victimization.[31]

The prolific legal literature dedicated to statelessness in the 1920s and early 1930s reinforced the handicap attached to the notion of stateless refugee. This scholarship emanated for the most part from Continental Europe. In Great Britain and the United States, safely sheltered from mass influx of refugees by the restrictive Aliens Acts of 1905 and 1919 or the quota-based Immigration Act of 1924, the phenomenon of statelessness did not raise similar concerns. "With very few exceptions," observed the interwar jurist Mark Vishniak, "Anglo-American scholarship, like Anglo-American judicial practice, has paid little attention to the problem."[32] The opposite was true in France, where a rich body of literature conceptualized statelessness as a form of delinquency contrary to international law and public order.[33] International jurists warned against the disruptive nature of statelessness, a "civic death" contradictory to a healthy system of law. "The juridical respiration of an individual," wrote the legal scholar Albert Geouffre de la Pradelle, "is conditioned by a state and depends upon a nationality."[34] Even for the jurists who had personally experienced exile and loss of citizenship after World War I, such as Jewish refugee scholars from World War One or the Bolshevik revolution, the orphans of the nation-state order suffered from the "evil of statelessness" more than political abuse.[35] Most of the interwar period was therefore "a time of international resolve to assist the victims of the legal phenomenon of statelessness...with limited attention accorded to the social causes underlying the refugees' legal predicament."[36]

A resulting shift occurred in legal framings of statelessness when the Institute of International Law meeting in Brussels in April 1936 proposed that the absence of nationality should cease to constitute the essential feature of refugees: more salient in the context of Fascism and Nazism was the notion of persecution. Contrary to the League of Nations' concern with persons deprived of citizenship, the discipline's flagship institution defined a refugee "as an individual who because of political events which occurred in the country of his origin...left the territory of that country."[37] To be sure, the Institute still acknowledged that "the distinctive criteria for the stateless and the refugees are not mutually inconsistent." Indeed, most refugees from the Third Reich lacked passports and legal status or were denationalized while already outside Germany or Austria. But the automatic portrayal of refugees as legal anomalies was now seriously challenged; it was first and foremost as victims of "political events" that refugees should be seen by the international community.[38] That political violence trumped statelessness in the conceptualization of refugees was also apparent in John Hope Simpson's survey of European forced displacement published in 1939. "Other features of the existence of the refugee," wrote the British politician and humanitarian, "may be incidental but are not essential to his quality as refugee."[39] Thanks to the emigration of German refugee scholars to the United States, this new definition also crossed the Atlantic Ocean. The forcible abandonment of a country for "political reasons," stated Louise Holborn in 1938, was the main characteristic of refugees, irrespective of their lack of state protection.[40] This change of approach did not of course fully alter the deeply rooted pathological dimension of statelessness, particularly so in xenophobic Vichy France. "The refugee is a category of the vast class of stateless persons," wrote a contributor to the review *Esprit* in November 1940, "and the stateless is ill."[41] Although perceptible in legal internationalist circles at the end of the 1930s, the marginalization of the stateless in favor of the political refugee only took effect after the end of World War II.

Europe's displaced persons played a crucial role in this evolution. As opposed to the "international tramps" of the post-1919 period, the displaced persons did not raise fears of mass statelessness. As the acronym "DP" clearly indicated, the most immediate challenge presented in the spring of 1945 by European refugees was their displacement from their countries of origin.[42] After the repatriation of most of the civilians assisted by UNRRA and the Allied armies, the "last million" of permanent Polish, Jewish, Baltic, and Ukrainian refugees raised a political problem more than a juridical one. Tellingly, there was no postwar equivalent to the "Nansen Passport," even if official travel documents recognized by several countries were occasionally issued to displaced persons. Indeed, the concept of statelessness lost much of its salience in the categorizations of refugees from World War II and its immediate aftermath. "Such people," an American observer pointed out, "may be deprived of citizenship...if they do not return. Some people may have citizenship restored, but nevertheless not want to go back home."[43] Paradoxically, it is a concern for the human rights of non–stateless people in a strict juridical sense which made the redefinition of statelessness in international law possible.

A first step in this direction was the recommendation issued on February 12, 1946, by the UN General Assembly to examine the problem of statelessness "in all its aspects."[44] Three years later, the Economic and Social Council issued a "study of statelessness" focused on refugees and displaced persons.[45] The

magnitude of the DP crisis indeed brushed aside the problem of nonrefugee
stateless people, such as women married to foreigners who were denationalized
as a result. The UN study relied on the expertise of the international jurist
Mark Vishniak, a Russian Socialist-Revolutionary exiled in France who subsequently emigrated to the United States. Vishniak's main concern since the
1920s was the place of stateless persons and ethnic minorities in international
law. Commissioned in 1944 by the American Jewish Committee to report on
the legal status of stateless persons and to recommend ways to improve their
lot, Vishniak reviewed the denationalization policies enacted by Nazi
Germany and its satellite countries.[46] Yet even if in his writings statelessness
was clearly the result of political or racial persecution, it essentially remained
"a problem of law" as well as a "pathological condition" not different from the
one previously decried by interwar jurists. The *Study of Statelessness* reiterated
this view: "Normally every individual belongs to a national community and
feels himself a part of it," it stated, "and the stateless person is an anomaly."[47]
Indeed, references to the "abnormality" of statelessness remained frequent in
postwar legal discourse. The IRO legal counsel and future bestselling novelist
Albert Cohen, for instance, typically distinguished between the normal alien
enjoying the "indivisible force of the state protecting him" from the abnormal
type, "weak and without support."[48] The UN study nonetheless introduced
innovative classifications. The DPs and other non-German refugees in postwar
Europe were stateless because they "themselves renounced the assistance and
protection of the countries of which they are nationals." As such, they were
now "stateless persons *de facto*," a category complementing that of "stateless
persons *de jure*."[49] The category of stateless de facto, faithfully mirroring the
situation of Europe's displaced persons, broadened the traditional scope of
statelessness while at the same time diminishing its singularity: the essential
feature of the stateless now had less to do with "national handicap" than with
"fear of persecution" in the country of origin.

Relegated to a lesser role as a legal category, statelessness was thus equated
to a loss of fundamental rights. A memorandum presented by the American
Jewish Committee to the participating nations at the San Francisco
Conference of June 1945 was among the first documents to convey this new
meaning: statelessness was not merely a condition "injurious to the existence
of the national state" but also "to the human community and to the dignity of
the human personality."[50] The 1948 Universal Declaration soon ranked statelessness among the violations deemed reprehensible by the international
community. As Article 15 stipulated, "everyone has the right to a nationality,"
and "no one shall be arbitrarily deprived of his nationality." Accordingly, the

reintegration into the realm of citizenship of all stateless persons was tanta-mount to human rights redress. The right to a nationality, however, neither conferred minority protection nor self-determination, both concepts notice-ably alien to the "human rights revolution." Its main purpose was to alleviate statelessness, a phenomenon "contrary to the rights of man and to the interest of the human community," in the words of René Cassin.[51]

Through Article 15, therefore, the Universal Declaration implied, not unlike Hannah Arendt, that rights are abolished in becoming stateless. But contrary to Arendt's lack of confidence in the ability of nation-states to guarantee the rights of stateless persons, postwar liberal internationalism optimistically viewed citizenship, safeguarded in time of crisis by interna-tional organization, as the natural guardian of human rights. As such, the stateless condition was repairable through reinstatement into a community of rights, the sovereign nation-state kept in check by international guaran-tees. Arendt's assessment was of course much more pessimistic: statelessness did not just amount to a loss of political and civic rights retrievable in a proper liberal internationalist polity. It was also a terrifying denial of something essential in life "a place in the world which makes opinions significant and actions effective."[52] Yet while Arendt dramatized the "trauma" of statelessness, she never bothered charting a clear path out of the night-mare. Several scholars have for this reason criticized Arendt's opposition to standards and fundamental norms, a position making rights impossible to uphold.[53]

The United Nations's unfettered faith in therapeutic nationality was also at odds with the idea of "world citizenship" briefly espoused in the late 1940s by eminent Western intellectuals, philosophers, writers, and scientists. Signed by Albert Einstein, Bertrand Russell, George Bernard Shaw, John Dos Passos, Aldous Huxley, Rebecca West, and François Mauriac, among others, a public letter sent in February 1949 to Secretary General Trygve Lie urged the United Nations "to reconsider their attitude to the refugee problem." In particular, the signatories demanded that stateless people should not be under obliga-tion to apply for new nationalities: "By sheer force of events they have acquired the feeling of belonging to a community larger than one nation. Indeed, History made them citizens of the world, and they should be treated as such." The postwar refugee problem was thus a unique opportunity to "let the ideal of world-citizenship subsist not exclusively in theories and programs, but also in courageous experimenting and in a genuine respect for the human person." This initiative was strongly criticized by the IRO: "Here are people to whom you say: be proud of your statelessness, remain this way and become the first world citizens!...But stateless persons know all to well what they desire: to stop being stateless. Not out of sentimentality, but to obtain asylum, a passport, a work permit or access to a hospital." In a direct jab at the signatories, the IRO press office charged that the dire situation of stateless intellectuals and professionals around the world was caused precisely by the ostracism of peers "still fortunate enough to have a homeland."[54]

As this exchange makes clear, the humanitarian advocates of DPs believed in the healing powers of citizenship. But their insistence on the protective dimension of citizenship bonds stemmed from the realization, commonplace among international jurists such as the IRO chief legal adviser Paul Weis, that "it is through his connection with a particular state by the ties of nationality that the individual finds his place in international law." Citizenship was therefore "one of the most effective means to safeguard and to ensure the human rights of the individual."[55] Whereas Mark Vishniak portrayed statelessness as a taint on "the whole political organism," Paul Weis placed the "human rights of the individual" above any concern for the health of the body politic: the DP question served indeed as a test case for the affirmation of individual rights in international law.

The 1948 Universal Declaration proclaimed the equality of all human beings but not of all human rights doctrines; although homage was paid to the social and economic rights championed by Soviet bloc countries or to the Christian-personalist conception of human dignity theorized by the French philosopher Jacques Maritain, the majority of its thirty articles were couched in the language of liberal individualism. The Declaration is often portrayed, including in the writings of its main "visionaries," as a carefully crafted compromise among a diversity of political and cultural traditions. The idea of a plural origin was indeed popularized by the famous questionnaire on the nature of human rights distributed in 1947 by UNESCO to seventy world thinkers asked to contribute their thoughts to the drafting process.[56] But once finalized, the Declaration was chiefly concerned with civic and political rights. Articles 1 through 21 expand upon negative liberties (what must not be done to people) already enshrined in the American Declaration of Independence of 1776 and the French Declaration of the Rights of Man and the Citizen of 1789. Additional rights to social security, education, work, or to an adequate standard of living, as well as references to the "free and full development" of the human personality certainly echoed socialist or personalist ideas but were safely confined to the last eight articles of the Declaration.[57] The covenant also carefully avoided any reference to group rights and self-determination; above all, the "Magna Carta for Mankind" heralded the rights of individuals against the prerogatives of states.

The postwar turn to individualism has been explained either by long-term historical trends or short-term causation. The French Revolution scholar Lynn Hunt contends that the 1948 Universal Declaration "reaffirm[ed] the eighteenth-century notion of individual rights" and "crystallized 150 years of struggle for rights" in the Atlantic world. The campaigns against slavery, torture, and cruel punishment launched since the late eighteenth century thus culminated in the reappearance of individual rights after 1945. The only difference between the Atlantic Revolutions and the "human rights revolution" was the fact that by 1948 "everyone knew, presumably, what human rights meant."[58] More interested in the international politics of the 1940s, Mark Mazower offers a more sobering assessment: "Behind the smokescreen of the rights of the individuals, the corpse of the League's minorities policy could be safely buried."[59] Moreover, Soviet hegemony in Eastern Europe made any enforcement of Wilsonian minority rights impracticable in the region. Above all, however, nonbinding "individual rights" looked particularly attractive to the Great Powers because of the ineffective challenge they actually mounted to state sovereignty and colonial rule. As Brian Simpson showed in detail, the outspoken American, French, and British defenders of individual human rights at the United Nations also ensured that third parties would not be able to interfere in domestic or colonial affairs.[60] In 1945, only one Western constituency openly supported the resurrection of minority rights: before quickly abandoning this idea in favor of Zionism, spokesmen of American Jewish organizations called for the perpetuation of interwar collective rights for Holocaust survivors in Eastern Europe. Marginal and short-lived, this plea for collective rights was also strictly limited to the near-extinct Yiddishland: in Western Europe, Jews were expected to fully recover the civic and political rights lost during the war.[61]

Prevalent in the postwar human rights project, the concept of individual rights also owed its resurgence to nearly three decades of forced displacement on the European continent: the appearance of mass statelessness since 1919 glaringly exposed the weakness of the individual in international law. A theme dear to Anglo-American lawyers during World War II, the "desacralization" of sovereignty had already been championed in the interwar years by the future human rights actors of the postwar era. When René Cassin claimed in 1930 that the "law of domicile" should in many cases trump the "law of nationality," the French lawyer turned the refugee problem into the basis of his legal individualist doctrine: the fact that stateless persons now resided in host countries entitled them to rights equal to those of nationals, thereby challenging the exclusive competence of the state.[62] In interwar France, the most influential scholars advocating a higher place for individuals in international law were similarly committed to the cause of asylum seekers. The fame constitutionalist Boris Mirkine-Guetzevitch is representative of this convergence: a legal counsel for refugees assisted in France by the League of the Rights of Man, the Russian émigré designated "man" as the "new direction of the juridical science."[63] In opposition to the doctrine of minority protection, the League of the Rights of Man and its European branches perceived human rights as individual guarantees. Yet for Hannah Arendt, this individualist conception hindered the protection of interwar pariahs. The League's main fault, she contended, was to behave "as though the question [of the right of asylum] were still merely the saving of individuals persecuted for their political convictions and activities. This assumption, pointless already in the case of millions of Russian refugees, became simply absurd for Jews and Armenians."[64] Arendt nonetheless identified a crucial trend: for the international lawyers and activists confronting the refugee exodus of the 1930s, individualism had become the gateway to universal human rights.

René Cassin is here again emblematic of this evolution. Frustrated by the League of Nations' inability to prevent discrimination, statelessness, and forced displacement, Cassin sought to transcend the shortcomings of minority rights. The League's central flaw, he argued, was its limited focus on "men who belong to certain collectivities" as opposed to "man himself."[65] A clear "path to universality" was needed to protect the victims of political and racial persecution, a rights system in which the individual would become the "common denominator of humanity."[66] The definition of refugees hammered out in April 1936 by the Institute of International Law reflected this vision. For the first time in the interwar period, the condition of the refugee was defined individually and universally: "any individual who because of political events which occurred in the country of his origin...left the territory of that country." No mention was made of group membership or specific nationalities; this new conception directly challenged the League of Nations' collective definitions of refugees based on ethnic or national origin, whether Russian or Armenian prior to 1936 or "refugees from the Reich" later. To be sure, the transformation of the individual into a subject of international law primarily remained an academic concern. Throughout the 1930s, opposition to totalitarianism was predominantly expressed in terms of human dignity, freedom, and democracy, and "almost never in a reassertion of the human rights idea itself."[67] Moreover, the recommendations issued by the Institute of

International Law in 1936 only came into force in 1951 with the signature of the Geneva Convention Relating to the Status of Refugees. But these recommendations already indicated that by the end of the "Twenty Years' Crisis," the individual formed the cornerstone of human rights in legal internationalist thought. The task at hand, René Cassin wrote in April 1940, was the protection of "man and the human community" from the oppressive "Leviathan State."[68]

An ideological response to fascism, individual rights prominently figured in the blueprints for peace devised during the war by international jurists envisioning the postwar order. Before the return of Great Power politics, the wartime era provided a unique window of opportunity for proponents of individual human rights. "The problem of minorities, of refugees, of backward peoples and of underprivileged classes... will be of immediate importance in the postwar years," wrote the American law professor Quincy Wright confidently in 1943. This prospect compelled international lawyers to devise "new procedures to accomplish the end sought, that of assuring basic freedoms to everyone."[69] Offering a similar rights-based platform, Karl Popper's "open society" envisioned a world in which "human individuals and not states or nations must be the ultimate concern not only of international organization, but of all politics, international as well as national and parochial." For the Austrian-born philosopher and social theorist, exiled during the war in New Zealand, one of the preconditions for "open society" was precisely the definitive abandonment of the Wilsonian experiment, which was "inapplicable on this earth."[70] Although kept in check by the return of Machiavellian international politics, the concept of individual and universal rights was not merely the product of cynical calculations or, alternatively, the culmination of Enlightenment principles and sensibilities. Its prevalence also owed much to the intellectual and legal groundwork laid during the interwar and wartime years by sympathizers of refugees convinced that individual rights provided the most adequate response to state persecution and political violence. At the end of World War II, this idea found an immediate concretization in the individualization of refugee definitions established in the course of the DP crisis: an "individualist perspective" replaced (with important consequences for asylum seekers today) the traditional group approach favored in the past by the League of Nations.[71]

This major institutional innovation signified that refugees were now defined as individuals with "valid objections" to returning to their country of origin due to fear of racial, religious, or political persecution. This notion formed the centerpiece of the IRO constitution adopted by the UN General

Assembly in December 1946 and hailed by commentators as an example of "enlightened individualism."[72] Valid fear of persecution became then the decisive criteria for obtaining DP status; despite many qualifications, it was as individuals and not as members of national groups that refugees in occupied Germany were afforded legal and humanitarian protection. For some analysts of refugee policies, this individual perspective was mainly a stratagem "affording governments yet one more level of control and regimentation—the individual level."[73] Others have claimed that this individual approach, more aligned with the famous political exiles of the nineteenth century than with the masses of displaced persons seen in Europe since 1919, exemplified Cold War perceptions of refugees.[74] But while the individual level enabled better screening procedures and romanticized the political dissident fleeing Communism, it indicated above all that the "fundamental incompatibility" between an individual and a government had become the essential characteristic of modern refugees.

To be sure, the individualist approach did not eliminate the significance of groups in the granting of political asylum. The DP universe was not made of abstract individuals but of Jews, Poles, Estonians, Latvians, Lithuanians, and Ukrainians collectively recognized by the Cold War West as persecuted or threatened groups. But the IRO definitions left a decisive imprint on the 1951 Geneva Refugee Convention, according to which "any person which owing to a well-founded fear of persecution is outside of his country" could benefit from international guarantees. At the end of the DP crisis, the transition from minority rights to individual rights was most visible in the realm of refugee protection in Europe: nonbinding in the 1948 "Magna Carta for Mankind," individual rights were inscribed into international law by the 1951 *Magna Carta for Refugees.*[75] Moreover, the 1951 Convention uniquely infused juridical substance into international rights otherwise merely declared at the United Nations. Alongside basic survival and dignity rights, asylum seekers were afforded an expansive range of binding civil and socioeconomic rights. Signatory states, as always, could refuse to enforce substantial articles besides survival and asylum rights. But the Convention is today widely recognized in international law as an enforceable human rights instrument.[76] Paradigmatic "rightless" for Hannah Arendt, Europe's refugees nonetheless obtained in the Convention fundamental guarantees against persecutor states.

At the end of the 1940s, therefore, proponents of a higher legal status for individuals could safely declare victory. "International law, like national law, must be directly applicable to the individual," opined the Columbia University professor Philip Jessup in 1948.[77] The dean of French legal internationalists,

Georges Scelle, was unequivocal: "Today this doctrinal battle has been won and the immense majority of authors recognize individuals as subjects of international law."[78] Hersch Lauterpacht was equally confident: "The individual has acquired a status and a stature which have transformed him from an object of international compassion into a subject of international right. The time is now ripe for assessing the significance of these changes…in the functioning of international society."[79] A thorough inventory of legal opinions in the mid-1950s confirmed that most Western scholars of international law held this opinion. But that a vast number of international jurists recognized the legal personality of the individual did not add much binding power to human rights law. Writing at the height of the Cold War, the French-Polish scholar Marek St. Korowicz found that in practice "the traditional concept of international law reigns decisively in spite of all the opinions and hopes expressed by theorists before and following the last World War."[80] Peripheral to the superpower struggle, the international human rights project was cast aside until the opening of the détente era. Yet even if they remained mere "texts," the seminal covenants adopted between 1945 and 1951 laid the foundations of modern human rights law. The pressing DP problem deeply impacted this standard-setting phase: promoted at the United Nations by the IRO legal staff, refugee rights gave much-needed substance to the "human rights revolution."

In instructions to a team of IRO experts advising the Commission on Human Rights in the drafting of the Universal Declaration, the legal adviser Paul Weis outlined the ambitious objective of his organization: "We are interested that the positive right of persecutees to seek and find asylum should be recognized and not the almost meaningless 'right to escape persecution' contained in previous drafts. It is essential that the principle of the right of asylum—an innovation in international law—should be laid down."[81] The Austrian-born Jewish lawyer scored a partial victory: a few months later, Article 14 of the Universal Declaration declared the right of everyone "to seek and enjoy in other countries asylum from persecution," although this provision did not require states to grant it. Like the IRO, numerous other NGOs with consultative status at the United Nations were called upon to participate in the elaboration of the Universal Declaration. This practice allowed UN organs—especially the Commission on Human Rights during its year-and-a-half efforts to shepherd an acceptable draft through approval process—to "tap into expert information and advice from competent and qualified organizations."[82] The International Labor Organization, for instance, pleaded for the inclusion of the rights of workers into the Declaration.[83] The Anti-Slavery Society naturally focused on forced servitude and women's organizations on what was not yet called gender rights. Other consultative NGOs represented special interests groups such as war veterans, journalists, or religious communities. On the basis of its expertise in the assistance and resettlement of displaced persons, the IRO became the principal interlocutor of the United Nations in refugee matters. There was a significant difference, however, between the IRO and the rest of United Nations consultants. Whereas other NGOs defended the interests of specific constituencies, IRO spokesmen believed that refugee protections supported the entire edifice of human rights. Their goal was not only to protect stateless or displaced persons but also to "enforce a new standard of international conduct."[84] The detailed memorandum sent by the IRO to the Commission on Human Rights in December 1947 exemplified this broad agenda. Alongside the right to a nationality and to asylum, the IRO offered wording on the right to fair trial and protection against double jeopardy and retroactive justice, as well as freedom from arbitrary interference with privacy, family, home, or correspondence.[85] The fulfillment of IRO demands, Paul Weis hoped, "may prove a landmark in the development of international law and in the history of suffering humanity."

To attain this objective, IRO representatives emphasized the unique vulnerabilities of refugees. Their weak status, explained Albert Cohen, exposed them to discrimination and xenophobia: "It is an undeniable fact in mass psychology that the behavior of a community towards an alien varies according to whether he is a normal alien or an abnormal one."[86] For this reason the IRO recommended minimal lag time between the absence of citizenship and its recovery. Its spokesmen also advocated the prohibition of arbitrary denationalization: "Loss of nationality by unilateral act of the state should be prohibited without simultaneous acquisition of a new nationality."[87] Article 15 of the Universal Declaration—"No one should be arbitrarily deprived of his nationality"—vindicated their position. With memories of Bolshevist, Kemalist, and Nazi denationalization policies still fresh, the collective deprivation of citizenship appeared to many the main cause of forced displacement. The ban on arbitrary denaturalization also allowed the United Nations to shame perpetrator states in the court of world public opinion: theoretically at least, governments who withdrew the citizenship of nationals for arbitrary reasons could be found in breach of international law. To be sure, the human rights instruments adopted in the course of the "revolution" carefully refrained from directly naming perpetrator states. As stated in its preamble, the purpose of the 1951 Refugee Convention was to find suitable solutions for refugees so as

"to prevent this problem from becoming a cause of tension between States."
Article 15 of the Universal Declaration similarly sought to limit international
frictions. Adopted in 1948, this provision forbade mass denationalization, an
arbitrary practice which already belonged to the past, but remained silent on
the more urgent question of mass deportation. The 1948 Genocide Convention
and the 1949 Geneva Convention indirectly referred to forced population
transfer and ethnic cleansing, but these infractions remained under the individualist radar of the Universal Declaration.[88]

Unlike victimized minorities and expelled populations, therefore, Europe's
refugees and displaced persons informed the design of the "Magna Carta for
Mankind." Their untenable situation, the IRO stressed, warranted a commitment by the United Nations to guarantee the right of asylum when the bond
between individuals and states was broken: "All persons who do not enjoy the
protection of any state shall be placed under the protection of an international organization established by the UN."[89] Like the League of Nations, the
United Nations would take refugees and stateless persons under its umbrella.
But as opposed to the interwar era, this responsibility would now be universal:
"all persons" not protected by a government would be sheltered by a temporary "replacement state," the United Nations.[90] On this point, the IRO found
in René Cassin a valuable ally. The French vice president of the Commission
on Human Rights was indeed a strong supporter of universal safeguards for
refugees: "Any declaration," he told the New York Times in June 1948, "must
state the duty to protect statelessness and to extend protection to all persons
not protected."[91] Cassin also relayed another key demand expressed by the
IRO: refugees should not only have the right to "seek and enjoy" asylum but
were also entitled to "be granted" it.[92] This radical escalation was in line with
the daring provisions penned by the future Nobel Peace Prize laureate in his
draft of the Universal Declaration submitted in June 1947. Cassin's blueprint
envisioned the granting of cultural rights to ethnic or linguistic minorities
(but characteristically remained silent on the right to self-determination),
required the incorporation of the Declaration into municipal law, and recognized the right of individuals "to petition the United Nations for the redress
of grievances."[93] Most of these provisions were curtailed or abandoned in the
course of the approval process, including by Cassin's own colleagues at the
UN Commission on Human Rights. "The immediate goal," countered
Eleanor Roosevelt, "is not individual petition but early adherence of a
substantial number of nations."[94] Cassin's far-reaching ideas on political
asylum, echoing those of the IRO, similarly probed the limits of the "human
rights revolution": by placing upon the United Nations the responsibility for

refugee protection and on states the unprecedented obligation to admit individuals fleeing persecution, Cassin not only affirmed the right of persecuted persons to seek asylum but also their natural right to obtain it.

Like other provisions of the Cassin draft, this proposal stirred up strong opposition among governments. British and American delegates at the United Nations were under instructions not to portray the right of international protection for stateless people as a fundamental human right.[95] With regard to the right of refugees to "be granted" asylum, the United Kingdom feared that such a provision would reduce the ability of states to control their immigration policies. Speaking on behalf of the United States, Eleanor Roosevelt similarly asserted that an obligation on states to grant asylum would interfere with unilateral American refugee programs. With its policies of "calculated kindness," the United States was not inclined to leave the strategic question of Eastern European anti-Communist refugees in the sole hands of an international body.[96] With perfect symmetry, the USSR rejected the idea of automatic asylum on "anti-Fascist" grounds: this practice would enable "quislings" and anti-Soviet propagandists in the DP camps to benefit unduly from the protection of human rights. In debates in the last phase of the Arab-Israeli war of 1948, Cassin's idea was also met with the opposition of Arab governments. While Lebanese, Egyptian, and Saudi Arabian representatives supported the United Nations humanitarian efforts on behalf of Palestinian refugees, they vehemently opposed the provision that refugees "be granted" asylum. In their mind, the proper solution to the Palestinian refugee problem was not permanent asylum in neighboring countries but "the right of everyone to return to his country" proclaimed in Article 13 of the Declaration. Condemned at birth, the right to "be granted" asylum was diluted into a right to "seek and enjoy" protection in a host country. [97] Due to the "tenacious resistance of state authorities," as Cassin put it, only "partial progress" was accomplished.[98]

Despite these setbacks, the impact of refugee advocacy on human rights law should not be overlooked. The IRO was also closely involved in the passing of the Fourth Geneva Convention of August 12, 1949, the Convention Relative to the Protection of Civilian Persons in Time of War. Its representatives argued that refugees in conflict zones should not be categorized as enemy nationals by belligerent parties and should be shielded from arbitrary internment. On this point, the IRO received the support of World Jewish Congress spokesmen similarly lobbying for the protection of refugees in wartime.[99] The Fourth Geneva Convention ultimately recognized the explicit "rights" of noncombatants and aliens in time of hostilities, a landmark improvement in the language of the law of war.[100]

Another decisive contribution made by the IRO was the elimination of group-based definitions of refugees. As participants in the drafting of the 1951 Geneva Refugee Convention, IRO legal experts advocated the adoption of the individual and universal refugee definitions tested in the course of the DP crisis. In their mind, Cold War tensions warranted drastic transformations in the framing of the refugee concept. As an IRO jurist diplomatically pointed out, "The present state of the world is in its essentials not similar to the state of affairs which ruled when the previous conventions were adopted."[101] Tailor-made for anti-Communist refugees, the 1951 Geneva Convention subsequently recognized as a refugee any individual with a "well-founded fear of persecution" in its country of origin. It also committed signatory states to ensure the safety of asylum seekers in their midst: even if initially curtailed by temporal and geographical restrictions favoring European refugees, the Convention was the most effective covenant born out of the "human rights revolution." As an American diplomat observed at the time, the European refugee crisis played a critical role in the emergence of enforceable international rights: "It is a curious paradox that out of a postwar clean up job, out of the wreck of the refugee's fundamental freedoms, there had arisen the first widespread and binding international agreement for the advancement of human rights."[102] The United Nations Department of Information was of course unreasonably optimistic when it proclaimed that the "Magna Carta for Refugees... marked a new level of world morality."[103] But contrary to what Hannah Arendt so powerfully claimed, European refugees did not just symbolize the end of the "rights of man": they also facilitated their frustrating, often hypocritical, but in many respects revolutionary beginnings.

5

Surplus Manpower, Surplus Population

ON OCTOBER 22, 1951, a forty-seven-year-old Slovak refugee named Alexander Ranezay stood at the center of an unusual ceremony. Under a "barrage of cameras and newsreels," the International Refugee Organization celebrated that day the "resettlement" of its millionth DP. Presented to the press at the IRO headquarters in Geneva, the United States–bound emigrant was ready to embark upon a "magic journey" to his final destination, Midland, Texas. After six trying years spent in a DP camp in Austria, Ranezay and his family were finally "leaving behind the mounting fears which had driven them from their home in Slovakia one day in January 1945, only three days before the Communist armies overran that district." The press release issued by the IRO for the occasion provided additional information on the future American. As a state employee in the city of Poprad Ranezay had left his post in 1941 "so as not to represent the Nazi party," a loose reference to the collaborationist Slovak's People Party led by Jozef Tiso. He then worked as a butler until the arrival of the Red Army, whose advance toward Berlin in the first months of 1945 was now described, in typical Cold War fashion, as "Communist armies overrunning districts." Framed this way, the life story of the "millionth DP" featured the perfect credentials: a European victim of Fascism and Communism, Alexander Ranezay epitomized the ideal type of political refugee heralded by the West in the aftermath of World War II.[1]

In the boastful words of the last IRO director general, J. Donald Kingsley, this "millionth" milestone represented "the most successful large-scale international cooperation in history." A higher-echelon official at the Social Security Administration prior to his appointment to the IRO in 1949, Kingsley was one of several New Dealers placed at the helm of postwar international organizations, the pillars of the post-1945 "global community."[2] Like

Herbert K. Lehman at UNRRA or David Morse at the International Labor Office, Kingsley simultaneously championed American leadership and multi-lateralism in order to solve refugee and migratory problems. As such, the coordinated emigration of Europe's displaced persons away from the conti-nent enabled the internationalization of New Deal methods of governance.[3] Tellingly, and despite the near extinction of New Deal policies in the United States, the population scholar Eugene Kulischer concluded his important study of displacement in Europe published in 1948 with a vibrant call for "a TVA of human migratory currents."[4]

Above all, the "millionth" DP resettled under the aegis of the International Refugee Organization marked the peak of centralized international migration. "For the second time within the memory of adults living today," wrote J. Donald Kingsley in September 1951, "the West is faced with the same dilemma: an excess of people in Europe whose very presence constitutes a threat to political and economic stability; a vast and growing demand in other parts of the world for the labor, the skill and the political and cultural assets possessed by these fretfully idle men and women."[5] In a departure from the interwar years, during which national immigration laws exclusively regulated the movement of migrants, the IRO was the "first experiment in cooperative international action employing selective procedures on a multilateral basis." Thanks to its efficient machinery, Kingsley boasted, "new prospects for population movements on a large scale have thus been opened." The fact that an international organization now enjoyed an "authority comparable to the government of an emigration country" largely accounted for the impressive results achieved: throughout its short operational life (July 1947–December 1951), the agency directly trans-ported or helped resettle over one million displaced persons in some forty-eight countries. "In no earlier world migration," wrote the official historian of the IRO, Louise Holborn, in 1956, "have so many uprooted people in an orga-nized effort been resettled in foreign countries."[6]

Although first implemented on a widespread basis in the context of the DP crisis, the idea of population redistribution under international auspices was not entirely new. A not too distant point of reference was the notorious address delivered in 1927 by the French Socialist politician Albert Thomas, then director of the International Labor Office (ILO), at the World Population Conference in Geneva. "An attempt should be made to tackle the migration problem," the French official urged, "and this attempt should be made internationally."[7] In particular, Thomas challenged the exclusive right of nation-states to control migratory flows. "Has the moment yet arrived," he asked provocatively, "for considering the possibility of establishing some sort of supreme supranational authority which would regulate the distribution of population on rational and impartial lines"?[8] Against the right of immigration countries to independently pursue their population policies, Thomas opposed the right of unspecified "overpopulated communities" to settle their surplus labor in foreign countries through emigration mechanisms accepted by all parties. Delivered at a key moment in the history of international population control in the twentieth century, Thomas's address echoed anxious debates over fertility rates, with the specter of overpopulated Asia already haunting the minds of Western demographers and population experts.[9] As opposed to eugenics or compulsory birth control, the redistribution of "surplus persons" advocated by Thomas was not a biological solution to the uneven growth of world population. Neither was his plan an attempt to send white settlers to colonial areas, exemplified by the Empire Settlement Act passed by the British parliament in 1922. Nonetheless, such a model of population redistribution was clearly intended to counter, through the regulation of migration, the negative effects of population increase in Asia. Enforceability was a different matter: Thomas himself recognized that his idea was "premature and Utopian" (as was his call for of a "supreme migration tribunal" to settle disputes among countries) and acknowledged that for the time being, "practical internationalism is still too weak."

Echoing some of Thomas's proposals, the secretive "M Project" conducted under the authority of Franklin D. Roosevelt between 1942 and 1945 sought to put into practice the idea of organized population redistribution. This mammoth plan, deemed by FDR "potential dynamite" if revealed to the public, envisioned the massive resettlement of displaced persons to Latin America, an area long considered by Roosevelt the last frontier of human migration.[10] The long list of people falling under the label "displaced persons" was indicative of M Project's revolutionary ambition. Wary of the disruptive effect of unstable populations on the post-1945 world order, FDR had in mind the relocation of millions of war refugees, "surplus populations" in Europe and Asia as well as "geopolitical problem children," i.e., members of political or cultural minorities at odds with nation-states. But despite his interest in these questions, it is doubtful whether FDR intended to proceed with such a controversial program. Fearing its "dangerous aspects," his successor, Harry Truman, abandoned the project in October 1945. Never implemented, this little-known initiative only resulted in 665 eclectic studies on human settlement penned by a team of population experts, geographers, and anthropologists.[11] Yet although these surveys were rapidly shelved M Project was not inconsequential: by situating "the refugee" at the center of long-range plans for international migration, the project influenced the philosophy and practice of postwar population redistribution efforts. One of the plan's recommendations was indeed the establishment of an "International Settlement Authority," a specialized United Nations agency in charge of the regulation of migration flows. Disgruntled former associates of the terminated project could therefore find solace in the operations carried out in Germany and Austria by the IRO, one of the first special agencies established by the United Nations. As a former M Project researcher wrote in 1947, the removal of displaced persons from refugee-crowded Europe fulfilled the scheme's vision and fostered, at last, "the lasting peace envisaged by FDR."[12]

While the IRO viewed the resettlement of DPs as a "safety-valve for over-population pressure," its methods were less radical than those envisioned in earlier blueprints. The organization pressed governments to accept refugees but never superseded national immigration policies. Its main task was to orchestrate migration movements according to the manpower needs or humanitarian proclivities of host countries. Yet despite several precedents, such as population exchanges between Turkey, Greece, and Bulgaria in 1923 or the role played the Intergovernmental Committee on Refugees in the evacuation of Jews from Nazi Germany, the IRO was the first "supranational authority" to regulate refugee migration on a worldwide scale. Advertising the mass of DPs as a reservoir of skillful and industrious workers, the agency organized the emigration of "surplus manpower" to countries in need of labor migrants.[13] When the Cold War intensified, the IRO additionally portrayed the DPs as symbols of democracy and propagators of anti-Communism. Toward the end of the 1940s, however, the European DP crisis was presented as a problem of "surplus population" hampering the stability of the continent and the prospect of European integration. Completed in the early 1950s, the resettlement of the "last million" paved the way for grand designs of population redistribution and for international institutions created to that effect in the early Cold War era.

"Is this not an insult to common sense," asked an IRO official in 1949, "that hundreds of thousands of people reduced to idleness neither consume nor produce at a time when all men and women should be associated with the tasks of reconstruction and production?"[14] This preoccupation with "DP idleness" was not a novelty: Allied military and civilian authorities had tried since the end of the war to put inactive refugees to work. This policy was first introduced in November 1945 in the French occupation zone. In charge of approximately fifty thousand DPs, the French military government assigned refugees to various tasks inside and outside DP camps.[15] Saddled with the bulk of the DP population, British and American authorities similarly tried to utilize, using various levels of compulsion, large numbers of displaced persons. Their employment as UNRRA auxiliaries or in the German economy, it was hoped, would accelerate their "moral rehabilitation" and prepare them for emigration elsewhere. However, the large number of DPs refusing to work, as well as scarce job opportunities outside the DP camp system, gravely hindered this effort.[16] "The amount of work [the DPs] contribute," concluded a report issued by the US army in 1946, "is only a fraction of the effort necessary to maintain them."[17] As a pool of "idle" manpower, the DPs offered instead a source of labor supply to countries engaged in economic and demographic reconstruction.

Chief among them were the Eastern European nations reeling from colossal losses of material and population incurred during the war. In order to support rebuilding efforts, the Soviet Union, Yugoslavia, and Poland adamantly insisted on the compulsory return of their displaced nationals. Yet as the dramatic fall in repatriation rates already indicated in late 1945, the prospect of socialist reconstruction at home failed to lure back the vast majority of the remaining DPs. This available pool of laborers immediately appealed to Western European governments in need of a replenished workforce. In France, Belgium, and England, wrecked industrial facilities and a dire lack of coal warranted the urgent recruitment of miners and other hands badly needed to win the "battle of production." Rural exodus and fears of depopulation, especially in France, similarly justified the importation of new bodies from neighboring Germany.

The French minister of population, Robert Prigent, was among the first Western European public figures advocating the immigration of DPs. A visit to Polish DP camps in the French occupation zone convinced him of the value of DP labor. "Having witnessed their clean and skillfully arranged interiors in these ruined barracks," Prigent declared in December 1945, "we are convinced that they could restore our abandoned villages and revive dying lands." Unlike interwar Polish immigrants "who lived with the legitimate hope to one day return to their country," the DPs offered "long-term demographic solutions."[18] Interest in DPs was equally strong in Great Britain. On February 14, 1946, the Labour Cabinet allowed the immigration of displaced persons to remedy shortages in key industries. But this decision was not devoid of racial considerations: as potential "white Britons," the DPs were deemed preferable to black immigrants from the West Indies.[19] Industrial workers were also in high demand in Belgium. In an attempt to recruit a substantial contingent of miners for collieries near Mons, Liege, and Charleroi, Belgian representatives entered in negotiations with Allied occupation authorities.[20] By 1947, the DP population had become an essential source of potential European migrants. "The chief hope of production increase," stated the sixteen members of the Committee on European Economic Cooperation, "lies in the employment of DPs, some Germans...and unemployed Italian workers."[21] The "last million" presented a considerable advantage over other type of migrants, however. As Robert Prigent presciently understood in 1945, refugee camps in Germany offered the convenient possibility of individual selection while affording manpower recruiters undisputed autonomy. While trusting his country's ability "to absorb and assimilate foreign laborers," Prigent also recommended that France "chose them adequately": for countries interested in laborers, the DP camps would soon provide an ideal terrain for the unhampered scrutiny of candidates for work." As the French minister rightly predicted, "it will be easy to examine the refugees regrouped in the camps according to their professional ability, physical shape, social background and behavior."[22]

Evocatively named "Operation Black Diamond" in Belgium, "Westward Ho!" in Great Britain, and the "French Metropolitan Scheme," three Western European plans launched the first phase of organized DP emigration. Initiated in May 1946, the Belgian recruitment drive raised the hopes of Polish, Ukrainian, and Lithuanian DPs awaiting a country of destination. "In our seven camps," recalled Kathryn Hulme, "we saw in microcosm what was happening all through the DP world of Germany at that moment: the lifted faces as to a fresh breeze, the tense debating wherever men were gathered...and the stricken look of the men over forty years, sad spectators of the first opening of a door to a new life to which they were already too old to qualify."[23] Eileen Egan, a volunteer for the Catholic Refugee Service, realized, however, that the Belgian labor scheme was not motivated by humanitarianism: "Cattle market deals, said welfare workers as truckloads of able-bodied males rolled out of the camps. But realism told us that war-depleted countries could not begin immigration schemes with a welfare approach."[24] In an effort to entice 35,000 male workers, the Belgian mission offered a standard contract that later served as a reference for British and French competitors: a commitment of two years of labor in the mines, with the promise of a salary equal to the wages paid to Belgian workers. Yet the full completion of the two years specified by the "freedom clause" was required in order to work later on in a field less strenuous than mining.[25] To the dismay of IRO representatives, the Belgian government also "reserved the most difficult areas of mine operations for the refugee workers." These harsh conditions explain the scheme's relative failure. By 1949, Belgium had only obtained 32,000 immigrants, out of which 8,000 soon opted to return to Germany.[26]

"Westward Ho!" proved more successful. With 82,000 Polish, Ukrainian, and Latvian DPs, England remained until 1948 the leading destination for DP emigrants.[27] Like the Belgian plan, "Westward Ho!" was not a charitable endeavor. "The Ministry of Labour officials stated outright that it was a cool-blooded labor recruiting campaign," recalled the UNRRA worker Marvin Klemme. Britain needed "good, healthy workers to mine coal, make bricks, work on the farms and do other heavy work and that those who volunteered would be used for that purpose."[28] The "European Volunteer Workers," labeled as such to emphasize their cultural proximity to the British population, were first recruited in the British occupation zone of Germany, which they left at an average pace of 1,500 workers a week in 1948. The vetting process carefully verified the refugees' marital status: single men had priority over married workers. Families accompanied by children under the age of sixteen were accepted if both parents were considered "productive." As Marvin Klemme pointed out, "The British did not want a lot of sickly or crippled relatives coming in later on." Like its Belgian predecessor, the British plan also confined the DPs to specific fields—in this case mining, textiles, agriculture, and "domestic hospital work."[29] It was only after 1951 that these restrictive measures were lifted, initially for DPs having resided in England at least three years.[30] Despite these constraints, numerous postwar commentators considered "Westward Ho!" a landmark success. "The British example," wrote one of them, "set a pattern which, although defective in some ways, broke down much of the initial resistance of many countries to refugee immigration."[31]

Despite its initial interest, France was the last European country of immigration to actively seek workers among the DPs. Preference for Italian workers, the presence in France of 450,000 German POWs employed at low cost, and denunciations of "Fascist" anti-Soviet DPs by the Communist Party caused this delay.[32] The French reluctance to accept displaced persons particularly angered American officials: "French policy results in a double charge against the American taxpayer who must pay deficiencies in the German economy and pay through the IRO the major share in the care of DPs."[33] As a consequence, members of the US congress threatened to withdraw Marshall Plan assistance from "any European nation refusing to open its borders to a reasonable number of DPs."[34] In addition to American pressure, the fear of losing valuable laborers to England prompted a change of course in French immigration policy: "The British are currently recruiting 120,000 workers," Le Monde reported in February 1948, "and they evidently want to reserve the best for themselves."[35] Finally, the high cost of bilateral immigration agreements signed with Italy, involving the export of precious coal in exchange for

200,000 workers, made the DPs cheaper to bring in.[36] In the spring of 1947, the French government was finally ready "to accept a large number of DPs, its immediate needs of labor being estimated at approximately 300,000 or 400,000 workers."[37]

Initial hopes for large numbers of suitable workers were quickly dashed. The French plan was marred from its inception by particularly high medical and professional selection criteria, at times yielding a 50 percent rejection rate.[38] "The French clearly want to handpick their DPs," a British observer of French selection practices pointed out. "Single men and women are preferred, working potential of dependants is an important factor to the French, managerial type not required, priority to industry; it seems clear that the French want DP labor to supply demands of least attractive industries; most interested in DPs between 16 and 25."[39] Indeed, French industrialists feared that the healthiest and most productive male workers had already been culled by Belgium and Great Britain: "What remains available," representatives of the French extractive industries bemoaned, "looks to be of bad quality."[40] The limited employment opportunities offered by France further diminished its appeal among DPs. Although the French Metropolitan Scheme was more liberal than others in terms of family reunification, it still gave priority to miners and industrial workers. In negotiations with British authorities, "the French said that any other course would upset their economic planning: if too much labor goes to attractive occupations, unattractive jobs would be left short."[41] Moreover, the presence of card-carrying Communists in the selection teams decreased the popularity of the French scheme. "Candidates are asked about their political opinions," noted the French military command in Germany, "and the rumor is that one must be a Communist sympathizer in order to immigrate to France."[42] Above all, however, the French plan only attracted 38,000 workers because of the scant interest of refugees to go to a country severely damaged by the war. A latecomer on the scene of DP resettlement, France suffered from the competition of more appealing destinations. "In most places," complained a French visitor to the DP camps in 1949, "the walls are covered with maps, flyers and photographs advertising the charms of Australia, Canada or the United States. Nothing indicates that a French plan exists."[43]

Although their yield was limited to 150,000 emigrants, the Western European schemes transformed the DP camps into battlegrounds for laborers. This "true manhunt," observed the French historian and demographer Louis Chevallier at the time, turned the labor migrant into a "rare and costly commodity...lured by economic, political and sentimental pressure."[44] This scarcity was not only caused by a shortage of candidates for hard industrial labor; it was also the product of rigorous selection criteria based on physical condition and ethnic origin. Refugees from the Baltic states stood at the top of this hierarchy of desirability. "The authorities of the different zones," a French report stated, "shared the view that from a moral standpoint Balts topped the ladder, ahead of Yugoslavs, Ukrainians and finally, Poles."[45] The morality of Baltic DPs was in contrast to the rampant alcoholism observed in Polish DP camps, where "on average 400 liters of vodka were consumed every Sunday."[46] The hygiene, athleticism, and productivity of Lithuanians, Latvians, and Estonians were also singled out. British labor officials were particularly impressed by the "good appearance" of Baltic women, "scrupulously clean in their persons and habits."[47] French social workers praised them as "an overall healthy and beautiful race" and admired the work ethic of Baltic DPs employed in UNRRA warehouses.[48] A desirable category of workers for Western European recruiting teams, "the gentry of the DPs" also appealed to transatlantic countries of immigration. Baltic DPs showed "every sign of having come from good stock and good breeding," reported an American congressman, and were "unmistakably intelligent, conscientious, industrious and energetic."[49] After the IRO stepped up its resettlement operations, the search for suitable "human material" was conducted by dozens of governments interested in the productive and ethnic value of DP immigrants.

August 20th, 1948, was an important date in the brief history of the IRO. That day, the agency officially became operative when the quorum of fifteen member countries, required in December 1946 by the UN General Assembly, was finally met. Although more that 50 percent of its budget was financed by the United States, the IRO was now empowered to promote the resettlement of displaced persons throughout the world.[50] Theoretically, the agency still "gave priority to repatriation" and publicly stated that when "a refugee has no valid objection to returning, home is the best place for him to go."[51] But this was mostly lip service to Soviet-bloc countries resentful of an international organization dedicated to the emigration of their nationals overseas. Indeed, the IRO functioned, in its own words, as "the largest mass transportation system in the world": soon equipped with a fleet of thirty vessels (many of them troopships used by the US army during World War II) in addition to many chartered seats on regular ships, the IRO facilitated the emigration of DPs "to destinations on five continents." From "staging camps" set near the ports of Bremerhaven and Hamburg, the agency was already moving "19,000 persons per month at a daily cost of just under $160,000" in November 1948.[52]

Kathryn Hulme vividly described this efficient process: "Call forward, in processing, final shipment...the new language of the Resettlement Center was exciting to hear, a functional phrasing descriptive of...the great emigration mill which changed the faces of everyone who entered it and the fates of everyone who got through it."[53]

The realization that Europe alone would not be able to settle the postwar refugee question explains the global reach of the IRO. Eastern Europe failed to attract enough "repatriants," but Western Europe did not absorb significant numbers of emigrants. Existing alternatives did not seem promising. The compulsory return of DPs to their homeland, explained the US secretary of state George Marshall in July 1947, would "violate our American traditions and standards of international conduct." Another option, "the abandonment of DPs to the German economy," was impracticable due to the millions of ethnic Germans expellees already clogging the local employment market. And the indefinite maintenance of DP camps would unfairly perpetuate the burden placed on American taxpayers. The only solution, concluded Marshall, was the resettlement of "these people in the various countries willing to receive them."[54] Western Europe, in his mind, had already filled up its room for immigrants. Like other American policymakers, Marshall worried that overcrowding in "the Western areas of Europe" undermined reconstruction and political stability. Moreover, the core premises of the Marshall Plan implied a lesser role for Western Europe in the absorption of DPs. The American aid package announced by Marshall a month earlier encouraged productivity and efficiency over raw production, with important consequences for the immigration projections of Western European countries: "their needs, economists tell me, are not primarily for additional manpower.... Some expert and experienced top-level assistance from the outside might be helpful to them, but so far as it might be drawn from displaced persons it would not be numerically important." The success of the Marshall Plan, in other words, depended less on the quantity than on the quality of the European work force. Instead of a hazardous influx of refugees and displaced persons, the European Recovery Program fostered rational modernization "so that available manpower can again effectively produce and the product be effectively distributed."[55]

New channels of international migration fortunately counterbalanced the limited absorptive capacities of Western Europe. Although the creation of the State of Israel in May 1948 triggered the birth of the Palestinian refugee problem, it also provided a permanent home for Jewish DPs. The ongoing military hostilities between Israeli and Arab armies temporarily forced the IRO Executive Committee to suspend its assistance to Jewish emigration until January 1949. Yet even without IRO support, the Jewish Agency for Palestine in collaboration with the American Jewish Joint Distribution Committee "moved a considerable number of Jews to Israel" throughout the War of 1948: 132,000 Jewish DPs registered under the IRO ultimately settled in Israel.[56] Although Harry Truman signed it "with very great reluctance" due to its many restrictions, the passing of the DP Act by the US Congress in June 1948 afforded Europe's displaced persons a chance to emigrate to the United States.[57] While allowing the entrance of 205,000 DPs, the law's stipulations, such as the issuance of 30 percent of all visas to persons with agricultural background, discriminated against Jews.[58] Still, the DP Act of 1948, later amended in 1950, sparked significant transatlantic movements: spearheading the migration of nearly 400,000 immigrants over the next four years, the first group of DPs left Bremerhaven for New York on October 21, 1948, with 813 passengers, including 161 Jewish refugees. Canada also opened its gates to DPs under programs for "close relatives" and laborers, including domestic workers. Both policies were initiated earlier, but emigration to Canada, totaling 123,500 DPs, significantly picked up pace in 1948. Departures to Australia similarly increased: after 1948, the shipping capabilities of the IRO enabled an overall number of 182,150 DPs to embark on the long journey across the Indian Ocean. In addition, seventeen Latin American countries took 100,000 emigrants from the DP camps between 1947 and 1952.[59] Overall, nearly fifty national resettlement missions, composed of immigration officials, doctors, and labor specialists, were present in Germany, Austria, and Italy at the peak of IRO operations.[60]

The advertising campaign launched by the IRO to market its refugee population contributed to the magnitude of this international response. In newspapers and pamphlets, the agency drew worldwide attention to the DP cause. Public information officers, however, were warned not to "make use of extravagant emotional appeals ... and should avoid undue emphasis of themes of acute distress, privation and horror" so as not to adversely affect immigration possibilities. Accordingly, the IRO portrayed the DPs as an energetic community of hard workers and "freedom-loving people." An official "Guide for Publicity on Displaced Persons" issued in November 1948 extolled their numerous qualities.[61] Against the common perception of DPs as "idle" and "apathetic," the IRO stressed their industriousness and strong physical and mental dispositions. Moreover, as "people with strong family ties" and religious values, the DPs had impeccable moral credentials. First and foremost, the IRO framed the DPs as an admirable "antitotalitarian" population: "Displaced Persons are democratic. The suffering they have endured under totalitarian rule has reinforced their devotion to democratic ideals." Life in IRO camps had adequately prepared the DPs for democratic citizenship: "They have their own elected camp leaders and conduct their own policing services."[62] In this light, the dispersal of DPs throughout the world would not only solve a humanitarian problem but also help propagate liberal democracy.

More than advertising campaigns, the "preparation" and "presentation" of DPs to international selection missions made a decisive contribution to the redistribution of the refugee population. A small portion of resettled DPs were "nominated migrants" sponsored by family members or friends in the United States, Canada, and Latin America in particular. In this case, the IRO mediated between sponsors, consulates, and emigrants.[63] But "placement on the basis of qualifications" remained the dominant mode of emigration. A first step toward the success of this program was the production of reliable figures on the occupational backgrounds of refugees. An IRO labor census of men and women of working age divided DPs into three main groups—skilled, agricultural, and professional—and revealed that refugees offered "youth and skills to the world: countries actively seeking persons in order to diminish their labor shortages will find that refugees can be of tremendous value in aiding in the solution of manpower problems."[64] Indeed, 83 percent of the DPs who lived in IRO camps were under forty-five years of age. Additionally, a sample of 330,000 males showed nearly 75 percent of them to be skilled or semiskilled workers, a remarkably high proportion "for any group of workers in any modern society."

In order to increase acceptance rates by governmental missions, the IRO developed its own preselection process within the camps. Eager to ensure a proper "presentation of candidates to selection missions," the IRO evaluated credentials and professional qualifications and conducted various medical exams so as to offer only healthy and productive refugees to labor selectors. In an experiment "with no precedent in the field of international migration," according to J. Donald Kingsley, the IRO sent comprehensive dossiers to potential recruiters around the world. In most cases, however, the DPs were directly presented to national representatives in resettlement centers located in the occupation zones. Manpower experts there could evaluate the refugees' skills and qualifications with the help of tools and machines made available to them. At the end of this selection pipeline, candidates left for a "staging center" before reaching a final "embarkation center." Unsuccessful DPs were sent to retraining programs with the goal of a more successful "presentation" in the future. Yet it was soon apparent that there were large numbers of rejected candidates. Touring Germany in late 1947, members of the US Congress observed the first signs of this: "The selection process tends to single out the best human material in terms of training, family situation and age."[65] In May 1948, the IRO criticized the "present recruitment programs which treat labor solely as a commodity."[66] Its director at the time, the American Quaker philanthropist William Hallam Tuck, called upon the international community to humanize selection practices. In particular, Tuck asked governments to take in whole families as well as the less able-bodied.[67] Alongside the so-called hard-core refugees, "intellectuals" and Jewish DPs did not smoothly fit into the machinery of population redistribution.

Revived during the war by the brutal "slave-labor" policies enacted by the Nazi regime, the image of slavery also came to mind for postwar observers of civilian displacement in Europe. The IRO director general J. Donald Kingsley, always keen to describe the organized emigration of DPs as "one of the great sagas of our time," told the United Nations in November 1949 that the courageous actions of his agency had prevented the return of bondage. "The IRO," he declared, "has not, and will not forcibly resettle those persons entrusted to its care: that indeed, would have constituted slavery."[68] The veteran British welfare worker Francesca Wilson went even further. "What [UNRRA and the IRO] did for the DPs in the seven years of their operations," she told the BBC in 1952, "was perhaps the greatest humanitarian achievement since the emancipation of the slaves." Comparisons between DPs and slaves were indeed common among relief workers. The British Quaker Grigor McClelland, for instance, thought that the "closest parallel" to the displaced persons was "the transshipment of Africans to work as slaves in American plantations."[69] Yet for Francesca Wilson, the DPs were worse off than African captives: "Slaves were needed, whereas large numbers of refugees live in enforced idleness, and their presence is resented." Mass migration under the auspices of the IRO amounted therefore to a new abolitionist movement: "If we have not lost the vision of our forebears who worked to free the slave, we will not forget his modern counterpart—the refugee."[70]

This potent metaphor was also used for other purposes. As the multiple references to "slavery" made by Western commentators indicate, the comparison of resettlement practices to "indentured servitude" was not merely a habit of Soviet-bloc spokesmen denouncing the use of DPs as cheap labor in the West.[71] Across the German border, the French newspaper *Le Monde* described the DP camps as "a slave market in the heart of Europe" and compared recruiters to slave traders "palpating muscles."[72] A French writer visiting the DP camps used a similar image when he portrayed selection missions as "animal dealers…tearing open the chops of horses in order to check the coating of their teeth."[73] A former leader of the French resistance, Claude Bourdet, compared screening methods to Nazi slave-labor practices: "Finicky governments, including French authorities…separate the 'fit to work' from the 'worthless,' just like Hitler did."[74] In the United States, anti-Communist advocates of (non-Jewish) DPs also depicted international manpower schemes in a derogatory fashion: "Governments may thumb through IRO's DP 'catalogue' like farmers through a Sears, Roebuck annual; their representatives prowl in the camps as if in department-store bargain basements, where the marked-down price tags feature race, size, family status, age, skill, muscles."[75] At times, readers of the American press were invited to directly sift through the inventory. Urging the American public to sponsor DP emigrants, newspaper articles emphasized the benefits of refugee labor: "Do you want a displaced person as a domestic? Perhaps you want a very young woman. Get an affidavit proving you're financially able to prevent the woman from becoming a public charge. You may make other requests too. You may prefer a Latvian, a Yugoslav, a Pole."[76]

These multiple allegations of "slavery" pertained to various patterns of exclusion at work in the redistribution of the DP population. A poor physical condition, for instance, brought a high risk of rejection. The Hambro-Williams report commissioned by the UN Economic and Social Council confirmed this trend: "The percentage of old people, sick, mutilated and maimed invalids is constantly rising," a fact confirmed by American visitors in Germany worried that the United States "will only receive the aged, indigent, infirmed or the very young."[77] To remedy this situation, the IRO urged countries to consider humanitarian gestures unrelated to manpower needs: "Unless each nation accepts its fair share of these people, there is no hope that they can ever leave their present disheartening situation."[78] To that end, IRO officials around the world tried to secure visas for so-called residual refugees. Still, tens of thousands of "institutional cases" joined the 230,000 "homeless foreigners" with limited opportunities handed over to West German welfare agencies after the formal termination of the IRO in December 1951.[79]

Alongside those with weakened bodies, "refugee intellectuals"—academics, specialists, managers, or members of the professions—were not in a favorable position in the screening of labor migrants. As an infuriated French journalist wrote from Germany, "A congenital imbecile, if robust and docile, is a premium piece for the Gentlemen Selectors.…Bring us healthy brutes! But this musician? This painter? What shall we do with them? Doctors? No thank you, we have ours. And we already have too many."[80] The retraining of

professionals for more desirable occupations was one measure proposed by
the IRO to overcome this handicap: visiting the American zone for the *New
Yorker*, the journalist Janet Flanner reported that in IRO vocational schools,
"intellectuals are learning to be garage mechanics, brick layers, and so forth."[81]
But according to Louise Holborn, 40,000–60,000 displaced intellectuals
still lingered in IRO refugee camps by the end of 1948.[82] The highest proportion
was found among the Balts (one out of nine), followed by Ukrainians (one
out of sixteen), Jews (one out of twenty-three) and Poles (one out of thirty-
one).[83] These figures, however, did not take into account various strategies
employed by "intellectuals" to pass themselves off as manual workers: "The
bank clerk or journalist, having been rejected by one or more selection boards
who wanted only farm laborers or artisans, at the next interview became a
cowman or a plumber."[84] In order to increase the chances of specialists to be
accepted by receiving countries, the IRO Placement Service issued a compilation of DP biographies revealingly entitled *The Forgotten Elite*. The brochure
profiled refugees with intellectual background turned down by selection
teams. "Ruefully," the IRO lamented, "they have watched hundreds of thousands of their fellow refugees gain acceptance for immigration as manual
workers... while they, the forgotten elite, have been passed over."[85] This "ban
on the brain," charged the IRO, was detrimental to "vast populations in dire
need of the very services [intellectuals] have to offer for the right of freedom
and citizenship."[86]

Unlike in the 1930s, postwar Jewish refugees were not significantly affected
by the anti-intellectual bias of immigration policies. The "rescue of learning"
carried out between 1933 and 1939 by Western European and American organizations had been prompted by the high proportion of academics and professionals among German and Austrian refugees from the Third Reich. In
1945, the Geneva-based Comité International pour le Placement des
Intellectuels Réfugiés (CIPIR), established in 1933 to assist "intellectuals having lost their professional occupations at the onset of the Nazi regime," still
sought to place 2,443 such refugees—half of them Jews—in Western European
countries.[87] Across the Atlantic, the Emergency Committee in Aid of
Displaced Foreign Scholars similarly tried to secure positions for German
Jewish émigrés in American colleges and universities.[88] But the Jewish displaced population in and outside IRO camps was not affected by these efforts:
unlike their German-speaking predecessors, Jewish DPs (predominantly of
Polish background) did not for the most part originate from the ranks of the
"cultivated bourgeoisie" (*Bildungsbürgertum*). In fact, there was little need to

rescue Jewish DPs from the constraints of manual labor: within the large Zionist segment of the Jewish DP population, "productivization" was in high demand. Vocational organizations such as ORT prepared Jewish refugees for skilled industrial life. And in small communities resembling the collective farms of Palestine, Zionist youth organizations fashioned young Jewish survivors into future "pioneers" for the state of Israel.[89] Jewish DPs only formed a small part of the "forgotten elite" of professionals, specialists and intellectuals. Instead, it was as candidates for emigration that Jews were deliberately "forgotten" by countries selecting newcomers among the DPs.

"Without openly declaring their unwillingness to accept Jewish immigrants," United Nations investigators in Germany reported, "the various missions invariably reject all the Jewish candidates."[90] Other reports described a similar pattern: "Jews are not being resettled in proportion to other DPs.... There is evidence that recruiting officials of receiving countries have practiced discrimination," a fact also deplored by advocates of Jewish refugees.[91] The physical condition of Holocaust survivors also explained the absence of Jews from the lists of DPs enrolled in labor schemes. A large segment of the Jewish population, United Nations visitors noted, was "not well equipped for manual or physical work in mines or factories."[92] But labor migration to Belgium or France, let alone reviled England, hardly appealed to Jewish DPs overwhelmingly bent on leaving Europe for Palestine. This lack of interest was mutual: Holocaust survivors had no desire to remain on the continent, and Western European manpower missions combing Germany for miners and hard laborers rarely considered the recruitment of Jews. The historian David Cesarani, among others, produced evidence showing that Whitehall did "all it could to bar Jews from British territory or areas under British control."[93] French representatives, however, tried to establish contact with Jewish DPs. They were, in their own words, "only interested in getting labor" irrespective of ethnic considerations. They also responded to the request of American occupation authorities urging the inclusion of Jews in the French Metropolitan Scheme. The US command, however, acknowledged that the "Jewish element" was not likely "to permanently settle in France nor did it exercise the professions sought by the French plan."[94] This is precisely what a French scouting mission discovered in the Jewish camp of Lampertheim in June 1947. "Few professions of interest can be found among them," concluded the French officials. After some questions were asked, "one of the DPs stood up and declared that everybody wanted to go to Palestine. All applauded. The only thing left was for us to leave."[95]

Opposition to Jewish immigration was, however, overt among officials of non-European countries. To be sure, few went as far as the Brazilian minister Jorge Latour in airing anti-Semitic views. "Jews only buy within their circles and sell at large profits," Latour told visitors exploring resettlement possibilities for displaced persons in Brazil. He was therefore determined "to fight to the last ditch against the granting of permanent visas to Jews."[96] His strong-mindedness paid off: in April 1947, a group of forty-seven Holocaust survivors whose entrance visas had lapsed by a few days were denied permission to land in the country.[97] In most cases, however, discrimination was indirect: as a study of DP immigration policies indicated in 1947, "the various restrictive techniques used included geographical quotas, financial requirements, literacy tests, occupational priorities, etc." The findings of this survey did not bode well for the swift departure of Jews from the camps. The entrance regulations of the British Dominions heavily favored "white stock," a label seldom applied to Jews. Indeed, Australia only took 8,172 Jewish DPs registered under the IRO (out of 182,150 DPs accepted), and Canada 16,021 (out of 123,479). In South Africa, Prime Minister Ian Smuts declared in March 1947 that his country "was not a solution to the Jewish problem" (but supported, at little cost, the establishment of a Jewish National Home in Palestine).[98] Latin American policies were equally unfavorable to Jews. Preference for agricultural workers of Catholic and Latin background seriously limited the prospect of Jewish immigration, as did a strong anti-Semitic bias among Argentinian and Brazilian officials: out of 100,000 DPs relocated to Central and South America, only six thousand were Jews.[99] Last but not least, the United States kept a restrictive approach toward wide-scale Jewish immigration until the DP Act of 1948 was amended for this purpose in 1950. In total, 65,000 IRO-registered Jewish DPs, approximately 25 percent of the total displaced Jewish population covered by the IRO, had emigrated to the United States by 1952.[100] Perhaps the solution to this dearth of opportunities, the New York based Freeland League proposed in 1948, was the settlement of Jews in Surinam. The Dutch government was said to welcome "the Jewish homeless on this sparsely populated territory...and with proper health and sanitary measure, Surinam can become a productive tropical paradise."[101] Other ideas similarly revived territorialist solutions for Eastern European Jews. The president of Warner Bros., for instance, proposed to Harry Truman that Jewish DPs be relocated in Alaska. The Hollywood tycoon sent camera crews to the northern territory in order to demonstrate the feasibility of such scheme. The "Hambro-Williams" report on displaced persons issued by the UN Economic and Social Council in June 1948 arrived at a different conclusion: "Outside Palestine [then already Israel], Jewish immigration will be a mere trickle, not even sufficient to offset the number of births in the Jewish camps."[102]

With the Old World and the New closed off to Jewish resettlement, the state of Israel was indeed the only safety valve for postwar Jewish migrants, regardless of their sympathy for Zionism. Various historians have recently argued that the leaders of the Yishuv (the Jewish community of Palestine) prior to May 1948 and of Israel afterwards regarded weak and "diasporic" Holocaust survivors with contempt and only encouraged the immigration of "good human material."[103] But by taking an overall number of 132,000 IRO refugees (alongside other unregistered Jewish refugees in Central Europe), Israel became the third largest country of DP immigration after the United States and Australia. In contrast to most selection missions, Israel adopted liberal admission guidelines praised by IRO officials: "Thanks to its acceptance of the most difficult cases (tuberculosis patients and the mentally insane), Israel contributed to a very large measure to solve the Jewish refugee problem faced by the IRO."[104] In November 1950, J. Donald Kingsley personally thanked the government of Israel for its "great humanitarian contribution" after 5,200 Jewish "hard-core" refugees requiring costly institutional care were allowed into the country. This indiscriminate approach, of course, largely stemmed from the need to populate the new state with Jews as Palestine was being forcibly depopulated of most of its Arab indigenous inhabitants. In fact, as historians of the first Arab-Israeli conflict have documented, the course of the 1948 war and the eviction of Arab Palestinians from areas and houses targeted for new Jewish immigrants was also dictated by the pace of Jewish DP emigration from Central Europe.[105] Nevertheless, the proven absorbency of the new country provided sufficient guarantees for the adequate resettlement of refugees, the primary task assigned to the IRO by the United Nations in 1946. Indeed, the integration of refugees and migrants from different backgrounds helped Israel gain valuable sociological legitimacy. In the 1950s, not coincidentally at the peak of the "melting pot" paradigm in migration studies, the Israeli experience was commonly hailed, including by international organizations such as UNESCO, as a model for the "cultural assimilation" of immigrants in various parts of the world.[106] For the IRO, eagerly searching for countries willing to accept refugees, Israeli immigration know-how crucially contributed to the settlement of the European DP problem as a whole. Emigrants to Israel, therefore, did not only help consolidate the population of the new Jewish state: as part of the "last million" of displaced persons redistributed across the world between 1947 and 1951, they also contributed to ridding the western part of the European continent of its alleged "surplus population."

"What started out as a movement of displaced persons...also made a beginning at easing the tensions that resulted from overpopulation in Germany, Austria, Italy, Greece and other countries," the final report of the US Displaced Persons Commission stated in 1952.[107] Initially, the emigration of displaced persons sought to alleviate overcrowded conditions in the Western occupation zones of Germany flooded with millions of destitute ethnic German expellees. Yet as the 1940s drew to an end, the displaced persons reflected a broader pattern of European overpopulation. "Behind the present problem of war refugees," wrote the demographer Eugene Kulischer in 1948, "is reappearing in Europe the specter of its overpopulated countries."[108] As the tip of a "surplus population" iceberg, the DPs were evidence of a deeper phenomenon. "The presence of millions of unsettled and dissatisfied people," warned the IRO director general J. Donald Kingsley in 1951, "creates dangers which threaten the political stability of Europe and constitutes a menace to the security for the whole western world."[109] The successful emigration of the DP "surplus" therefore had contradictory consequences: although the vast majority of DP camps in Germany, Austria, and Italy had finally closed, Harry Truman solemnly declared in 1952 that "one of the gravest problem arising for the present world crisis is created by overpopulation in parts of Western Europe, aggravated by the flight and expulsion of people from the oppressed countries of Eastern Europe."[110]

Indeed, as experts, journalists and welfare professionals often pointed out in the early 1950s, IRO resettlement operations had only relieved Europe of a small portion of its homeless population: "The assertion sometimes publicly made that when IRO's work is completed the refugee problem in Europe will be 'solved' is a tragic misstatement," wrote one observer; and while "carefully devised systems of migration have been moving a million people out of the IRO camps," the *Times* claimed, "political events have been creating ten times that number of refugees."[111] Underlying this anxiety was the vexing situation of German expellees in West Germany. The abundant literature produced by expellee groups and German social scientists studying this issue drew an alarming picture: with 9.5 million expellees in its midst (including recent arrivals from the German Democratic Republic), the population of West Germany rose, despite the civilian and military deaths incurred by the war, from 39 million in 1939 to 48 million in 1951.[112] For the World Council of Churches, overseeing the work of Christian charities on behalf of expellees in the Federal Republic, the plight of ethnic Germans proved to the world that the European refugee problem was not in the past: "How can it be otherwise when every sixth person in Germany is a refugee?" Tightly compressed into the Federal Republic of Germany, the "heirs of Potsdam" represented "two thirds of the homeless refugees of Western Europe."[113] In addition, Austria sheltered in 1953 approximately 330,000 foreign-born ethnic German refugees (many of them expelled from Communist Balkan countries), about 5 percent of its overall population.[114] "This vast problem seethes in Germany and also in Austria," warned the World Council of Churches, "and the world will soon hear about it." The estimated 445,000 Eastern European political refugees who by the end of 1952 had crossed from the other side of the Iron Curtain into those two countries certainly helped dramatize the "surplus population" woes of postwar Central Europe.[115]

Other instances of civilian displacement exacerbated these worries: Karelian exiles in Finland, Italian refugees from Venezia Giulia (the Julian March under Yugoslav control since June 1945) and the 700,000 internally displaced persons from the Greek civil war added themselves to the "hapless procession" of uprooted civilians. Moreover, the two million European refugees officially registered by the United Nations High Commissioner for Refugees in the early 1950s reinforced the impression that large swaths of Europe had become a "DP Land." Although many of them, like Spanish Republicans in France, were prewar refugees successfully resettled in a new country, the large numbers of individuals with UNHCR refugee status demonstrated to the world that Europe was chronically saddled with "people adrift."[116] The case of Italy and the Netherlands, however, reminded observers that "overpopulation" on the continent was not entirely the result of a plethora of refugees and displaced persons. With close to two million unemployed workers, Italy was once again categorized as a chronically overpopulated peninsula with a need to divest itself, through emigration, of a significant part of its surplus inhabitants. In the Netherlands, plagued by high population density and the return of expatriates from the Dutch Indies, it was assumed that 60,000 people needed to leave every year to offset demographic and economic pressures. Including both refugees and inactive workers, European overpopulation was generally estimated at five million "surplus men" at the beginning of the 1950s. But whereas the existence of "surplus workers"—in Italy in particular—was a well-known phenomenon, the cohorts of refugees scattered throughout Western Europe strongly enhanced the perception of overpopulation. Fresh memories of the postwar DP crisis strongly affected this diagnosis. "A new kind of DP plagued the conscience of the West after the Displaced Person had become an historical phenomenon," an American immigration expert pointed out in 1957; "it was the 'Disinherited Person,' the

FIGURE 5.1 In its final year of operation, the IRO projected the emigration of 5,000,000 "surplus Europeans" over a period of ten years. International Refugee Organization, Migration from Europe (Geneva, Switzerland: IRO, 1951).

national of overcrowded Western Europe who was surplus to the economy in which he lived."[117] Indeed, the DP experience stimulated a powerful "over-population" discourse unexpectedly aligning Europe with other "overpopu-lated" areas across the world.

The American-dominated population-control lobby did not, however, weigh in on the European overpopulation debate. Two of its most active members, the demographer Dudley Kirk and the Princeton social scientist Frank Notestein, had already (wrongly) concluded at the end of World War II that the population of Europe had peaked and was destined to decrease.[118] In 1948, another influential proponent of population control placed Western European countries and the United States in the same demographic category. Still unaware of the baby-boom effect, Warren S. Thompson claimed that these nations "were now growing slowly and will probably soon cease to grow."[119] For the postwar birth-control lobby, the most preoccupying over-populated area remained teeming Asia "where neither the birth rate nor the death rate has come under reasonably secure control." A trio of differential growth rates sustained this argument. Behind "Class 1" areas (the stagnant West) and "Class 2" countries (the moderately growing Soviet-bloc and Latin American countries), "Class 3" types ("the remainder of the world") presented by far the highest risk of "population explosion"; this included, of course, the "Third World," to use the notorious expression coined by the French demog-rapher Alfred Sauvy in 1952. Europe, however, was not entirely absent from the list of demographic danger zones. In the aftermath of World War II, Western advocates of regulatory population policies could easily justify their motivations by simply pointing to millions of displaced persons and expelless crowding refugee camps in central Europe. But concerned, if not obsessed, with India, Southeast Asia, and soon Africa, the population control establish-ment did not anguish over the question of European overcrowding. A much taller order for demographers and population analysts was the "unsustain-able" growth rates of Asian countries, a scientific argument thinly veiling deep existential worries over the decline of the West.

Anxieties over Western European overpopulation originated instead from overlapping American and European political concerns. Gathered in London in May 1950, Dean Acheson, Ernest Bevin, and Robert Schuman jointly expressed their preoccupation: "The excess of population from which several countries in Western Europe are suffering is one of the most important ele-ments in the difficulties and disequilibrium of the world."[120] The alarming tone of this declaration, issued at a meeting of twelve foreign ministers con-vened to finalize NATO aims, was not incidental. Ridding the continent of its refugees and surplus population was essential to "the maintenance of peace and the defense of freedom," the loose strategic aim to which NATO members subscribed. Breeding poverty and Communism, overpopulation in Europe endangered this goal. "A solution to this problem," declared Harry Truman in 1952, "becomes vitally necessary to strengthen the defense of the North Atlantic Community." At stake was the "very outcome of the Cold War, in which the character, scope and sincerity of the free world's treatment of refugees and…overpopulation may be crucial factors."[121] Although the Korean War brought the superpower struggle into Asia, Western Europe still remained the epicenter of the Cold War. Issued in April 1950, the National Security Council Report 68 (NSC 68) outlined a comprehensive doctrine to contain Soviet power; a turbulent and overpopulated European continent posed a vital threat to success of this grand strategy.[122]

Overpopulation woes also overlapped with the prospect of European integration. On May 9th, 1950, the French foreign minister Robert Schuman presented his famous plan for a "European Coal and Steel Community." A first step toward a European community under French and German leadership, the pooling of extractive resources envisioned by the plan did not explicitly address the problem of excess population. Schuman was nonetheless worried about its detrimental effect on his European vision. "A solution to the problem of refugees and population surplus," he wrote in 1951, "is a precondition to the success of European integration policies."[123] French officials reiterated this position at various times: excess population, they contended, impeded "the building of the European community and the liberalization of exchanges."[124] Yet with a large part of the "surplus" located in the refugee-flooded Federal Republic, this argument echoed traditional French fears of German demographic superiority. At the Moscow Conference of Foreign Ministers held in April 1947, Schuman's predecessor, Georges Bidault, had already insisted that any settlement of the "German question" should include a reduction of the German population. To that end, Bidault envisioned the emigration to France of a large number of *Volksdeutsche* in the hope of depleting Germany of a part of its inhabitants.[125] A proponent of French-German reconciliation, Schuman framed this contentious issue in more conciliatory terms: the economic constraints imposed by overpopulation, even if most visible in Germany, stood in the way of European unity.

As Europe's first flagship institution, the Council of Europe added its voice to the overpopulation chorus. In 1951, its committee of experts counted "4.5 million refugees who have neither finally nor temporarily been absorbed into their economy of their country of residence" in addition to several million unemployed surplus workers.[126] "The problem raised by the presence of refugees and surplus elements of population on the territory of Member States is greater than any that European statesmen have so far had to solve," the Council stated in 1953 while calling Europeans to task: "The conscience of the peoples of Europe should revolt at the fact that among them are living millions of persons bearing the label of 'surplus.'"[127] In a fashion reminiscent of earlier descriptions of DPs in occupied Germany, the Council of Europe drew attention to the dangerous abnormality of the unfortunate surplus: "What of the mental outlook of these beings cast out by society? What of the young people, whose earliest impressions are of the wretchedness of refugee camps or of permanent unemployment?" The remedies proposed to solve this problem, such as integration in host countries or intra-European migration, were initially continental: "The future of Europe depends on the solution to be found by us Europeans to the population problem." But a reinstitution of IRO resettlement operations seemed unavoidable: "We must first endeavor to bring about a better distribution of population and then, in agreement with the peoples of other lands, to seek openings outside Europe for those who cannot be absorbed." Planned international migration, based on the recent achievements of the IRO, appeared once again to be the best "safety valve" to relieve European overpopulation.

As in the interwar era, the International Labor Office actively championed such a solution. Like Albert Thomas in 1927, its longtime director David Morse advocated a supranational regulation of migratory movements, a proposal already issued by the ILO in the midst of World War II.[128] For Morse, the "tragic paradox of the present epoch" was the simultaneous existence of "countries with too many hands and brains and of countries where those hands and brains could contribute to the development of unexploited resources."[129] From the point of view of the ILO, the countries "with too many hands" were those of refugee-ridden and overpopulated Western Europe. To orchestrate the orderly redistribution of excess population, the ILO convened an international conference on migration held in Naples in October 1951. Its ambitious aim was to organize the transfer overseas of no less than 1,700,000 Europeans over a period of five years. "The ILO," reported the *New York Times*, "continues the momentum which has taken place under the auspices of the IRO."[130] With the termination of IRO operations at the end of 1951, the ILO remained the only international body devoted to the cause of planned migration. But reluctant to devolve large powers to an international organization with Communist governments among its members, the United States refused to sponsor the ILO project and instead called its own international migration conference in late November 1951. Gathered in Brussels, Western

European governments heard the US delegate George Warren—a long-time refugee policy adviser at the State Department—significantly scale down the initial objectives of the ILO. What Europe needed, declared Warren, was the departure of approximately 700,000 persons over a period of five years. The IRO was designated as the model to follow: the system put in place to relocate the DPs was "applicable to the larger problem of European overpopulation," and its fleet of ships was still available to transport emigrants.[131]

The Intergovernmental Committee for European Migration (ICEM), the predecessor of the current International Migration Organization, was established to carry out this plan. This agency was under full American control and deliberately placed outside the orbit of the United Nations.[132] From 1952 to 1957, ICEM "assisted the movements" of nearly 572,000 Europeans, most of them originating from Italy, Germany, and Austria and predominantly moving to Australia, the United States, Canada, and Argentina.[133] These emigrants, however, were already independently slated for departure overseas and seldom required additional help—with the exception of the Hungarian refugees of 1956 transferred from Austria to other countries under the auspices of ICEM. Yet unlike the IRO, this little-known international body based in Geneva only indirectly facilitated the departure of European migrants, even though it was well funded by the United States, joined by sixteen governments, and staffed by 124 international civil servants. Its more limited role was to coordinate and "supplement national efforts," not to serve as the "largest mass transportation agency in the world." Still, ICEM proudly celebrated the departure from Europe of its own "millionth migrant" in September 1960, in this case an eleven-year-old Latvian child born in a DP camp in Bavaria and relocated to Kalamazoo, Michigan.[134]

Despite this apparent success, interest in coordinated population movements rapidly dwindled. At the first meeting of ICEM in February 1952, George Warren already noticed a clear "loss of enthusiasm" among the participants. Indeed, countries of emigration and immigration hardly needed such an international mechanism. In the United States, the McCarran-Walter Act and the presidential Escapee Program of 1952, followed by the Refugee Relief Act of 1953, maintained the immigration of European "escapees" within the exclusive—and, for a short while, surprisingly restrictive—realm of American sovereignty.[135] In Germany, the "economic miracle" helped the absorption of greater numbers of refugees and expellees, ultimately putting to rest any fear of surplus.[136] Elsewhere in Europe, economic recovery removed much of the pressure to emigrate overseas: the fierce pace of economic growth relegated fears of a demographic "gangrene" to the past.[137] At the World Population

Conference held in Rome in 1954, migration experts (including former IRO officials now employed by ICEM) continued to praise the merits of transcontinental migration as a means to relieve overcrowding in parts of Europe. Demographers quickly dismissed their views. "Overseas migration is essentially a palliative, not a cure, for problems of population pressure," argued Dudley Kirk at the same meeting.[138] For the director of the influential Population Council financed by John D. Rockefeller, Sr., the lowering of fertility rates remained the most effective remedy to overpopulation. This battle was to be waged in Asia, not in Western Europe: irrespective of temporary population pressure, the combined low mortality and fertility rates of postwar Western Europe still offered the best model for Third World countries urged by American demographers to "transition" toward modern patterns of Western demography. By abandoning its efforts to oversee wide-scale population movements emanating from Europe, ICEM acknowledged the end of the planned migration era: at the start of the 1960s, the organization turned to "migration for development" programs limited to the emigration of experts and highly skilled workers to Latin America.[139] While still confident in "multinational efforts to provide rational directions for the planned movements of people," Louise Holborn admitted in 1965 that "to a considerable degree, the cycle is being closed."[140]

From the DP crisis to the late 1950s, however, population redistribution remained a cardinal feature of the early Cold War period. At the peak of the "displacement continuum" initiated three decades earlier by the end of World War I, American and European policymakers, relying on a network of international organizations, firmly believed that democratic liberalism, economic integration, and prosperity hinged on the removal of "excess Europeans" from allegedly overcrowded areas. Whether as displaced persons under the IRO or other types of refugees afterwards, large numbers of emigrants were shipped out of the continent under elaborate international schemes. This significant episode of population control was made possible by the unchallenged Western monopoly on the organization of international migratory flows. Orchestrated by the Cold War West under American leadership, the redistribution of "surplus manpower" and "surplus population" exclusively focused on Europeans: no equivalent scheme was ever envisioned to relocate Asians or Africans in Western areas. Until the emergence of south-north population movements, transoceanic crossings continued to originate predominantly from Europe: culminating around 1960, the organized exit of "excess" displaced persons and refugees marked the final episode of the Great Atlantic Migration.

6

Extraterritorial Jews

HUMANITARIANISM, PHILOSEMITISM, AND THE ADVENT OF JEWISH STATEHOOD

A HISTORICAL ACCOUNT of Jewish refugees in Allied-occupied Germany must start with a reminder of an astounding fact: in the weeks and months following the fall of Hitler's regime, the cradle of Nazism unexpectedly offered a humanitarian shelter to the survivors of the Final Solution. Indeed, the demise of the Nazi order enabled the surprising return of Jewish life on the "blood-soaked soil" of Germany: in 1947–48, the "surviving remnant" numbered approximately a quarter million Jewish displaced persons, predominantly concentrated in American-controlled Bavaria and Hesse.[1] Initially composed of liberated inmates of concentration camps and survivors of death marches, the Jewish DP population in Germany was reinforced by the arrival into the American zone of approximately 150,000 "infiltrees," most of them Polish Jews. Saved from death at the hands of the Nazis by harsh but timely exile in the Soviet Union, they were repatriated by the USSR to Poland in early 1946. This return proved temporary: the complete destruction of families and homes combined with instances of anti-Semitic violence culminating with the Kielce pogrom of July 1946 provoked a mass departure of Polish Jews to occupied Germany. Joined by a small number of Romanian, Czechoslovak, and Hungarian brethren, these "post-hostility" refugees, as they were officially known, steadily converged, spontaneously or in organized fashion, on the Jewish DP camps of the American zone and the Western-occupied sector of Berlin. Altogether, "infiltrees" from Poland and eastern European countries came to represent two-thirds of the overall Jewish DP population.[2]

Although they were no strangers to intense physical and emotional suffering, most displaced Jews in Germany were indirect victims of the Final Solution. Lumped together, however, the emaciated faces encountered by

Allied troops in the spring of 1945 and the subsequent waves of "infiltrees" constituted the most conspicuous group of "Holocaust survivors" on the European continent. Such a definition, according to Israeli historian Dalia Ofer, "not only reflected the Zionist understanding of what constituted a survivor, but was also used by the survivors themselves in their writings, public declarations, and private correspondence."[3] This visibility contrasted sharply with the discreet presence of Jewish survivors in postwar European polities. In the Soviet Union, the principal site of the "Holocaust by bullets" perpetrated between 1941 and 1943 by the Wehrmacht and local helpers in the Ukraine, Belarusia and the Baltic States, memories of the Great Patriotic War encapsulated Jewish victimization within a scripted "national-Communist" narrative. In East-Central Europe on the verge of Communist takeover, official "anti-Fascism" similarly played down the singularity of Jewish wartime experiences. In France, Belgium, and the Netherlands, the small number of Jews fortunate enough to return from Nazi death camps was absorbed into the broader category of labor and political deportees.[4] In the "DP Land" of Germany, however, Jewish survivors were on full display, their presence magnified by the establishment of separate Jewish camps throughout the American zone. Contrary to the collective invisibility and silence of Holocaust survivors elsewhere in Europe, Jewish DPs loudly asserted their identity in front of military authorities, German civilians, welfare professionals, and a cohort of journalists and foreign dignitaries.

The transient experience of Jews in occupied Germany is therefore hardly reducible to a suffocating "waiting room." The temporary sojourn of Jews in the land of their former tormenters did not simply symbolize the last chapter of the Holocaust or, alternatively, the first chapter of Israeli history: it also enabled a formidable cultural, political, religious, and educational drive toward regeneration and normalization. In particular, Zeev Mankowitz's meticulous analysis of prayer books, rituals of public remembrance, and the writings of Jewish leaders amply confirmed what a Yiddish song popular among DPs vigorously announced: "Now one must live because the time has come!"[5] Atina Grossmann has described how deeply aggrieved Jewish DPs rebuilt their lives in constant negotiation with American soldiers, German civilians and the world at large.[6] Seen from this "regenerative" angle, the warm Zionist feelings shared by Jewish DPs were part of a complex rehabilitation process. Therapeutic and utopian more than staunchly ideological, Zionism was the main available language of hope for survivors longing for relatives and a sense of home. "The yearning for Palestine," explained the chief rabbi of Poland to Anglo-American visitors in 1946, "was a basic human instinct and had nothing political in it."[7]

Undeniably, the scars on body and soul left by the Holocaust and its aftermath shaped the collective identity fashioned by Jewish DPs. "What distinguished the Surviving Remnant in Germany," wrote one of its historians, "was the articulated group awareness that their singular situation prompted."[8] Indeed, the constitution of an autonomous Jewish collectivity is certainly one of the most striking consequences of the postwar European refugee crisis. To be sure, the affirmation of Jewish cultural and political distinctiveness prolonged an already rich history of Jewish separatism in East-Central Europe. Advocates of Folkism, Bundism, and different strands of Zionism had since the beginning of the twentieth century argued that Yiddish-speaking Jews formed a separate national-cultural entity. Moreover, prewar interethnic relations in East-Central Europe bore a certain resemblance with the "borderlands" conditions later experienced by Jewish DPs: in occupied Germany, the last heirs of the vanished Yiddishland continued to live alongside and yet apart from their immediate neighbors. However, the exceptional circumstances created by the Final Solution and the resurgence of anti-Semitism in Poland placed Jews in a unique position within the constellation of uprooted people in the Western occupation zones. In contrast to the millions of ethnic Germans evicted from Czechoslovakia or Poland, Jewish refugees could not conceivably be resettled in Germany, although approximately 30,000 of them eventually stayed in the Federal Republic.[9] And unlike anti-Communist Polish, Ukrainian, or Baltic displaced persons branding themselves as the vanguard of "captive nations," Jews in Germany sought shelter more from the *society* than from the *government* of their previous countries of residence (Poland in the case of most Jewish DPs). A "diaspora" only in the biblical sense, the remnants of East-Central European Jewry that regrouped in the Jewish camps near Munich and Frankfurt was more akin to a nonterritorial nation placed under American protection.

Jewish observers took notice of this evolution. Touring occupied Germany, the rabbi and lawyer Zorach Warhaftig marveled at the rise of a "Jewish ethnological nationality." Members of the Anglo-Jewish Association similarly reported in 1946 that "the consciousness of nationality within European Jewry is more widespread and perhaps even more intense than before."[10] A defiant affirmation of hope and life reborn, the remarkable rise of an autonomous Jewish collectivity was not, however, born exclusively from resilience and political savvy. Although their transitional existence in self-ruled DP camps allowed Jews to recover historical agency, external factors also shaped the Surviving Remnant into a nation. During and after the war, American Jewish organizations dismayed by the refusal of Allied armies and UNRRA to treat Holocaust survivors as a separate group of refugees forcefully pleaded for the recognition of a distinctive Jewish nationality. Following the decisive Harrison Report of August 1945, the statelessness of Jews was finally recognized by Allied relief policies and United Nations agencies. As refugees and migrants subjected, like other displaced persons, to international categorizations, Jews in occupied Germany obtained the status of extraterritorial collectivity entitled to political and migratory rights. In 1948, the IRO fully backed their emigration to Israel despite its official refusal to interfere in the first Arab-Israeli conflict. By acknowledging the legitimacy of Jewish nationhood claims, the postwar refugee regime fostered the emergence of philosemitism in international politics.

"The world at large does not have in its international thinking and international law a political term with which to designate us," lamented one participant in the American Jewish Conference, which convened for the first time in New York in August 1943. Worried about the lack of a "concept or category that will give us international status," he urged fellow delegates to clarify the international position of Jews in anticipation of the postwar era: "The fact that we have not had such status heretofore should not hinder us from defining it now, when the historical moment demands it."[11] Contrary to his wish, however, a precise and all-encompassing label applicable to Jews—whether they constituted a political nation, a cultural minority or a religious community—remained, like in the past, open to debate. Yet the American Jewish Conference, the first unified federative Jewish body ever formed in the United States, placed the legal and political position of Jews in the postwar world at the core of its agenda. This concern for the future of Jews outside of the United States, while not new to American Jewish institutions, announced a turning point in their relationship with the rest of the Jewish world. Unofficially serving as the wartime spokesperson of the American Jewish community, the American Jewish Conference also marked "American Jewry's recognition that it had been charged by history to assume leadership of world Jewry."[12] Undoubtedly, the ongoing mass murder of Jews within the Nazi orbit facilitated the adoption of this transnational and hegemonic role. "The elimination of Continental Jewry as an active factor," the legal expert and director of the Institute of Jewish Affairs, Jacob Robinson, stated in 1943, "strengthens the responsibility of those sections of the Jewish peoples which have not been engulfed."[13] Consequently, the most detailed blueprints on "the future of the Jews" emanated between 1943 and 1945 from the myriad of Jewish leaders and organizations loosely unified under the American Jewish Conference. Particularly active in this

regard was its Committee on Postwar Europe, tasked with guiding the rehabilitation, indemnification, and citizenship rights of surviving Jews. As the examination of its proceedings reveals, the prospect of Allied victory prompted
strong demands for Jewish political and legal particularism. In the midst of
World War II, this large constellation of American Jewish organizations presciently sensed that Holocaust survivors, whose number was still impossible to
assess, foreboded a decisive shift in Jewish history. For the victims of Hitler,
they argued, "a return to the *status quo ante* is hardly conceivable."[14]

The short-lived American Jewish Conference (1943–49) is mostly remembered today as the first instance of collective identification with Zionism by
large segments of the American Jewish community. Although its embrace of
the Biltmore-Jerusalem Program of 1942 calling for a Jewish commonwealth
in Palestine provoked a rift with the powerful American Jewish Committee,
which was more cautious about statehood, the Conference successfully ral-
lied to the Zionist platform the vast majority of its delegates, who were elected
by 2,235,000 voters across the United States.[15] Less noticed, however, was the
strong attention it paid to the related question of "uprooted Jews in
the immediate postwar world."[16] Besides the "implementation of the right of
the Jewish people with regard to Palestine," the Conference was in fact specifically created for the purpose of planning the rescue of European Jewry and
"taking action upon Jewish postwar problems in Europe." The latter issue was
thoroughly debated in the course of two sessions respectively held in
New York (August 1943) and Pittsburgh (December 1944). That the bulk of
surviving Jews from East-Central Europe would not return to their countries
of origin after the war was abundantly clear to wartime Jewish organizations.
The World Jewish Congress, for instance, warned as early as 1943 that the
majority of survivors "will have to migrate, because they were ousted from
their homes and driven to different localities." Even if at that time the situation
of the Jews in Axis Europe was still subject to "swift and catastrophic change,"
the prospect of significant Jewish displacement appeared certain. By the end
of 1944, it could be categorically established that many surviving European
Jews "will not want to live in the same places where they and their kinsfolk
have suffered or witnessed the indescribable horrors of Nazi persecution."[17]
Ultimately, the assumption of looming Jewish displacement fueled insistent
demands for the "extraterritorialization" of future Holocaust survivors.

Indeed, the construction of surviving European Jews into a nonterritorial
nation predated the end of the Nazi extermination program. Jews in Axis-ruled
territories, the World Jewish Congress argued in 1944, formed a "co-belliger-
ent nation" deserving of full Allied recognition. After the Nazis mercilessly

treated European Jewry as a belligerent nation, Jewish victims were owed by the future liberators a similar label guaranteeing their rights and status in the approaching postwar period.[18] Speaking on behalf of the Institute of Jewish Affairs created in New York in 1941, Jacob Robinson espoused a similar view. The situation of future survivors, he contended, "could not be considered in relation to a limited territory or to each country separately, but it was a universal, or at least a European continental problem."[19] The Lithuanian-born émigré lawyer advocated, therefore, the full disentanglement of Jewish survivors from national polities and jurisdictions, particularly in matters of citizenship, property claims, and international representation. Although conceived with the last remnants of Yiddishland in mind, this supranational blueprint did not solely apply to East-Central European survivors. The status of "deported Jews from Western European countries who were only residents but not nationals of those countries" also constituted a genuine "extraterritorial problem."[20] Unaware that foreign Jewish refugees who lived in France and the Low Countries prior to the war would be swiftly reintegrated as resident aliens in 1944–45, Robinson believed that from Eastern to Western Europe, the vast majority of Jewish survivors formed a juridical category extraneous to domestic law. "What is to be their status, who will represent them or take care of them," he wrote, "must be decided on the basis of Jewish rights and status as a whole": the main consequence of the Final Solution was the severance of the bonds uniting European Jews to their former countries of residence. To counteract this loss of state protection, the American Jewish Conference recommended the establishment of a "Jewish Reconstruction Commission of a general character to take care of the problems of European Jewry on a continental scale." It also asked that this body, which ultimately never saw light, "be given the right to participate in the deliberations of the United Nations" so as to negotiate on an equal basis with sovereign nation-states.[21] Writing in the New York émigré publication *Aufbau* in April 1945, Hannah Arendt championed the same view: the "Jewish people," she claimed, stood on equal footing with the forty-four members of the United Nations in having the right "to take part in the organization of the victory and peace."[22]

The assisted emigration of Jewish survivors was another issue through which Jewish particularist claims were expressed in wartime America. "While there is no definite information on the numbers of persons involved," the American Jewish Conference predicted in 1944, "the resettlement of European Jews will no doubt have to be carried out on a mass scale."[23] By "resettlement," American Jewish leaders meant the emigration of Jewish survivors to countries willing to receive them in addition to Palestine, which was "ready and

best suited for Jewish colonization." However, the "principle of selection"
inherited from restrictive interwar immigration policies greatly limited the
relocation possibilities of Jewish refugees. Palestine, on the other hand, "had
been prepared through decades of Jewish pioneering effort to absorb large
masses of Jewish resettlers."[24] This demand was carefully presented as "a practical solution apart from all ideological considerations": the much-debated
"absorptive capacity" of Palestine, assiduously measured since the 1920s by
British administrators and Zionist geographers, made its territory "the only
place where Jewish settlement for colonization is possible" and the natural
destination for Jewish displaced persons in the near future.[25] But even if the
emigration of Holocaust survivors to Palestine was publicly urged by American
Jewish organizations, this issue remained at that time subsumed into a broader
demand for the right of Jews to leave East-Central Europe through international assistance. To that end, the Conference summoned UNRRA to help
future Jewish resettlers with "transportation to the new countries and aid in
their first stages of adjustment," just like the agency helped non-Jewish "repatriates of the United Nations to return home."[26] At the end of the war, Jewish
survivors were already seen by their American supporters as a category of
migrants bound to leave the European continent, in opposition to the millions
of other displaced civilians who would reintegrate their countries of origins.

Between April and June 1945, the San Francisco conference presiding over
the birth of the United Nations Organization presented a unique opportunity for Jewish leaders to propagate this view. Granted by the US government
special advisory status alongside fifty other non-Jewish organizations, the
American Jewish Conference joined forces with the World Jewish Congress
and the Board of Deputies of British Jews to offer a "Jewish position" to the
drafters of the United Nations Charter. Reminiscent of the Committee of
Jewish Delegations at the Paris Peace Conference of 1919, this unified Jewish
representation—"the largest and most representative Jewish delegation ever
to attend an international conference," according to its chairman, Louis
Lipsky—sought the protection of Jews in the new postwar order.[27] But
whereas the Jewish lobbyists of 1919 wanted the Great Powers to recognize
the separate national existence of Jews within successor states, the "Jewish
position" of 1945, cautiously but openly promoting the Zionist cause, emphasized a definitive fracture between Jews and East-Central European polities.
Increasing knowledge about the extent of the Final Solution as well as the
visible presence of liberated concentration camps inmates in Germany and
Austria gave particular substance to this claim: "Surviving European Jews
who are now in countries of refuge or temporary asylum," a memorandum

presented at San Francisco declared, "will neither wish nor be able to return to their former homes." As such, the appearance of Jewish displaced persons on the international scene altered the equilibrium between the individual rights enjoyed by Jews in the United States and western Europe and the collective minority rights granted to eastern- and central-European Jews after 1919. The Jewish delegation at San Francisco certainly wished to perpetuate and even strengthen both forms of protection: one of its main goals was to promote an enforceable human rights jurisdiction grounded in individual rights while safeguarding those of cultural and religious groups. Jewish DPs, however, did not easily fit into this dual system of rights. In extraterritorial limbo, the Surviving Remnant embodied instead the quest for territorialized national rights: the American Jewish Conference, together with other Zionist organizations, would soon draw an explicit link between Jewish refugees and Jewish nationhood, later summarized in a memorandum presented in 1947 to the United Nations Special Committee on Palestine.[28] In June 1945, however, the most immediate agenda of the American-led Jewish delegation concerned with "the future of the Jews" was to press the United Nations and its main refugee agency to recognize the distinctive predicament of Holocaust survivors in occupied Germany.

Despite repeated entreaties by American Jewish groups in 1944 and 1945, the first United Nations institution entrusted with the care of civilian displaced persons in liberated Europe did not acknowledge Jews as a nationality. "UNRRA has indicated that it will make no special provisions for handling Jewish war victims in liberated territories," reported two analysts of Jewish affairs in 1945: "It was felt that appropriate plans for dealing with specific Jewish problems can be worked out within each nation."[29] At its second session, held in Montreal in September 1944, the UNRRA council nonetheless prompted the organization to extend help to "enemy or ex-enemy nationals" who were victims of Nazi persecution because of race or religion; this clause entitled Jewish "persecutees" from ex-Axis countries to be identified as "United Nations nationals."[30] For Hannah Arendt, a keen observer of international refugee policies during and after the war, the fact that UNRRA "was allowed to care for Jews formerly of enemy nationality was only a compromise between the benevolent attitude of the governments represented and the unaltered principle that stateless Jews are still citizens of the countries from which they had been banished."[31] Arendt's observation was accurate: in the weeks following the end of the war, Jewish survivors ranked among the recognized victims of World War II but were not treated as a separate collectivity by the Western Allies in charge of their care.

Various reasons accounted for this situation. The overall (and correct) assumption within UNRRA and the Displaced Persons Branch of the Supreme Headquarters Allied Expeditionary Forces (SHAEF) was that Allied troops sweeping into Germany would only encounter a small number of Jewish survivors. Accordingly, Anglo-American planners did not think that special provisions for Jewish displaced persons were necessary. In the spring of 1945, the liberation of concentration camps confirmed their views: "With only about 20,000 Jews in Western Germany and another 7,000 in Western Austria," wrote the expert Malcolm Proudfoot later, "the Jewish problem understandably appeared to be minor when compared to…the millions of other displaced persons requiring care and repatriation."[32] Another factor prompted UNRRA to absorb Jewish refugees into the larger mass of European DPs: its permanent subordination to the policies devised by Allied military authorities. Before the liberation of Europe, SHAEF handbooks on displaced civilians stipulated that special treatment of Jews would "perpetuate the distinction of Nazi racial theory." Consequently, "Jewish" was not listed in the classification of DP nationalities established by military planners; for their liberators, Jews still formally belonged to their former countries.[33] In June 1945, Jews began to be referred to as "stateless" in SHAEF directives, a term endorsing the disconnection of Jewish survivors from their prewar countries of citizenship. This designation, however, only entitled Jews to share the uncertain status of displaced persons who refused to go home and were allowed to remain in camps until a solution could be found.[34] Compared to the particularist demands formulated by American Jewish organizations since 1943, the protection granted to Jewish DPs in the weeks following the liberation of concentration camps was unexceptional: by August 1945, Holocaust survivors had only earned the protective label of "United Nations nationals" and a de facto status of "non-repatriable" refugees.

The well-known Harrison Report handed to Harry Truman in August 1945, a scathing indictment of the mistreatment of Jews by the US military, is generally considered a turning point in the short history of Jewish DPs. As Leonard Dinnerstein pointed out, this damning survey of conditions prevailing in the DP camps located in the American zones of Germany and Austria played the role of the "progenitor of almost every controversy and policy suggestion of how the Western powers should disperse DPs and minimize their woes while so doing."[35] The study, conducted in July 1945 by Truman's envoy, Earl G. Harrison, at that time the dean of the University of Pennsylvania Law School, was indeed of crucial significance for the future of Jewish displaced persons.[36] After being handled by American soldiers "just like Nazis treated

Jews, except that [they did] not exterminate them," Jewish refugees received improved humanitarian care in autonomous camps separated from the rest of the DP world. At the root of this consequential shift was Harrison's unique understanding of the historical predicament of Jewish survivors: "Jews as Jews" had been singled out by the Nazis and consequently deserved "separate and special recognition." Harrison's statement seemingly contradicted his recent support for ethnic-blind categorizations of Jewish migrants. As the commissioner of the United States Immigration National Service between 1942 and 1944, Harrison had indeed courageously removed the appellation "Hebrew" from the list of "races and peoples" used by American immigration agents, thus making Jews theoretically invisible within the quota system based on national origins.[37] In his report to Harry Truman, however, Harrison argued that the tragedy of the Holocaust called for renewed Jewish distinctiveness: not based, to be sure, on the dubious concept of "Hebrew race" but on the peculiarity of the Jewish wartime experience: "While admittedly it is not normally desirable to set aside particular racial or religious groups from their nationality categories, the plain truth is that this was done for so long by the Nazis that a group has been created which has special needs."[38] One such need was for the creation of separate Jewish camps policed by the US army, administered by UNRRA and opened to the American Jewish Joint Distribution Committee and other Jewish relief organizations. Another special need outlined by the report was the necessity to relocate Jewish survivors to Mandatory Palestine. Unlike Zionist leaders, however, Harrison only spoke of the "evacuation" of "some reasonable number of Europe's Jews" and not of national rights for Jews as a whole. This limited form of emergency Zionism, championed by Harrison without any consultation with Arab Palestinian representatives, was not without benefits for the United States. The swift departure of Jews from Germany would relieve the US army from a costly burden and exempt the US government from having to liberalize its quota-based immigration policies. Nonetheless, the Harrison Report fulfilled the main demands expressed by Jewish DPs and their American Jewish supporters. "Subjectified" as a national collective, Holocaust survivors became from then on central actors in the sequence of events leading to the partition of Palestine, approved by the United Nations on November 29, 1947. Moved by several encounters with Jewish survivors in DP camps and in Poland, the Anglo-American Committee of Inquiry appointed in November 1945 by Ernest Bevin and Harry Truman supported in its final report of April 1946 the emigration to Palestine of 100,000 DPs. Even though the committee opposed Jewish (and Arab) statehood in Palestine, its recommendation further reinforced the status of Jewish refugees as a national entity entitled to self-determination. As the historian Dan Diner pointed out in a study of Jewish DP camps in American-occupied Bavaria, "It is arguable that the immediate founding of the State of Israel had its beginnings in southern Germany."[39]

Triggered by the Harrison Report, the reversal of American policies toward Holocaust survivors also upgraded the position of Jewish refugees within UNRRA regulations. The fact that the US army eventually allowed Jewish "infiltrees" to enter DP camps until April 2, 1947, instead of the initial cut-off date of December 20, 1945, compelled UNRRA to adjust its criteria regarding Jewish "post-hostility" refugees. "Every humanitarian argument was on the side of extending help to these unfortunate people who had suffered so much," explained UNRRA's official historian. "The Administration," he continued, "solved the problem by invoking the doctrine of 'internal displacement'": despite their delayed entrance into Allied occupied areas, what mattered was the displacement of Jews from their homes during the war, either to the Soviet Union or to concentration camps. UNRRA instructions consequently stated, in December 1945 and again in July 1946, "that all Jews were automatically considered eligible unless positive proof to the contrary was produced."[40] Not surprisingly, this ruling was met with strong resistance by British authorities wary of a swelling tide of Zionist activists intent on illegally reaching Mandatory Palestine. "Polish Jewish immigrants," the British command ordered in February 1946, "will not be admitted to DP centers in the future. They will be treated as refugees and absorbed in the German population."[41] Most of them, however, purposefully avoided the unwelcoming British zone. In November 1946, the number of Jewish DPs registered by UNRRA in the American zone rose to 157,000, a clear indication that southern Germany had become the surrogate homeland of choice for Jews on the move.[42]

The lenient American position on Jewish "infiltrees" was tantamount to preferential treatment. As opposed to other "post-hostility" refugees, Jews were not required to provide any "concrete evidence" of internal displacement during the war. "Things began to run smoothly," a refugee camp director, recalled, "because an order was issued from above, I think from Washington, that every Jew for the very reason that he is a Jew, is eligible for UNRRA assistance."[43] Non-Jewish refugees who entered Germany after the war, on the other hand, had to prove that they had been victimized at the hands of the Nazis or their associates. However, the fine semantic distinctions of UNRRA directives had a limited effect on non-Jewish entrants: prior to the Czechoslovak coup of February 1948, the vast majority of "infiltrees" crossing from behind the Iron Curtain into Allied-occupied Germany and Austria were Jews bent on leaving their former places of residence behind. In keeping with the trajectory of American policies toward Jewish refugees and Zionism, a complex web of military directives and UNRRA instructions treated Jewish DPs as a separate collectivity. However, the more traceable deliberations held at the United Nations in 1946 on the status of displaced persons reveal with greater clarity how Holocaust survivors became the object of unprecedented philosemitism in the international arena.

Outside of Germany, various organs of the United Nations debated the condition and status of Europe's displaced persons. The DP question, indeed, occupied a particularly high place on the agenda of the new world organization. The purpose of these negotiations, conducted from February to December 1946, was to solve a thorny issue: should the "last million" DPs be returned to their home country or remain in occupied Germany under international guardianship? "Non-repatriable" refugees for the West and "quislings and enemies of democracies" for Soviet-bloc countries, the non-Jewish Poles, Balts, Yugoslavs, and Ukrainians displaced in Germany stood at the center of rising Cold War tensions. Yet in 1946, the emerging Eastern and Western blocs shared similar views on the status of Jewish displaced persons. As opposed to other types of DPs suspected of wartime collaborationism, Eugene Kulischer observed, "the Jewish refugees met no such antagonism."[44] That Jews formed the least problematic category of refugees was undoubtedly a sharp reversal of prewar conditions. Across the spectrum of participating delegations, knowledge of the Final Solution provoked strong public pronouncements in favor of Jewish victims. If the International Military Tribunal at Nuremberg (November 1945–October 1946) was the first distinctive international effort "outside of Jewish circles to grasp the awful significance of the murder of European Jews," so too were the less publicized discussions on the future of Holocaust survivors held simultaneously at the United Nations.[45] As "victims of the Nazi or fascist regimes," "victims of persecution for reasons of race," "persons considered refugees before the outbreak of the war," or "persons outside their country of nationality...as a result of the Second World War," Jews unquestionably qualified as both "refugees" and "displaced persons." Although the prospect of Jewish emigration to Palestine remained a contentious issue, the right of Jews to international protection was unanimously accepted. The first "great humanitarian experiment to approach the refugee problem in totality," in the admiring words of an American political scientist in the 1950s, the newly created IRO also specifically vindicated

Jewish suffering: "In that sense, the blood, tears, and despair of Buchenwald, Auschwitz, and Bergen-Belsen had perhaps not been entirely in vain."[46]

Prominent among the pro-Jewish advocates at the United Nations were the representatives of the USSR (including the Soviet Republics of Ukraine and Belarusia) as well as Soviet-bloc countries (then limited to Poland and Yugoslavia). Indeed, a unique brand of anti-Fascist philosemitism paralleled the favorable American policy toward Jewish survivors generated by the Harrison Report. For the USSR and its first satellites, Jews also constituted a special case among the displaced persons and deserved more than others to be granted international status. This position was stated from the onset of the negotiations: the duty incumbent upon the United Nations, declared a Soviet Ukrainian delegate was to assist "those million of Jews who have so horribly suffered at the hands of our common enemies."[47] His Polish colleague went substantially further: "The Jewish problem," he declared, "can not be treated without consideration of the Palestine problem."[48] In early 1946, the Soviet Union was still "careful to avoid involvement with any controversy over Zionism," an American observer of the deliberations recorded.[49] Still, from the opening remarks of Andrey Vyshinsky in February 1946 to the closing arguments made by Andrey Gromyko ten months later, the USSR overtly supported the extraterritoriality of Jewish DPs: due to their past sufferings, the Soviets repeatedly insisted, Jews formed the only acceptable category of "non-repatriable" refugees in occupied Germany.

The sympathetic stance contradicted of course the resurgence of anti-Semitism in the USSR and Poland. Although in 1946 organized Stalinist campaigns against "rootless cosmopolitans" had yet to be launched, the Soviet Communist Party "kept strangely silent...about the new anti-Semitic talk, about the Kiev pogrom of September 1945, and about what had happened to Soviet Jews under the Nazis."[50] In Poland, the return in early 1946 of nearly 150,000 exiled Jews from Siberia and other parts of the Soviet Union generated a deep antagonism toward them, bloodily expressed in Kielce in July 1946. As symbols of "Judeo-Communism," unwelcome claimants on property, or the "feared" incarnation of Polish wartime guilt, Jewish returnees from the USSR or from concentration camps formed an "endangered species" in postwar Poland.[51] There was therefore a clear correlation between the Soviet-bloc position toward Jewish DPs at the United Nations and the situation of Jews in the USSR and Poland in the immediate aftermath of the war. In both cases, they represented a separate nationality: extraneous to ethnicized Soviet and Polish polities yet compassionately presented as a collectivity deserving of national rights elsewhere.

The Polish position on the status of Jewish DPs particularly illustrates this ambiguity. More than any other Eastern European country, Poland insistently requested the immediate return of its displaced nationals. The indescribable destruction wreaked by the Nazis during the war created gigantic economic and demographic needs. In addition, Poland's new western frontier, thoroughly emptied of Germans, required large contingents of settlers for the "recovered territories" east of the Oder-Neisse line. In this context, the large Polish refugee population in occupied Germany was a vital human reservoir. At least 450,000 non-Jewish DPs of Polish origin received UNRRA care in March 1946, while at the time the overall number of Jewish survivors and (predominantly Polish) "infiltrees" was still limited to approximately 50,000 registered refugees. In December 1946, however, the number of Jews on UNRRA rolls had swelled to 185,000, while 250,000 ethnic Poles still remained in the DP camps.[52] This chronology is important: the negotiations over the fate of Europe's displaced persons held at the United Nations coincided with the peak of the Jewish exodus from Poland. As the records indicate, the diplomats sent to the UN by the Communist-dominated National Unity Government fully acknowledged the definitive dimension of this departure. Polish Jews, explained in May 1946 by J. M. Winiewicz, Poland's delegate to the United Nations, suffered from a "psychological fear of returning to a country where they lost their dear ones."[53] Although Polish speakers at the UN never alluded to the anti-Semitic climate as a cause of the exit of Polish Jews, they nonetheless spoke warmly of Jewish DPs tragically facing closed gates throughout the world: "No country welcomes them," bemoaned an official, "in spite of a general lack of manual labor."[54] Echoing the Soviet line, Poland unambiguously ranked Jews, alongside Spanish Republicans, among the few postwar asylum seekers exceptionally entitled to emigrate with international assistance.

Clearly there was more to this position than a mere expression of anti-Fascist solicitude: the murder of nearly three and a half million Polish Jews by the Nazis, the transfer of a half million ethnic Ukrainians to the USSR, and the mass expulsion of Germans from the "recovered territories" radically transformed Poland's ethnic landscape. In 1946 and 1947, the exodus of Jewish survivors capped off this astonishing process of ethnic homogenization.[55] The displacement of various categories of "Poles" in Germany was indeed a valuable opportunity to reshape the Polish nation along narrower ethnic lines. The Polish government, for instance, was eager only for the return home of a refugee population adequately purged of "Polish-Ukrainians," i.e., ethnic Ukrainians who resided in eastern Poland prior to the Soviet occupation of September 1939.

The object of numerous Allied directives and policies, members of this uncertain category of displaced persons hoped to avoid repatriation to the USSR by passing theselves off as ethnic Poles blending in among fellow nationals in the DP camps. To counteract this, Polish authorities explained to UNRRA and IRO camp personnel "how to recognize Ukrainians who represent a drag on repatriation" by asking precise questions pertaining to their geographical, religious, or linguistic background.[56] A bishop serving Polish DPs in Germany later described the welcome effects of this homogenization: "Now that the other groups who had Polish citizenship were removed…Polish DPs constitute a very cohesive group from a national and religious point of view."[57]

In contrast to Polish-Ukrainians, Jews were hermetically separated from ethnic Poles within the DP camp system. Moreover, the large Polish segment of the Surviving Remnant, even if they had been pushed out by the reappearance of anti-Semitism, had also deliberately severed ties with their former homeland. Little effort was required, therefore, to expunge Jews from the Polish national community in exile. At the United Nations, the unremitting Polish support for a separate international status for Jewish DPs endorsed this postwar divorce. "Communist authorities," charged Jan T. Gross in his study of postwar anti-Semitism in Poland, "acquiesced in society's violently expressed desire to render the country *Judenrein*."[58] Yet public statements on the return of Jewish DPs to Poland were less peremptory. As the first Jews displaced into the Soviet Union started to repatriate, Polish officials reassured Western visitors that the "government was anxious to keep them in Poland" and predicted that within five years 250,000 Jews would live in the country.[59] Following the Communist electoral takeover of January 1947, IRO envoys in Warsaw tempered this optimism: "The Polish authorities welcome back all Jews of Polish origin who wish to return but they do not wish to publicize any encouragement of their mass repatriation."[60] Other observers noticed this ambivalent stand. "Politically," a Joint representative from Warsaw reported, "the government does everything to make the life of Jews comfortable yet re-emigration to Poland would cause extreme difficulties and complicate the political situation."[61] This delicate balance was already identifiable in the declarations made by Polish officials at the United Nations in 1946. While undeniably attuned to Jewish suffering, they never formally claimed Jews as their own displaced nationals: the sympathetic recognition of "extraterritorial Jews" was made all the more easier by the unchallenged exodus, soon after the Holocaust, of the last visible Jewish minority in Poland.

Another revealing episode exemplifies the broad acceptance of Jewish supranationality at the United Nations. In May 1946, the Special Committee on Refugees and Displaced Persons appointed by the Economic and Social Council addressed the situation of approximately twelve thousand German and Austrian Jews who had recently returned from deportation. In August 1945, Law No. 1 issued by the Control Council of Germany had revoked the Nuremberg Laws as well as other Nazi denationalization decrees and called for the automatic restoration of German and Austrian Jews to their previous citizenship. This policy was, however, met with strong opposition from Jewish organizations and international jurists. For the distinguished Cambridge scholar Hersch Lauterpacht, this "forcible regermanization of stateless persons" was contrary to international law. In keeping with his individualist vision of human rights, Lauterpacht argued that the right of states to confer citizenship ought to be limited by the "interests and desires of the individuals concerned." International morality was also invoked: German and Austrian Jews had not merely been denationalized but also "cut off, amidst calculated and prolonged indignities and humiliation, from any sort of community."[62] Their compulsory "regermanization," the American lawyer and refugee expert Joseph. P. Chamberlain concurred, "would be offensive to a sense of decency," an argument repeated in various memoranda presented to the United Nations by the World Jewish Congress and the Jewish Agency for Palestine. The following question, therefore, stood before the Special Committee: should the United Nations grant refugee status and recognize the statelessness of German and Austrian Jews who were opposed to reintegration into their former countries?

The United States and Eastern European countries favored such a measure. "Although antisemitism had now disappeared in Austria and its disappearance in Germany could be looked forward to," their representatives maintained, "if they could not enjoy international protection and assistance the Jews would be obliged to live in the same localities where they had suffered so much and would be kept in contact with their former prosecutors."[63] Initially focused on a small number of German and Austrian survivors, these discussions soon broadened to include Jewish DPs as a whole. The Dutch chairman of these meetings, in particular, resolutely stressed the distinctiveness of the Jewish predicament, even if in 1945 returning Holocaust survivors in the Netherlands enjoyed neither special status nor specific rights to food, clothing, or money.[64] "By reason of the suffering inflicted on them and the inhumane treatment they had received," he declared, "Jews constitute a category absolutely apart which should receive different treatment."[65] Wary of this indirect support for Zionism, the United Kingdom delegation challenged this view: "Terribly as the Jewish people have suffered at the hands of their

Nazi oppressors, it is generally recognized that they were by no means the only victims of Nazi persecution." Treating nationals of Jewish origin as international refugees would create an "inequitable and difficult situation" among other types of victims, such as non-Jewish Germans deported by the Nazis. The British also added that "His Majesty's Government cannot subscribe to the policy so strongly advocated by the Nazi regime, that there is no place for Jews in central Europe, or as citizens of the states which will eventually be established there."[66]

Siding with Britain on this issue were the representatives of Lebanon, Iraq, and Egypt. While they conceded that German and Austrian Jews had endured great suffering, international acceptance of Jewish extraterritoriality would "put a premium on emigration" to Palestine against the will of its native population. On behalf of the Arab League and with unusual Soviet support, the Lebanese delegate Charles Malik asked that the "new refugee organization will not be required to concern itself with refugees and displaced persons who have returned to the countries of nationalities they hold or in which they had habitual residence": a reference not only to German and Austrian Jews but also, more importantly, to Jewish "infiltrees" into Germany.[67] The Western majority replied that this was not "the right place to express an opinion about the future place of Jews in central Europe, but we should like to state that these Jewish survivors from concentration camps have in fact no opportunity as a group to re-establish a normal life in their own country." The American representative, George Warren, admitted that an international status for German and Austrian Jews "not yet firmly resettled" in their own countries created an exceptional precedent. He nonetheless urged the committee to "err on the side of generosity and justice." Ultimately, the constitution of the IRO adopted by the General Assembly in December 1946 applied the term "refugee" to repatriated German and Austrian Jewish "victims of Nazi persecution."[68] This little-known provision had little effect besides the possibility for destitute survivors to obtain international aid and access American Jewish welfare organizations operating in Berlin, Munich, or Vienna. But its meaning transcended the mere case of German and Austrian Jews returned "home" after 1945. If Holocaust survivors could be deemed extraterritorial refugees in their own countries, the United Kingdom feared, "the new provision might well involve the new International Refugee Organization in schemes for Jewish immigration into Palestine." This forecast was prescient: even if, as the American delegation suggested in a conciliatory move, the IRO was to "give due weight to any evidence of genuine apprehension and concern...by the indigenous population of the non-self governing country in question," it also greatly facilitated the emigration of the Surviving Remnant to the state of Israel.

The officially recognized disentanglement of Jewish refugees from existing polities had indeed one important consequence: the acknowledgment of Jewish extraterritoriality normalized the idea of Jewish self-determination in international politics. Diplomatic and international historians have described how between 1945 and 1948 the Jewish DP problem, central to the Zionist struggle, elicited favorable attitudes toward Jewish statehood among Western and Soviet-bloc nations.[69] Yet under the shadow of Great Powers diplomacy, United Nations humanitarianism also played a decisive part in "post-Holocaust politics." It is often forgotten that the mass emigration of Jewish refugees to Israel after 1948 (more than 300,000 Holocaust survivors, not all of them DPs, were absorbed in the new state by 1952) was facilitated and financed by the postwar refugee regime. Indeed, the secretive Bricha organization and the Jewish Agency for Palestine were not the sole protagonists in the relocation of the majority of the Surviving Remnant to the Jewish state. In operation during the crucial years of 1947–49, the IRO significantly backed Jewish emigration to Israel. To be sure, the "largest travel organization in the world" did not officially support Zionism. Jewish refugees undoubtedly formed "one of the principal groups for whose resettlement the Organization was established," its director general at the time, the philanthropic Quaker businessman William Hallam Tuck, declared. But from the start of its operations in July 1947 to the proclamation of the state of Israel on May 14, 1948, the IRO only facilitated the legal emigration of six thousand Jewish immigrants to Mandatory Palestine.[70] When war broke out between Israel and Arab armies on May 15, 1948, the IRO considered the region a dangerous "area of hostilities" and refused to use its funds to support the emigration of refugees to belligerent countries. In accordance with a UN Security Council resolution condemning the "introduction of fighting personnel" (Jewish and Arab) into the battlefield, the IRO limited itself to the assistance of Jews within the DP camps of Germany, Austria, and Italy. This position changed toward the end of 1948, particularly after the second truce of July 18–October 15, 1948. Although William H. Tuck did not want "to run the risk of the Organization's being a contributor to the intensification of the Arab refugee problem or the preemption of the return of Arabs to their home," he nonetheless made budgetary provisions to retroactively pay for the emigration of 50,000 Jewish DPs independently transported since May 1948 by the Jewish Agency for Palestine with the support of the American Jewish Joint Distribution Committee. In December 1948, the IRO director general still expressed his agreement with the principle of equity advocated in July 1948 by the UN mediator, Count Folke Bernadotte, two months before his assassination in Jerusalem. "It would be an offense against all principles of elemental justice," the Swedish diplomat had warned, "if these innocent victims [i.e., Palestinians] of the conflict were denied the right to return to their homes while Jewish immigrants flow into Palestine and offer the threat of permanent replacement of the Arab refugees."[71] Tuck nonetheless believed that the war no longer hampered the "firm reestablishment" of Jewish DPs in areas controlled by Israel. "There was no evidence," he contended in front of the IRO Executive Council, "that many thousands Jewish refugees who have entered Palestine since May 1948 have experienced difficulty in resettlement or in becoming firmly integrated."[72] For Tuck, the absorption and assimilation capacities of the new country provided sufficient guarantees for the adequate resettlement of refugees, the primary task assigned to the IRO by the United Nations in 1946. For the IRO, eagerly searching for countries willing to accept refugees, Israeli know-how in immigration and resettlement made a crucial contribution to the prompt resolution of the DP problem in Europe.

Although pragmatic factors explained this reversal of attitude, diplomatic considerations strongly influenced the policies of an organization headed by an American civil servant and predominantly financed by the United States. Prolonging the "Great Power discord" between Britain and the United States on the Palestine issue, Tuck's proposal to retroactively pay for the transportation of Jewish DPs to Israel was hotly debated within the IRO Executive Committee.[73] The American representative, George Warren, conceded that there was "no positive proof that no refugee who had gone to Palestine was living in a house previously occupied by an Arab and unquestionably some were doing so." He added, however, that "the immigrants who had moved to Arab houses could be almost counted on the fingers of one hand" and that the vast majority of Jewish newcomers "only worked in cooperatives and in areas where the Arab had not lived."[74] As recent research has established, this statement did not reflect the reality on the ground. The systematic resettlement of abandoned Arab towns and neighborhoods started in earnest soon after May 1948 when the city of Jaffa was repopulated with Jewish immigrants. As the war increasingly went the way of the Israeli army, tens of thousands of Jews freshly arrived from Europe occupied vacant Arab houses in Haifa, Acre, and Ramla. At the same time, dozens of Jewish settlements were created on Arab lands and destroyed villages long before the formal end of the war.[75] Stemming in part from the decision made in June 1948 by the Israeli authorities to obstruct the return of Palestinian refugees to their homes, the settlement of

Jews in former Arab areas was dictated by short-term housing necessities and long-term repopulation designs. The American delegate at the IRO Executive Committee nonetheless maintained that Jewish immigration did not violate the terms of the UN Partition Plan and, more importantly, vitally relieved American taxpayers from the expensive upkeep of Jewish refugees in Germany.

With several *New York Times* articles in hand, the British representative countered that immigration was a "key Zionist strategy" and not a neutral policy: "Who could say that none of those actual persons helped in that way would not occupy a refugee's house or land or join a strategic colony?"[76] In between was the majority view held by the Executive Committee: while sympathetic to the plight of Holocaust survivors awaiting emigration, most of IRO members supported the UN Conciliation Commission appointed by the Security Council on December 11, 1948, to secure the return of Arab refugees, as per UN Resolution 194 issued that same day. A compromise was reached on January 29, 1949, shortly before a series of separate armistices signed between Israel and Arab countries. The Executive Committee authorized the IRO director general to reimburse the Joint to the extent of four million dollars for the movement of 50,000 Jews to Israel between May 1948 and January 1949. The IRO also pledged to do "nothing which would interfere with the UN Conciliation Commission's mandate to bring about peaceful settlement of the Palestine dispute."[77] On April 5, 1949, the IRO released an additional five million dollars after the Conciliation Commission recognized Israeli sovereignty in immigration matters. This decision cleared the way for the transportation of a projected 120,000 IRO-registered Jewish DPs by the end of 1949. To that end, the IRO transferred ten million dollars to the Jewish Agency as payment for this operation. "By supporting a policy of clearing out a whole area thereby creating displaced persons in order to settle other persons there," the Lebanese representative, Karim Azkul, predictably argued at the UN General Assembly in May 1949, "the IRO was partly responsible for the fate of the Arab refugees from Palestine."[78]

Yet the organization did not ignore the dire situation of Palestinian refugees in the Arab-held areas of Palestine or in neighboring Lebanon, Jordan, Syria and Egyptian-controlled Gaza. In response to an emergency $32 million relief program launched by the United Nations on November 19, 1948, the IRO donated 100,000 blankets, secured "6,000 to 7,000 tons of flour," and made available its stores and vehicles located in the Middle East for more than half a million Palestinians displaced at that time.[79] The IRO also assigned experienced personnel to the program and later contributed additional supplies and funds.[80]

A year before the creation of the United Nations Relief and Works Agency (UNRWA), the IRO was among the first responders to the 1948 Arab refugee crisis.[81]

At the request of the UN Security Council, the IRO also examined the legal status of this new category of displaced persons. Until the creation of UNRWA in December 1949, it was indeed still unclear whether Palestinian refugees should be the responsibility of the IRO or of a separate UN agency: were they political refugees similar to Europe's displaced persons or humanitarian refugees of a new kind? The IRO legal division argued that "Arab refugees were the result of war operations and did not fall within the wording 'persecution or fear based on reasonable ground of persecution,'" the criterion otherwise used to evaluate the claims of DPs in Europe. But because they were "willing" to return home but "unable" to do so, Palestinian refugees could plausibly be considered political refugees: this inability, the IRO legal experts suggested, was potentially equivalent to "fear of persecution." Ultimately, however, the IRO concluded that the determination of a legal status for Palestinians was less urgent than the delivery of humanitarian help: "The need for material assistance is much greater."[82]

In his book *The Ethnic Cleansing of Palestine*, the historian Ilan Pappe has claimed, without any supporting evidence, that "it was Israel and the Zionist Jewish organizations abroad that were behind the decision to keep the IRO out of the picture."[83] For supporters of Israel, the international body that was assisting Jewish refugees in fulfilling their own "right of return" could not possibly extend the same support to Arab Palestinians. Zionist lobbyists, contends Pappe, "were keen to prevent anyone from making any possible association or even comparison between the two cases."[84] That Jews were more deserving of the label "refugees" than Arab Palestinians was indeed an argument made by prominent Israeli officials. Abba Eban, the long-time icon of Israeli foreign policy, hinted at this qualitative hierarchy when he pleaded the case of Jewish DPs at the UN Security Council in August 1948: "International agencies are appropriately forced to measure the plight of these new refugees [i.e., Arabs] against those who have endured refugee conditions, not for months, but for years."[85] But the institutional separation of Palestinians from Jewish and European DPs did not stem from Zionist pressure: unlike Holocaust survivors, Palestinians were seen by United Nations agencies as humanitarian refugees in need of material help more than European-style political victims.[86] For the first director of UNWRA, Herbert Kennedy, "the Arab refugee" was simply a "staunch individualist forcefully resisting the politicization of his plight."[87]

As a "relief and works" agency funded by large American subsidies, UNRWA drew direct inspiration from New Deal public works. Gordon Clapp, one of the agency's founders and the head of the Economic Survey Mission created in August 1949 to investigate the feasibility of large-scale water and forestry projects in the Middle East, had previously served as chairman of the Tennessee Valley Authority. As a result, UNWRA's official policy was to promote the integration of refugees into "developing" Arab countries over repatriation to Palestine.[88] In contrast to Jewish DPs in postwar Germany, Palestinian refugees were not perceived as being in conflict with their place of refuge. But like the Holocaust, the Palestinian "catastrophe" of 1948 had a profound, even if delayed, nationalizing effect: in the 1950s, the "burning of ration cards" urged by the rising Palestinian national movement rejected the "humanitarization" of Palestinian refugees in favor of political and violent struggle, and above all, the right of return.[89] Not unlike Jewish DPs between 1945 and 1948, the Palestinian diaspora forged its own extraterritorial identity within the confines of United Nations refugee camps. What Palestinians did not obtain from the refugee protection system was similar recognition as a nonterritorial nation. Seen from this angle, the Arab-Israeli conflict reveals alternative and interdependent roots: not only a face-to-face history of hostility but also an internationally mediated scramble over refugee categorizations.

The more successful Jewish path to extraterritoriality, critical for the legitimization of the State of Israel, nonetheless came to a close at the end of the 1940s. Here again, IRO eligibility guidelines illustrate the evolving status of Jews as refugees and international migrants. Following the Czechoslovak coup of February 1948, a small wave of Jewish "inflitrees" from Communist countries sought to obtain DP status in Germany. Yet unlike their predecessors, they underwent this time thorough "screening" by IRO agents. Indeed, the intensification of the Cold War normalized the status of the last Jewish refugees coming out of East-Central Europe: like anti-Communist political dissidents, Jews were required to provide valid objections of a political nature justifying their refusal to return home. "A Jewish refugee as any other must produce some evidence that he is a bona fide refugee," the IRO Manual for Eligibility Officers stipulated; "the mere desire to go to Palestine is not considered acceptable as a valid objection."[90] The IRO feared at that time that many border crossers from East-Central Europe were economic migrants passing themselves off as political refugees. The Communist seizure of power in the region had indeed disrupted traditional patterns of Jewish livelihood:

As most of the Jews from the eastern countries are self-employed (craftsmen, shopkeepers, etc.) and follow trades which are liable to disappear as a result of the measures applied there, their aversion to the regime is prompted by both political and economic considerations. Many of the Jews pleaded persecution, and with good reason, but economic reasons…contributed doubtless to the motives for their departure.[91]

Moreover, post-1948 Jewish refugees did not neatly fit the heroic image of anti-Communist "escapees" crafted at the height of the Cold War.[92] "When persons have left their country of nationality of former habitual residence with all plans made, such as passports and visas for other countries…they are emigrants," the IRO stated. According to Cold War logic, "a political dissident would not normally avail himself of the protection of his government."[93] The mention of "compelling family reasons," such as the loss of relatives in the course of "previous persecution," nevertheless allowed most Jews to bypass the rigors of IRO screening.[94] But as the 1940s drew to an end, the position of Jews as paradigmatic refugees was abruptly challenged. At that time, however, these fine nuances hardly mattered. Departure to the sovereign state of Israel was not hampered by the lack of DP status. Nor was emigration to the United States, an increasingly attractive destination for Jewish refugees after the amended DP Act of 1950 opened the gates of the *goldene medine* ("golden land" in Yiddish) to Holocaust survivors.

In a seminal article written shortly before the creation of the State of Israel but published soon afterward in 1948, Nathan Feinberg, a renowned international jurist at the Hebrew University in Jerusalem, argued that the Jewish people now constituted a "state-forming entity" recognized in international law.[95] To make his case, Feinberg enumerated a wide range of legal arguments mostly revolving around the "juridical validity" of the Balfour Declaration, on the decisive impact of the "minorities question" in the aftermath of Word War I, and on the legal status of the Jewish Agency for Palestine as a legitimate "nucleus of the Jewish government." Feinberg, however, started his study with an overview of humanitarian actions carried out on behalf of Jews from the eighteenth century to 1919:

> It was felt necessary to offer this cursory survey…because it is only in the light of these interventions that the fundamental, if not indeed revolutionary, change in the approach to the Jewish question during

the First World War can be adequately appreciated. Thereafter the Jewish question was raised to the level of a question involving a nation as a whole, an entity entitled to separate national existence and to the organization of its life within the framework of the State."

Writing at the end of 1947, Feinberg did not allude to the role played by Jewish DPs in this nationalization process. But as shown throughout this chapter, the particular place of Holocaust survivors in the postwar governance of displacement completed the "revolutionary" developments analyzed in this important essay.

The crucial contribution of international humanitarianism in establishing Jews as a nation had until then been downplayed in the historiography of Jewish nationalism. In early and mid-twentieth-century Zionist narratives of nationhood in particular, "contingency" carried less historical weight than "destiny."[96] International contributions to the rise of Jewish nationhood, decisive as they may have been, took the back seat to historical subjectivity, allegedly the real engine of Jewish self-determination and national redemption. This explains why, for David Ben-Gurion, touring Germany in 1945, Jewish survivors were not yet part of the national collective but remained "a mob and human dust without language and education, without roots and without being absorbed in the nation's vision and traditions."[97] Yet the opposite was true: the "Jewish nation" owed much to the extraterritorial predicament of Jewish DPs in occupied Germany between 1945 and 1948. As is often noted, without the visible presence of Holocaust survivors in the DP camps of Germany, Austria, and Italy, Jewish statehood may simply never have been achieved. Expounding on his ideas during the uncertain period leading to the UN Partition Plan of November 1947, Nathan Feinberg still had plausible reasons to doubt the "international recognition of the existence of the Jewish people and of its right to national life in Palestine."[98] But after a cataclysmic war during which Nazi and other anti-Jewish policies were taken to their most extreme levels without the interference of any major countervailing force, Holocaust survivors triggered an unprecedented philosemitic moment in postwar international politics. As much as the historical agency claimed by the survivors of the Final Solution, the skillful determination of the Zionist movement, or the political backing of the Western and Eastern blocs, refugee humanitarianism enabled the reterritorialization of the Jews, a formidable rise from catastrophe to power sadly accompanied by the deterritorialization of another people.

Epilogue

THE GOLDEN AGE OF EUROPEAN
REFUGEES, 1945–60

"WE LIVE UNDER circumstances which produce refugees day and night."
So wrote in July 1951 G. J. van Heuven Goedhart, the first UN high
commissioner for refugees.[1] By that date, however, most of World War II's
displaced persons had found new homes overseas. Although the last DP camp
did not close its gates until 1957, the DP episode officially came to an end in
April 1951 when West Germany absorbed approximately 140,000 IRO refugees. These newly designated *heimatlose Ausländer* (homeless foreigners)—
including 12,000–15,000 Jewish DPs willing to remain in the Federal Republic
of Germany—then became the responsibility of the burgeoning West German
welfare state.[2] In his statement, the UN commissioner was describing instead
a new cohort of European exiles. After the beginning of 1951, the number of
fugitives from the German Democratic Republic to West Germany hovered
around 1,000 daily, while the influx of Soviet-bloc escapees into Germany,
Austria, and Italian Trieste was estimated at 1,500 monthly.[3] UNHCR had
been created in December 1950 to provide permanent solutions to the problem
of refugees created by World War II, and its first commissioner was justifiably
worried about the ongoing displacement crisis still plaguing Central Europe.
To that effect, and despite its meager budget, UNHCR established field
offices in the area to assist border crossers from Communist countries.[4]

Other commenters on refugee issues, however, thought that the problem
now transcended the boundaries of Europe. Joseph P. Chamberlain, a legal
scholar at Columbia University and chairman of the American Council of
Voluntary Agencies for Foreign Service, reported in February 1949 that
"demands are ever increasing, not only in Europe but now in India there is a
new displacement in Kashmir, and there is the great problem of the Arab refugees which may be followed by another of Jewish refugees from some of the

Arab countries."[5] That same year, hundreds of thousands of mainland Chinese fled the newly created People's Republic to Hong Kong and Taiwan. In June 1950, the outbreak of the Korean War provoked another severe humanitarian crisis. After completing his European mission, the IRO director general, J. Donald Kingsley, applied his expertise to Korea, where he took over the United Nations Korean Reconstruction Agency (UNKRA) created in December 1950 to help displaced civilians in the southern part of the peninsula.[6] UNWRA, the UN relief organization formed in December 1949 to help dispossessed Palestinians, opened another important theater of aid operations at the same time. Five years after the end of World War II, the center of gravity of international refugee humanitarianism started to shift from Europe to the Middle East and Asia. "Within the humanitarian community in the United States and elsewhere," recalled the State Department adviser George Warren, "there was the first dawn of recognition of the fact that refugees were going to be a worldwide, not just a European problem."[7]

While millions of refugees around the globe overshadowed their European counterparts, the DP experience continued nonetheless to exert considerable international influence. Since 1945, the continuous presence of displaced persons in Germany meant that the concept of political refugee had been strongly shaped by the postwar European context. When the Conference of Plenipotentiaries representing twenty-six nations adopted the UN Geneva Convention Relating to the Status of Refugees on July 25, 1951, human rights law acknowledged the exemplarity of the European case. Although the convention introduced the universal concept of "fear of persecution" to the granting of political asylum, it nonetheless bound the condition of asylum seeker to Europe's geography and history.[8] A political refugee was now narrowly defined as an individual forced into exile as a result of "events occurring in Europe before January 1, 1951." Contrary to a draft originally adopted by the United Nations General Assembly in December 1950, the text of the 1951 convention sharply distinguished between Europe and the rest of the world. Signatory states could ultimately choose to extend asylum to refugees created by "events occurring in Europe or elsewhere" but acknowledgment of the rest of the world was half-hearted. "What started as a world convention," noted an observer of the proceedings, "ended up as a European one."[9] This imbalance was only rectified in 1967 when the New York Protocol relating to the Status of Refugees lifted the original temporal and geographical restrictions in order to include Third World asylum seekers.

The European bent of the so-called Magna Carta for Refugees has been often attributed to Cold War contingencies. "The drafters thought mainly of the refugees from Eastern Europe," a jurist who took part in the deliberations

commented, "and they had no doubt that these refugees fulfilled the definition they had adopted."[10] This mindset resulted directly from the experience
of displacement in occupied Germany: for several consecutive years, the DPs
formed the most conspicuous group of (non-German) refugees resulting
from "events occurring in Europe before January 1, 1951." It was on their behalf
that United Nations envoys visiting DP camps in early 1948 called for the
rejection of the 1933 Geneva Convention drawn up to deal with Armenians
and Russian refugees. Interwar legal arrangements, argued the officials, no
longer "correspond to the needs of the day."[11] Indeed, the complex origins of
the 1951 Geneva Convention, going back to a resolution issued by the UN
Commission of Human Rights in 1946, closely overlapped with the beginnings of the DP crisis.[12] Although by 1951 most of the displaced persons had
left Europe, they still provided the model for the elaboration of international
refugee protections.

This influence stands out unmistakably in the records documenting the
drafting of the Geneva Convention.[13] The main backer of DP operations since
1945, the United States insisted that the document pertain specifically to
the problems created by the war. As the American representative stated, "the
Convention should apply only to the IRO refugees." This meant leaving out
the non-European refugees already covered by other UN agencies, as well as
ethnic Germans who had been taken in by West Germany. "In view of unforeseeable happenings in the future," the United States feared, "too vague a definition would amount so to speak to signing a blank check."[14] It was therefore
preferable "to get something signable for Europe…[rather] than an unsign-
able convention for the whole world." Yet after these restrictions were introduced, the United States ultimately declined to sign the Geneva Convention.
Its provisions, it was alleged, were not "well adapted to the United States laws
and practices under which all refugees already receive rights shared by all other
legally admitted aliens."[15] More importantly, Cold War strategy remanded
retrenchment. In keeping with its rapidly diminishing enthusiasm for multilateralism, the Truman administration independently harnessed its refugee policies to the struggle against the Soviet Union. The Mutual Security Act, a
massive foreign aid bill submitted to Congress in May 1951, openly encouraged
the defection of Eastern European nationals and their enlistment to the
"defense of the North Atlantic area." It also allocated generous funding to the
United States Escapee Program launched by President Truman in March 1952.
Uniquely designed to assist broadly-defined "refugees from Communism," the
Escapee Program served American strategic interests without the burden of
open-ended commitments to international agreements.[16]

The American position received belated support from the French government. Like his American colleague, the French official involved in the drafting of the Geneva Convention, Robert Rochefort, advocated territorial limitations: "One region in the world was ripe for the treatment on an international scale. That region was Europe."[17] The fact that only a few countries expressed genuine interest in a system of international refugee protection justified a narrow, continental focus. "The project of the Convention," reported France's permanent representative at the United Nations, "is in fact only carried out by the United States, France, the United Kingdom, and Israel."[18] Rochefort, for his part, sarcastically compared the Conference of Plenipotentiaries convened by the United Nations in July 1951 to a "slightly enlarged version of the Council of Europe." Consequently, "one problem was ready to form the subject of an international convention, namely the problem of European refugees." In addition, France "was responsible for too great a number of refugees to seek to extend her generosity to parts of the world which took no interest in the solution of such problems."[19] This position also stemmed from France's concerns about its colonial territories. "The granting of refugee status to persons of non-European citizenship," the French Ministry of Foreign Affairs privately cautioned, "could provoke particular difficulties in the case of Middle Eastern agitators seeking entrance in our North Africa."[20] A universal convention would have dangerously allowed the recognition of anticolonial activists as genuine political refugees, a matter that soon came before the United Nations when National Liberation Front members and Algerian civilians sought asylum in Morocco and Tunisia.

The United Kingdom saw the situation in a rather different light. "The status of refugee," the British representative maintained, "should be granted to any person fleeing persecution."[21] Underlying this ostensibly liberal approach was an assumption disproved three decades later but credible enough at the beginning of the 1950s: namely, that refugee movements emanating from other continents were not likely to ever become "a serious burden on European countries." Because the prospect of mass refugee influx from Third World countries seemed implausible, temporal and geographical restrictions on the convention were unnecessary: "It was of utmost importance that a convention negotiated under the auspices of the United Nations...should provide minimum guarantees for all refugees, wherever they came from." The French immediately retorted that "it was too easy to be generous with words" if yours was an insular land: France's territorial continuity with refugee-producing countries—Germany and Spain in the 1930s and Eastern Europe in the early 1950s—imposed a heavier burden of asylum on the French government. The British position was also criticized by Australia and Canada, two countries of mass immigration wary of unforeseeable commitments. It nonetheless won the favor of Benelux and the Scandinavian countries, as well as the endorsement of Egypt and Iraq. The two Arab delegations present in Geneva supported the idea of a universal convention to ensure continued funding for the relief of displaced Palestinians. But they insisted that the only acceptable solution to the Palestinian refugee problem remained the swift implementation of the right of return.[22]

The result of the negotiations was less discriminatory than is often asserted.[23] After the Holy See hammered out a compromise between "Europeanist" and "universalist" delegations, it was agreed that future parties to the convention could opt for either formula (the majority of initial signatories preferred the restrictive version). Thanks to the flexibility and good offices of UNHCR, humanitarian assistance and legal protection were soon extended to Hungarian civilians who fled their country in 1956 and to anti-Communist Chinese refugees in British-ruled Hong Kong. By the early 1970s, most European countries of asylum had ratified the New York Protocol of 1967, expanding the scope of the original "European" convention. But when it was adopted in July 1951, leading nongovernmental organizations promptly attacked the convention for its Eurocentric bias. Elfan Rees, a Welsh theologian and a spokesman for the World Council of Churches, compared the convention to a "menu at an expensive restaurant, with every course crossed out except the soup—and a footnote to the effect that the soup might not be served in certain circumstances."[24] Other groups such as the International Red Cross Committee and the International Association of Penal Law deplored the "piecemeal treatment" of the refugee problem and the potential exclusion of millions of people from the scope of the convention. They demanded instead the "rehabilitation of all refugees, expellees and stateless persons in the world without distinction of race, religion or nationality."[25] The World Jewish Congress, however, applauded the convention for its far-reaching protections against the forcible return of refugees to their country of origins. Indeed, the protections drawn up in July 1951 were vastly superior to those secured by previous international arrangements. No "blank check" had been written—the main beneficiaries remained predominantly Europeans—but the convention should not be read as blatantly discriminatory against African or Asian asylum seekers who had not yet knocked at Europe's doors. Its Eurocentric outlook derived instead from the polarization of Cold War international relations. Although couched in carefully worded language, the convention designated the Soviet Union and its satellites as perpetrator states while framing Eastern European dissidents as archetypal sufferers of political oppression. In that sense, as the *New York Times* correspondent in Geneva noted, "European needs were met."[26]

Clearly inscribed in human rights law, the European identity of refugees was also forged by humanitarian expertise. The DP camps of postwar Europe not only served as emergency shelters for various categories of individuals made homeless by the war but also functioned as social laboratories in which experts in medicine, social work, child development, education, and occupational therapy came into close contact with displaced populations. As a result, according to the Scottish refugee expert H. B. M. Murphy in 1955, it became "fairly easy to define [refugees] and trace their history: we have quite elaborate data from the IRO reports and this covers most of the group."[27] Indeed, the European refugee emerged then as a "knowable, nameable figure and as an object of social-scientific knowledge."[28] The standardized administration of UNRRA and IRO camps had indeed enabled the accumulation of countless surveys, reports, and questionnaires collected by a wide array of welfare professionals. The result was an enduring perception of refugees as idle and helpless, unable to act on their own. The policies enacted by UNRRA and the IRO did not, however, deny refugees the possibility to independently handle their own affairs: in their official publications, at least, both agencies hailed self-government as the cornerstone of "relief and rehabilitation." But as the peculiar history of a syndrome known as "DP apathy" indicates, displaced persons were by default considered passive and powerless—stereotypes allegedly still prevalent among refugee aid workers today.[29]

A phenomenon initially attributed to long periods of internment in slave labor or concentration camps, "DP apathy" was routinely detected among refugees in occupied Germany. In one of the first studies surveying the psychological condition of displaced persons, the American scholar Edward Shils was struck by their "apathy about the external world and for a time, about one's personal fate."[30] In subsequent reports, apathy was commonly described as the central marker of DP existence and the unfortunate consequence of camp life and displacement. Refugees themselves contributed to the popularity of this diagnosis. Eduard Bakis, an Estonian DP and lecturer in psychology at the Baltic University in Exile in Hamburg, observed among his peers "a widespread symptom of procrastination and apathy." This "DP-Complex," in the words of a Polish refugee, led to a fatalistic state where "nothing can help us, and nothing can hurt us." The apathetic DP had therefore "surrendered completely: he has no spirit, no desire for a fight or for revenge left in him."[31] Originally limited to European displaced persons, "apathy" was soon used to characterize all refugees in the postwar world. In his landmark report, funded by the Rockefeller Foundation, Jacques Vernant concluded that "the refugee often shows a typical lack of drive." Compared to the resourceful and energetic labor immigrant, "the refugee has no longer the elasticity which enables a man when fortune has dealt him a hard blow to recover his poise and carry on."[32] Already a weak, stateless person in international law, the refugee also epitomized psychological feebleness and despondency.

At the start of the 1950s, the widely acknowledged frailty of the refugee elicited a new pattern of humanitarian compassion, with Christian organizations such as the World Council of Churches setting the tone for refugee advocacy in Western Europe. Constituted in 1948 by 147 North American and European churches, the Geneva-based ecumenical organization eagerly embraced the cause of refugees: "We face today as grave a trespass on the common rights of man as the world has ever witnessed and a unique responsibility rests on the Christian Church to respond to the claims of mercy and compassion." The work of Jewish relief agencies on behalf of Holocaust survivors was cited as the model to imitate: "It is to the honor of World Jewry that Jews in every continent united to succor their fellows under the harrow in Europe."[33] While the Jewish refugee problem was over, an estimated 300,000 "hard-core" DPs and other camp dwellers languished in German and Austrian camps. This caseload of aging, ill, or mutilated refugees unable to emigrate to Western countries became the focus of Christian humanitarianism. The Reverend Father Georges Pire, a Belgian priest awarded the Nobel Peace Prize in 1958, exemplified the Christian commitment to refugee welfare. Born in 1910 and displaced himself as a child by advancing German troops, Pire visited Austria in 1949 to acquaint himself with "the age of barracks and human distress." There he found a dehumanized world tragically devoid of "goodness and Christian radiance."[34] More than mere shelters, the seven "European villages" for refugees he established in Austria and Germany were meant to restore human dignity. Like other Christian humanists of the period, Pire appealed to a "Europe of the heart" to alleviate the ills of the postwar world: the refugee symbolized Europe's destructiveness but also the possibility of its renaissance. In exile in Paris, the Czech Catholic writer Jan Cep similarly described the "hard-core"—intellectual DPs, like him, deemed unsuitable for labor immigration—as the basis of European regeneration: "Out of our suffering the new community will rise, larger and freer than ever."[35] The predicament of this group of refugees also resonated with French Catholic intellectuals inspired by personalist philosophy. "Time may pass and statistics may improve," wrote the young writer François Nourissier, "but Europe remains in a state of mortal sin."[36] For the novelist Georges Duhamel, Europe's lingering refugees made the postwar years "the era of human residues." Indeed, Christian compassion for Europe's last refugees transcended the rigid fault lines of Cold War politics, prompting thinkers and intellectuals identifying with Christian humanism to call for spiritual revolt against "a world in chaos, tortured by hatreds and inhumane ambitions."[37]

More than any other defining feature, "uprootedness" encapsulated the displaced condition. "The word poverty does not fully capture his misery," stated the Reverend Father Pire. "Above all, the refugee is uprooted."[38] This arboreal metaphor equally appealed to other churchmen delivering assistance to displaced persons. "The refugee," said the head of the French agency Secours Catholique, was comparable to "a tree yanked out of its forest and lying on a boulevard." Extracted from its natural habitat, the refugee needed careful replanting in a favorable environment.[39] The trope of "uprootedness" was also particularly popular in the field of migration studies. In his famous book revealingly entitled *The Uprooted* (1951), the renowned immigration historian Oscar Handlin described the transatlantic migration of 19th century European peasants to America in terms strikingly applicable to the DP experience: "Thus uprooted, they found themselves in a prolonged state of crisis—crisis in the sense that they were, and remained, unsettled."[40] Writing in the midst of the European refugee crisis, Handlin conceived of mass migration to the United States as a process of absolute dislocation—a popular characterization only challenged by the softer "transplantation" paradigm in the 1980s.[41] Strikingly reminiscent of the Great Atlantic Migration, the relocation of displaced persons in the New World appeared indeed just as "uprooting" as previous waves of transoceanic crossings. For the foreseeable future, the Iron Curtain prevented the return of refugees to their countries of origin and made their exile permanent and definitive. At the onset of the Cold War, "uprootedness" became thus another distinctive refugee pathology and a metaphor widely embraced by humanitarian actors.[42] "Torn from his native land," Georges Pire wrote of the European refugee, "his personality dissolves into a mentality common to all DPs."[43] Used in this context, the "uprootedness" trope paradoxically depoliticized Cold War refugees: although political theorists such as Hannah Arendt still linked the refugee problem to the question of statelessness, the remaining European DPs exemplified instead the "age of the uprooted and the century of the homeless man."[44] Revealingly, the official emblem chosen for World Refugee Year, the campaign organized by the United Nations in 1959–60, was an uprooted oak tree symbolizing the forcible extraction of human beings from their original surroundings.

Not all European refugees, however, were described as victims of abrupt dislocation. In sharp contrast to the passivity and mental breakdown ascribed to the "hard-core" was the image of the vigorous, courageous, and politically active anti-Communist escapees. The 1956 Hungarian uprising marked in this regard a turning point in the expression of empathy for European exiles. Many of the 200,000 Hungarians who fled into Austria following the Soviet invasion were young, fit, and active, "the elite of a brave nation." Unlike idle DPs passively awaiting assistance, Hungarians courageously "braved minefields, barbed-wires, swollen rivers and brutal frontier guards to seek freedom."[45] Descriptions like this had regularly appeared in the American media since the late 1940s; stories of defection, captivity, and dramatic flight shaped the popular culture of the early Cold War era.[46] Unlike old camp refugees, escapees possessed the most desirable physical and political traits. Vice President Richard Nixon waxed especially eloquent: "I stood on the border between Austria and Hungary and I saw young people come across in spite of communist guns there to shoot them down. These were workers and students, not as the communist said enemies of the people, but people from all walks of life who loved freedom."[47] The humanitarian response to the Hungarian crisis reflected this sympathy. "Countries which accept these refugees," declared President Eisenhower, "will find that rather than having assumed a liability, they have acquired a valuable national asset."[48] Spokesmen for relief organizations were thoroughly impressed with the efficiency of international efforts: "No group of refugees," said Elfan Rees, "has ever been treated so well and so quickly."[49] Indeed, eagerness to avoid the negative precedent set by "hard-core" DPs influenced the fast-paced emigration of Hungarians to the United States and Western European nations. Countries of asylum and welfare agencies alike sought at all cost "to avoid housing [Hungarians] in camps to stagnate in the manner of older refugees."[50] Toward the end of the 1950s, Western humanitarianism distinguished therefore between two types of refugees: old remnants of World War II and new products of the Cold War. Whether passive or heroic, despondent or energetic, both nonetheless remained closely linked to the European postwar experience.

Western charitable groups did not, however, neglect refugees from other parts of the world. In a survey published in 1959, Edgar Chandler, the director of the Service to Refugees of the World Council of Churches, showcased the various programs initiated by his organization. Besides their work in Europe, the council's personnel worked alongside United Nations agencies in Hong Kong, Korea, and the Middle East.[51] In Lebanon, Syria, and Jordan, British and American evangelical missionaries maintained a strong humanitarian presence in the region dating back to the Near East Relief created in the

United States in the wake of the Armenian genocide. Together with the Quakers and the International Red Cross, the International Missionary Council and the World Council of Churches stood among the first nongovernmental responders to the humanitarian crisis provoked by the Palestinian exodus. During the Arab-Israeli war of 1948, boasted the WCC, "Christian agencies were, apart from the local Arab governments, almost the only bodies which took the refugee problem seriously."[52] As Elfan Rees readily admitted, the plight of Arab refugees in the Middle East was far "more pathetic" than the situation of DPs in Europe and required urgent intervention: "From the European point of view, if charity can begin at home Christian charity cannot stop there."[53] Rees portrayed relief missionary work on behalf of Arab Palestinians as a selfless and apolitical endeavor: "The Church comes in because no one else can, or will...and dare not take sides in what is after all an issue between the Muslim and the Jew."[54] More active in the Middle East than members of secular NGOs, Christian welfare volunteers were instructed to remain strictly neutral "over the basic rights and wrongs in the Palestine-Israel struggle."[55] Above all, Palestinian refugees appealed to the religious emotions of evangelical humanitarians. In Edgar Chandler's account of refugee aid in Lebanon and Jordan, photographs of Palestinian children in the pastoral outskirts of Beirut "could illustrate a story from the bible," while the delivery of food rations to hungry residents in the Old City of Jerusalem movingly reminded the author of the "sixth chapter of Saint John." But if depoliticized Palestinians evoked the Scriptures, European refugees continued to mirror the Cold War present: the political and cultural identification with DPs and anti-Communist escapees was not replicated with the same intensity in the Middle East and other non-European areas. In a moving investigation of the "refugee world" conducted in 1960, the British journalist Robert Kee acknowledged that Europeans only constituted "one small example of the total world refugee problem." Ultimately, however, the "refugee world" surveyed by this dedicated advocate of international relief programs only encompassed the network of camps and shelters spread across Germany and Austria since 1945. Despite its dwindling prominence on the map of international displacement, the European humanitarian theater still served "as an inspiration and a warning" and remained the most potent symbol of the refugee condition.[56]

The World Refugee Year, organized under the aegis of the United Nations between July 1, 1959, and June 30, 1960, significantly altered this pattern. Initiated in the aftermath of the Hungarian refugee crisis by four young English idealists, the first international year in the history of United Nations observances was initially prompted by the plight of 40,000 European displaced persons still living in barracks and another 100,000 "out-of-camp refugees" in need of assistance.[57] Its broader goal, however, was to encourage voluntary and governmental contributions and to find solutions for the "fifteen million human beings throughout the world who for one reason or another find themselves without a country." To that end, the United Nations sponsored national committees in various countries, issued pamphlets and books, launched advertising campaigns and appointed the Russian-born actor Yul Brynner as "special consultant."[58] Eager to make a "personal and positive contribution," Brynner participated in a documentary movie filmed in European refugee camps, anchored several radio broadcasts, and published a series of poignant photographs.[59] Other famous actors, among them Gregory Peck, Peter Ustinov, Charlton Heston, Audrey Hepburn, Grace Kelly, and Ingrid Bergman (who in 1950 had played an enigmatic Baltic refugee in Roberto Rosselini's *Stromboli*), also lent their names to the cause of World Refugee Year. In a radio program, Eleanor Roosevelt described the initiative as the most "pleasing" United Nations humanitarian endeavor since the days of UNRRA and called attention to the continuing existence of refugee camps, "those frightful places which I have seen, which still exist in Europe fourteen years after the war."[60] Even though President Eisenhower pledged to maintain the "traditional American leadership in the refugee field," the United States responded lukewarmly by contributing just five million dollars to the UN effort. The Eisenhower administration preferred to fund refugee programs independently—spending sixty-five million dollars in 1960 alone—in ways that were better suited to its foreign policy. "For the United States," the Department of State explained, "every year since the end of World War II has been a refugee year."[61] Deprived of substantial American backing and boycotted by Soviet-bloc countries, World Refugee Year nonetheless raised close to ninety-five million dollars in ninety-seven participating nations and territories. The high proportion of individual donations (contributions by citizens and charity groups outstripped government giving), the active involvement of eighty NGOs, the various statements issued by heads of state, and the patronage of European royal families suggest that the twelve-month campaign did not go entirely unnoticed. Felix Schnyder, the Swiss high commissioner for refugees in 1961, declared that "so much enthusiasm was aroused among the peoples of many countries that WRY became as much their concern as that of their governments."[62] This assessment was exaggerated; World Refugee Year certainly encouraged the demonstration of international goodwill, but outside of the United Kingdom the event drew scant public interest. It was largely ignored in the United States and only quietly celebrated—by state officials more than ordinary citizens—in France, Italy, Belgium, the Netherlands, and Germany. For Peter Gatrell, the author of a comprehensive history of World Refugee Year, this multifarious event was first and foremost a blueprint for modern sensibilities toward refugees.[63]

Conflicting representations of displaced persons further impeded the possibility of full-scale international mobilization. As the collection of postage stamps issued for the occasion clearly reveals, participating countries often extolled one particular type of refugees. Although numerous governments adopted the neutral uprooted oak emblem proposed by the United Nations, others inserted political statements into their philatelic designs. The commemorative stamp issued by Yemen depicted Palestinian refugees pointing to a map of Palestine, but the one released by Israel showed Yemenite Jews brought into the country by Operation Magic Carpet in 1949. Stamps issued by Western European countries displayed Hungarian border crossers (Austria) or emphasized the human tragedy of postwar European refugees: a refugee girl amidst ruins (France), a refugee woman sitting on a suitcase (the Netherlands), or a lonely child, an anxious man, and a distraught woman representing "hard-core" refugees (Belgium). Newly independent North African countries such as Morocco chose instead to showcase the plight of Algerian civilians and National Liberation Front sympathizers displaced by the ongoing Algerian war. The United States stamp was a thinly veiled anti-Communist statement: recalling the mass immigration of displaced persons after World War II, a refugee family walking into a new life asserted America's benevolence against Soviet tyranny.[64] Although it may have paved the way for subsequent humanitarian campaigns, World Refugee Year did not elicit much cosmopolitan empathy for the people it sought to help. In 1960, the "discourse of global compassion," later facilitated by televised fundraisers such as USA for Africa and Live Aid, remained a distant prospect.

By far the most tangible achievement of the campaign was the sizeable reduction of refugee settlements in Europe: "Camp-clearance programs are approaching their climax," a summary report proudly announced. But at the dawn of the 1960s, the humanitarian refugee crisis in Europe was already less severe than in other parts of the world. "Like a terrible disease which leaves its mark on the patient long after the climax is past," observed Robert Kee, "the refugee problem in Europe appears to slowly be coming to an end." The wide outreach of World Refugee Year exemplified this evolution: going far beyond the brief of the 1951 Geneva Convention, the program encompassed 2.5 millions refugees worldwide. Among its intended beneficiaries were Palestinian refugees, displaced Chinese in Hong Kong and Macao, and Algerians in Morocco and Tunisia. Few of these refugees saw their lives change: the "problem" remained as acute at the end of the year as it had been twelve months earlier. In fact, lamented the World Council of Churches, the situation of displaced persons around the world "was made worse because of disappointed expectations."[65] However, the long list of Asian, African, and Middle Eastern refugee hotspots drawn up at the conclusion of World Refugee Year showed that dislocated Europeans no longer constituted the bulk of global refugees in need of international assistance.[66] "In conceding the needs of non-European refugees," wrote Peter Gatrell, [World Refugee Year] entered a different realm from most campaigns that had been devised in the preceding decade and a half."[67]

Outside the orbit of the United Nations, unilateral American policies similarly contributed to the globalization of refugee humanitarianism. "Today," the Department of State boasted in 1960, "a hungry child waits in line for free milk in North Africa, a blind Chinese refugee from Communist China is learning to read in Macao and somewhere in Europe the first steps of freedom are being made a little easier for an exhausted man who has just crawled across the mine fields of the Iron Curtain."[68] For its part, the Soviet Union championed the new refugees displaced by anticolonial strife on the African continent. In contrast to anti-Communist displaced persons and Cold War defectors, African refugees were eagerly recognized by the Soviets as "refugees in the fullest sense, refugees from the persecution they had suffered for their participation in national liberation movements."[69] Having scorned UNHCR since its creation, the two superpowers reversed course at the beginning of the 1960s. For the United States, stemming Communism in the Third World demanded extensive refugee assistance—a doctrine first tested on European escapees in the 1950s. For the Soviet Union, African refugees provided a useful contrast to the Eastern European freedom fighters heralded by the West.[70] Whether harnessed to the cause of anti-Communism or to Third World anticolonialism, these new DPs hardly resembled the "uprooted" of the previous decade. Having been solved by mass emigration and Western economic expansion, the mid-century European refugee crisis rapidly receded into the past.

Yet the legacies of "Europe on the move" deeply affected the subsequent history of asylum seekers in the West. Inspired by the "last million" Europeans dislocated after World War II, the 1951 convention imposed a definition of refugees unchallenged for most of the of the Cold War era: persons outside their country of origin facing the reality or the risk of political, racial, or religious persecution. Conceived with European exiles in mind, this framework posited the existence of strong cultural bonds between refugees and predominantly Western host countries. Over the course of two decades, the protection system elaborated in the course of the DP crisis proved liberal and inclusive. It was also perfectly in tune with the Manichean political world of the Cold War: from the 1950s to 1970s, Gil Loescher pointed out, "recognizing persecution and the identifying perpetrators caused no headaches and the grant of asylum was generally used to reaffirm the failures of Communism and the benevolence of the West."[71] In the last twenty years, however, the sharp rise in the number of asylum applications in the West has exposed the limits of the European "persecution model" inherited from the immediate postwar years. This "crisis of asylum" originated in a discrepancy between the persecution requirement peculiar to the 1951 convention and the reasons for flight cited by predominantly non-European asylum seekers knocking on Western doors.[72] Today's refugees, Africans chiefly among them, are indeed overwhelmingly produced by civil wars, ethnic strife, or collapsing states. Unlike in the Cold War era, abusers of refugees are not simply oppressive regimes but third parties such as guerrilla or insurgent armies, criminal gangs, death squads, or even family members. Similarly, new patterns of persecution such as sexual and environmental violence have challenged the primacy of political oppression established in the wake of World War II.[73] To be sure, protection agencies have acknowledged these transformations. Shying away from the requirement of "fear of persecution," UNHCR has recognized the existence of a broad range of "humanitarian refugees," irrespective of the nature of the harm inflicted upon them. Similarly, courts in Australia, Canada, Britain, and the United States have adjusted their interpretation of persecution to include, among others, battered women or victims of ethnic conflicts.[74] Yet despite this evolution and the introduction of policies partially circumventing the limitations of the 1951 convention, the "Magna Carta for Refugees" remains the principal instrument used by liberal states to evaluate, and more often than not reject, the claims of asylum seekers. An outdated restrictionist device for its opponents, the last line of defense against "bogus" refugees for its supporters, the 1951 convention still largely regulates the attribution of political asylum in the West. The period known as "postwar Europe" may well have ended in 1989, but it enjoys a vibrant afterlife in the current governance of people out of place.

Notes

1. Quoted in "Long Range Plan for Refugee Care," *New York Times*, October 18, 1939.
2. Eleanor Roosevelt, *The Eleanor Roosevelt Papers*, vol. 1, *The Human Rights Years, 1945–1948*, ed. Allida Black (Detroit: Thomson Gale, 2007), 230.
3. Herbert Emerson, "Post-War Problems of Refugees," *Foreign Affairs*, January 1943, 211–20.
4. H. J. Laski, "The Machinery of International Relief," in *When Hostilities Cease: Papers on Relief and Reconstruction Prepared for the Fabian Society* (London: Gollancz, 1943), 30–42.
5. Cited by Zorach Warhaftig, *Relief and Rehabilitation: Implications of the UNRRA Program for Jewish Needs* (New York: Institute of Jewish Affairs of the American Jewish Congress and World Jewish Congress, 1944), 90.
6. Eugene M. Kulischer, *The Displacement of Population in Europe* (Montreal: International Labour Office, 1943), 163. Kulischer later estimated the total number of Europeans displaced between 1939 and 1945 at roughly fifty-five million people. See Kulischer, *Europe on the Move: War and Population Changes, 1917–47* (New York: Columbia University Press, 1948), 304.
7. On the origins of Allied refugee relief programs see Malcolm J. Proudfoot, "The Anglo-American Displaced Persons Program for Germany and Austria," *American Journal of Economics and Sociology* 6 (1946): 33–54.
8. Kenneth G. Brooks, "The Re-establishment of Displaced Peoples," in *When Hostilities Cease*, 99–124.
9. Hannah Arendt, "The Stateless People," *Contemporary Jewish Record* 8 (April 1945): 137–53.
10. Hannah Arendt, *The Origins of Totalitarianism* (1951; repr., New York: Schocken Books, 2004), 353.
11. At the end of 1946, the Allied military authorities estimated that 1,037,404 DPs lived in and out of camps in Germany, Austria, and Italy. When the IRO took over UNRRA operations in July 1947, it assumed custodianship of 707,000 DPs in DP

camps and extended assistance to an additional 366,000 "free-living" refugees. Archives Nationales (Paris), IRO Records, 43AJ-180.

12. "President's Message to Congress, July 7, 1947," Harry S. Truman Library (hereafter HSTL), Box 674, Official File 127; George Woodbridge, *UNRRA: The History of the United Nations Relief and Rehabilitation Administration* (New York: Columbia University Press, 1950), 3:423.

13. Anne O'Hare McCormick, "Abroad; UNO and the Fate of Europe's Displaced Persons," *New York Times*, January 16, 1946; Irene B. Taeuber, "Population Displacement in Europe," *Annals of the American Academy of Political and Social Science* 234 (July 1944): 1–12.

14. Edgard H. S. Chandler, *The High Tower of Refuge: The Inspiring Story of Refugee Relief throughout the World* (New York: Praeger, 1959), 220.

15. Gustavo Corni and Tamas Stark, eds., *People on the Move: Forced Population Movements in Europe in the Second World War and its Aftermath* (Oxford: Berg, 2008), 61–100; Jerzy Kochanowski, "Gathering Poles into Poland: Forced Migration from Poland's Eastern Territories," in Philipp Ther and Ana Siljak, eds., *Redrawing Nations: Ethnic Cleansing in East-Central Europe, 1944–1948* (Lanham, MD: Rowman, 2001), 135–154; Catherine Gousseff, "Evacuation versus Repatriation: The Polish-Ukrainian Population Exchange, 1944–6," in Jessica Reinisch and Elizabeth White, *The Disentanglement of Populations. Migration, Expulsion and Displacement in Post-War Europe, 1944–9* (New York: Palgrave Macmillan, 2011), 91–111.

16. Kathryn Hulme, *The Wild Place* (Boston: Little, Brown, 1953), 191.

17. Ibid.

18. Quoted in Steve Neal, ed., *HST: Memories of the Truman Years* (Carbondale: Southern Illinois University Press, 2003), 30.

19. Woodbridge, *UNRRA*; Louise W. Holborn, *The International Refugee Organization: A Specialized Agency of the United Nations; Its History and Work, 1946–1952* (London: Oxford University Press, 1956); Kulischer, *Europe on the Move*; Malcolm J. Proudfoot, *European Refugees: 1939–52; A Study in Forced Population Movement* (Evanston, IL: Northwestern University Press, 1956).

20. G. Daniel Cohen, "Remembering Postwar Displaced Persons: From Omission to Resurrection," in *Enlarging European Memory: Migration Movements in Historical Perspective*, eds. Mareike König and Rainer Ohliger, (Stuttgart: Horbecke Verlag, 2006), 87–97.

21. Wolfgang Jacobmeyer, *Vom Zwangsarbeiter zum heimatlosen Ausländer: Die Displaced Persons in Westdeutschland, 1945–1951* (Göttingen, West Germany: Vandenhoeck & Ruprecht, 1985); Kim Salomon, *Refugees in the Cold War: Toward a new International Refugee Regime in the Early Postwar Era* (Lund, Sweden: Lund University Press, 1991).

22. See among others Marta Dyczok, *The Grand Alliance and Ukrainian Refugees* (New York: St. Martin's, 2000); Lubomyr Y. Luciuk, *Searching for Place: Ukrainian Displaced Persons, Canada, and the Migration of Memory* (Toronto: University of Toronto Press, 2000); Anna D. Jaroszyńska-Kirchmann, *The Exile Mission: The*

Polish Political Diaspora and the Polish Americans, 1939–1956 (Athens OH: Ohio University Press, 2004); Thomas Lane, *Victims of Stalin and Hitler: The Exodus of Poles and Balts to Britain* (New York, Palgrave Macmillan, 2004). Zeev W. Mankowitz, *Life between Memory and Hope and Hope: The Survivors of the Holocaust in Occupied Germany*, (Cambridge, UK: Cambridge University Press, 2002); Atina Grossmann, *Jews, Germans, and Allies: Close Encounters in Occupied Germany* (Princeton, NJ: Princeton University Press, 2007); Margarete Myers Feinstein, *Holocaust Survivors in Germany, 1945–1957* (Cambridge: Cambridge University Press, 2010).

23. Ben Shephard, *The Long Road Home: The Aftermath of the Second World War* (London: Bodley Head, 2010); Silvia Salvatici, *Senza casa e senza paese: Profughi europei nel secondo dopoguerra* (Bologna, Italy: Mulino, 2008); Mark Wyman, *DPs. Europe's Displaced Persons* (Ithaca: Cornell University Press, 1998).

24. U.S. Army War Department General Staff, G-2, "The Displaced Persons Problem in Germany and Austria," *Intelligence Review* 43 (December 1946): 32–38.

25. United Nations, Summary Records of Economic and Social Council, August 12, 1948 and August 24, 1948.

26. Address to the United Jewish Appeal, April 15, 1947, Robert H. Jackson Papers, Box 44, Folder 10, Library of Congress, Washington, DC.

27. Louis K. Hyde, *The United States and the United Nations, Promoting the Public Welfare: Examples of American Co-operation, 1945–1955* (New York: Manhattan, 1960), 59.

28. Bruce Cronin, *Institutions for the Common Good: International Protection Regimes in International Society* (Cambridge, UK: Cambridge University Press, 2003).

29. Akira Iriye, *Global Community: The Role of International Organizations in the Making of the Contemporary World* (Berkeley: University of California Press, 2002); Stewart Patrick, *Best Laid Plans: The Origins of American Multilateralism and the Dawn of the Cold War* (Lanham, MD: Rowman &Littlefield, 2009).

30. Earl Harrison to Harry Truman, December 20, 1946, HTSL, Official File 127, Box 673. In July 1945, Harrison served as Truman's envoy to the Jewish DP camps and later served as chairman of the Citizens Committee for Displaced Persons.

31. United Nations General Assembly, Official Records, First Session, Second Part, 1421.

32. A thought-provoking attempt at rewriting the history of Europe "from the periphery inward" is Dan Diner, *Cataclysms: A History of the Twentieth Century from Europe's Edge*, trans. William Templer and Joel Golb (Madison: University of Wisconsin Press, 2008).

33. Himself a former UNRRA employee, the Austrian-born British writer Gitta Sereny drew a revealing comparison between the DP crisis and the tragedy of Kosovar refugees in the spring of 1999. See Gitta Sereny, *The German Trauma: Experiences and Reflections, 1938–2000* (London, Penguin, 2001), 26.

34. "Saved from Murder, Condemned to Death," advertisement in *New York Times*, February 11, 1948. This campaign, initiated by the Citizens Committee on

Displaced Persons, was endorsed by American liberal intellectuals including John Dewey, W. E. B. Dubois, John Dos Passos, and Reinhold Niebuhr. Jacob Pat Papers, Robert F. Wagner Labor Archives, Tamiment Library, New York University, Box 1, Folder 45.

35. Eleanor Roosevelt, *On My Own* (New York: Harper, 1958), 50.

36. Laski, "Machinery of International Relief," 38.

37. UNESCO, International Conference on Social Work, Paris, February 1947 (in IRO Records, AJ43–20).

38. Hyde, *United States and United Nations*, 79.

39. Peter Gatrell, *Free World? The Campaign to Save the World's Refugees 1956–1963* (Cambridge, UK: Cambridge University Press, 2011).

CHAPTER 1

1. *New York Times*, "The Human Side of UNO," February 2, 1946.

2. Ernest F. Penrose, "Negotiating on Refugees and Displaced Persons, 1946," in *Negotiating with the Russians*, ed. Raymond Dennett and Joseph E. Johnson (Boston: World Peace Foundation, 1951), 139–71.

3. Agnes Roman, "UNRRA in China," *Far Eastern Survey*, November 7, 1945, 61–74. Historians have since estimated that in China alone the Second Sino-Japanese War (1937–1945) caused the displacement of 95 million people. See Stephen MacKinnon, "Refugee Flight from the Outset of the Anti-Japanese War," in Diana Lary and Stephen MacKinnon (eds), *Scars of War: the Impact of Warfare on Modern China* (Vancouver: University of British Columbia Press: 2001), 118–35.

4. *Displaced Populations in Japan at the End of the War*, Department of State Bulletin 13, October 7, 1945.

5. *Refugees and Displaced Persons: An Urgent United Nations Problem*. New York: Russell Sage Foundation, 1946, 3.

6. Patrick Murphy Malin, "The Refugee: A Problem for International Organization," *International Organization* 1 (September 1947): 443–59.

7. Foreign Office (FO), *Proposed Transfer of Non-repatriable Refugees to UNO*, December 31, 1945, FO 371/57700-0003; *Seventeenth Meeting of the Executive Committee of the IGC*, November 6, 1945, FO 371/51139-0012.

8. George Rendel, *The Sword and the Olive: Recollections of Diplomacy and the Foreign Service, 1913–1954* (London: Murray, 1957), 253.

9. Rendel, *Sword and Olive*, 248.

10. Ernest Bevin to US Secretary of State Byrnes, January 8, 1946, FO 371/57700-0004.

11. FO 1049/416, undated.

12. Amikam Nachmani, *Great Power Discord in Palestine: The Anglo-American Committee of Inquiry into the Problems of European Jewry and Palestine, 1945–1946* (London: Cass, 1987).

13. Bevin to Byrnes, January 8, 1946, FO 371/57700-0004.

14. Rendel to Bevin, January 18, 1946, FO 371/57700-0007.

15. *Rapport de Marcel Livian* (undated, end of 1944), Archives Nationales (Paris), Records of the International Refugee Organization (henceforth IRO Records), 43AJ–48.

16. Direction des Conventions Administratives, Article 171, July 30, 1945, Centres des Archives Contemporaines (Fontainebleau, France; henceforth CAC), 77063.

17. Emmanuel Mounier, "Les nouveaux réprouvés," in *Œuvres*, vol. 4, *Recueils Posthumes; Correspondance* (Paris: Seuil, 1963), 95.

18. CAC 77063, Article 171.

19. Leonard Dinnerstein, "Harry S. Truman and the Displaced Persons 1945–1949," in *Harry S. Truman: The Man from Independence*, ed. William F. Levantrosser (New York: Greenwood, 1986), 151–56.

20. *Foreign Office to British Embassy in Washington*, January 5, 1946, FO 371/57700-004.

21. *Proposed Transfer of Non-repatriable Refugees to UNO*, December 31, 1945, FO 371/57700-0003.

22. Tommie Sjöberg, *The Powers and the Persecuted: The Refugee Problem and the Intergovernmental Committee on Refugees (IGCR), 1938–1947* (Lund, Sweden: Lund University Press, 1991), 211.

23. "Restatement of Policy on Germany," Speech by US Secretary of States James Byrnes delivered in Stuttgart on September 6, 1946. Department of State Bulletin, September 15, 1946, 496.

24. United Nations, General Assembly, Fourth Session of the Third Committee, January 28, 1946.

25. Eleanor Roosevelt, *The Eleanor Roosevelt Papers*, vol 1, *The Human Rights Years, 1945–1948, Vol. 1*, edited by Allida Black (Detroit: Thompson Gale, 2007), 172.

26. Amy Zahl Gottlieb, "Refugee Immigration: The Truman Directive," *Prologue* 13 (Spring 1981): 5–17. By mid-1946, the United States had received 3,500 DPs, the majority of them Jews, under the Truman Directive. 120,000 unused slots in prewar immigrant quotas still remained available. Fiorello LaGuardia to Harry Truman, June 26, 1946; Philleo Nash to Harry Truman, August 12, 1946, Harry S. Truman Library (HSTL), Official File 127, Box 67.

27. Oral History Interview with George L. Warren. Available at http://www.truman-library.org/oralhist/warrengl.htm.

28. Launched by UNRRA in the summer of 1946, "Operation Carrot" temporarily increased repatriation rates by offering sixty-day food rations to Polish DPs willing to return home. This UNRRA policy has been well documented. See among others Ben Shephard, *The Long Road Home: The Aftermath of the Second World War* (London: Bodley Head, 2010), 239–40.

29. Michael L. Hoffmann, "Millions Remain in DP Category," *New York Times*, February 3, 1946.

30. Malcolm J. Proudfoot, *European Refugees: 1939–1952; A Study in Forced Population Movement* (Evanston, IL: Northwestern University Press, 1956), 399.

31. Anne O'Hare McCormick, "Abroad; UNO and the Fate of Europe's Displaced Persons," *New York Times*, January 16, 1946.

32. Roosevelt, *Eleanor Roosevelt Papers*, 230.

33. Penrose, "Negotiating on Refugees," 141.

34. James Reston, "Negotiating with the Russians," *Harper's*, August 1947, 97–106.

35. Harold Karan Jacobson, *The USSR and the UN's Economic and Social Activities* (Notre Dame, IN: University of Notre Dame Press, 1963), 82.

36. Roger Nathan-Chapotot, *Les Nations Unies et les réfugiés: Le maintien de la paix et le conflit de qualifications entre l'Ouest et l'Est* (Paris: Pedone, 1949).

37. Eleanor Roosevelt, "An American View," *New York Times*, March 24, 1946.

38. George S. Marshall, "Concern Expressed on Resettlement of DPs; Statement by Secretary of State," *Department of State Bulletin*, July 27, 1947, 194–97.

39. Third Committee of the United Nations General Assembly (London, January-February 1946); Special Committee on Refugees and Displaced Persons (London, April-June 1946); Economic and Social Council (Lake Success, NY, September 1946).

40. Eleanor Roosevelt, *On My Own* (New York: Harper, 1958), 49.

41. Penrose, "Negotiating on Refugees," 142.

42. United Nations, *Official Records of the Second Part of the First Session of the General Assembly, Third Committee, Summary Record of Meetings, 24 October–12 December 1946*, November 9, 1946.

43. Roosevelt, *On My Own*, 51.

44. McCormick, "Abroad; UNO."

45. George Woodbridge, *UNRRA: The History of the United Nations Relief and Rehabilitation Administration* (New York: Columbia University Press, 1950), 3:339.

46. Woodbridge, *UNRRA*, 3:486.

47. Mark R. Elliott, *Pawns of Yalta: Soviet Refugees and America's Role in their Repatriation* (Urbana: University of Illinois Press, 1982); Carol Mather, *Aftermath of War: Everyone Must Go Home* (London: Brassey's, 1992); Georges Coudry, *Les camps soviétiques en France: Les "Russes" livrés à Staline en 1945* (Paris: Albin Michel, 1997).

48. United Nations, *The Question of Refugees: Documents for the Special Committee on Refugees and Displaced Persons*, E/REF/1, April 1946, 6–8.

49. E/REF/1, January 28, 1946. "The Yugoslav delegate," noted George Rendel, "overstated his case to such an extent that he lost the sympathy of the public and of the press. This greatly strengthened my hand in fighting the battle of the refugees." Rendel, *Sword and Olive*, 253.

50. E/REF/1, January 30, 1946.

51. Pavel Polian, *Deportiert nach Hause: Sowjetische Kriegsgefangene im Dritten Reich und ihre Repatriierung* (Munich: Oldenbourg, 2001); Vanessa Voisin, "Le retour et

la réintégration des rapatriés soviétiques dans la région russe de Kalinine en 1945–1956" in *Les réfugiés en Europe du XVIe au XXe siècles*, ed. Olivier Forcade and Philippe Nivet (Paris: Nouveau Monde, 2008), 253–72.

52. Penrose, "Negotiating on Refugees," 164.

53. David J. Dallin and Boris I. Nicolaevsky, *Forced Labor in Soviet Russia* (New Haven, CT: Yale University Press, 1947).

54. Pavel Polian, "The Internment of Returning Soviet Prisoners of War after 1945," in *Prisoners of War, Prisoners of Peace: Captivity, Homecoming and Memory in World War II*, ed. Bob Moore and Barbara Hately-Broad (Oxford: Berg, 2005), 123–39; Catherine Merridale, *Ivan's War: The Red Army 1939–45* (London: Faber & Faber, 2005), 310.

55. Claudena M. Skran, *Refugees in Inter-war Europe: The Emergence of a Regime* (Oxford: Clarendon, 1995), 102–3.

56. E/REF/1, February 4, 1946.

57. E/REF/1, February 1, 1946.

58. E/REF/1, February 4, 1946.

59. Alexandre Parodi to G. Bidault, June 24, 1946, Centres des Archives Diplomatiques de Nantes, Mission Permanente de la France à L'ONU 1945–1985, Article 94.

60. E/REF/1, February 6, 1946.

61. Christoph Schiessl, "Nazi Collaborators from Eastern Europe as US Immigrants and the Displaced Persons Act," *Michigan Academician* 35 (2003): 295–320; David Cesarani, *Justice Delayed: How Britain Became a Refuge for Nazi War Criminals* (London: Phoenix, 2001).

62. United Nations, *Documents of the Special Committee for Refugees and Displaced Persons*, E/REF/31.7.

63. Michael L. Hoffman, "UN Board to Sift Traitors Is Asked," *New York Times*, April 13, 1946.

64. Nancy MacLennan, "Two in U.N. Retort to Mrs. Roosevelt", *New York Times*, November 10, 1946.

65. United Nations, *General Assembly, Official Records (First Part of First Session), Report of Third Committee A/45*, Thirtieth Plenary Meeting, February 12, 1946.

66. On the "hortatory and vague" language of Article 55, see James C. Hathaway, *The Rights of Refugees under International Law* (Cambridge, UK: Cambridge University Press, 2005), 42–43.

67. E/REF/1, February 12, 1946.

68. United Nations, General Assembly, Thirtieth Plenary Meeting, February 12, 1946. "The Nations: Spasm of Aggression," *Time*, February 25, 1946. (no author listed).

69. E/REF/1, February 3, 1946.

70. Penrose, "Negotiating on Refugees," 158; Eleanor Roosevelt, "The Russians Are Tough," *Look*, February 18, 1947.

71. Quoted in John George Stoessinger, *The Refugee and the World Community* (Minneapolis: University of Minnesota Press, 1956), 75.

72. Quoted in Nathan-Chapotot, *Les Nations Unies*, 154.

73. Anna Holian, "Anticommunism in the Streets: Refugee Politics in Cold War Germany," *Journal of Contemporary History* 45 (January 2010): 134–61.

74. Committee on Foreign Relations of the U.S. Senate, *A Decade of American Foreign Policy: Basic Documents, 1941–49* (Washington: Government Printing Office, 1950), 934–36.

75. E/REF/1, February 12, 1946.

76. United Nations, *Economic and Social Council, Official Records, Summary Records, Second Session, Report of Special Committee on Refugees and Displaced Persons*, June 7, 1946, E/REF/75.

77. E/REF/1, January 30, 1946.

78. Reston, "Negotiating with the Russians," 105.

79. United Nations, *General Assembly, Official Records of the Second Part of the First Session, Third Committee, Summary Records of Meetings, 24 October–12 December 1946.*

80. E/REF/1, February 12, 1946; Diana Kay and Robert Miles, *Refugees or Migrant Workers? European Volunteer Workers in Britain, 1946–1951* (London: Routledge, 1992), 46.

81. E/REF/1, February 12, 1946.

82. Daniel Kanstroom, *Deportation Nation: Outsiders in American History* (Cambridge, MA: Harvard University Press), 2007.

83. Nathan-Chapotot, *Les Nations Unies*, 20.

84. Stoessinger, *The Refugee*, 74–75.

85. Proudfoot, *European Refugees*, 401.

86. The five Soviet-backed delegations that voted against it were the USSR, the Ukrainian Soviet Socialist Republic, the Belarusian Soviet Socialist Republic, Yugoslavia, and Poland.

87. United Nations, *General Assembly, Official Records of the Second Part of the First Session, Third Committee, Summary Records of Meetings, 24 October–12 December 1946.*

88. Woodbridge, *UNRRA*, 1:27.

89. In August 1945 the USSR presented UNRRA with a request for an aid package amounting to $700 million. Woodbridge, *UNRRA*, 1:101; Dean Acheson, *Present at the Creation: My Years in the State Department* (New York: Norton, 1969), 201.

90. This disengagement was virtually completed by 1949. See Charles Easton Rothwell, "International Organization and World Politics," *International Organization* 3 (November 1949): 605–19.

91. Constitution of the IRO, Annex I, Definitions.

92. Henri Monneray, "La condition juridique des réfugiés," in *Personnes déplacées*, ed. François Berge (Paris: Clermont, 1948), 72.

93. George Ginsburgs, "The Soviet Union and the Problem of Refugees and Displaced Persons 1917–1956," *American Journal of International Law* 51 (April 1957): 325–61.

94. Louise W. Holborn, *The International Refugee Organization: A Specialized Agency of the United Nations: Its History and Work, 1946–1952* (London: Oxford University Press, 1956), 185.

95. Elfan Rees, "The Refugee and the United Nations," in *International Conciliation* 492 (New York: Carnegie Endowment for International Peace, 1953): 265–314.

96. James Reston, "Negotiating with the Russians," 102.

97. Penrose, "Negotiating on Refugees," 167.

98. *Provisional Arrangement Concerning the Status of Refugees Coming from Germany* (July 4, 1936); *Convention Concerning the Status of Refugees Coming from Germany* (February 10, 1938).

99. Ivor C. Jackson, *The Refugee Concept in Group Situations* (The Hague: Nijhoff, 1999), 25.

CHAPTER 2

1. IRO Records, *Manual for Eligibility Officers* (1950), 43AJ–1251.

2. Roger Nathan-Chapotot, *Les Nations Unies et les réfugiés: Le maintien de la paix et le conflit de qualifications entre l'Ouest et l'Est* (Paris: Pedone, 1949), 127.

3. George Woodbridge, *UNRRA: The History of the United Nations Relief and Rehabilitation Administration*), 3 vols. (New York: Columbia University Press, 1950), 3:156.

4. Malcolm J. Proudfoot, *European Refugees: 1939–1952; A Study in Forced Population Movement* (Evanston, IL: Northwestern University Press, 1956), 243.

5. Arieh J. Kochavi, *Post-Holocaust Politics: Britain, the United States, and Jewish Refugees, 1945–1948* (Chapel Hill: University of North Carolina Press, 2001), 20.

6. Harry Truman to Byrnes, April 17, 1946, Harry S. Truman Library, Official File 127, Box 673.

7. Wolfgang Jacobmeyer, *Vom Zwangsarbeiter zum heimatlosen Ausländer: Die Displaced Persons in Westdeutschland, 1945–1951* (Göttingen, West Germany: Vandenhoeck & Ruprecht, 1985), 103. Laura Hilton, "Prisoners of Peace: Rebuilding Community, Identity and Nationality in Displaced Persons Camps in Germany, 1945–1952" (Ph.D. diss., Ohio State University, 2001), 191.

8. Michael L. Hoffmann, "Millions Remain in DP Category," *New York Times*, February 3, 1946.

9. Louise W. Holborn, *The International Refugee Organization: A Specialized Agency of the United Nations; Its History and Work, 1946–1952* (London: Oxford University Press, 1956), 203.

10. Henry Monneray, "La condition juridique des réfugiés," in *Personnes déplacées*, ed. François Berge (Paris: Clermont, 1948), 64–80. On the charge of "national indignity," see Anne Simonin, "L'indignité nationale, un châtiment républicain," in *Une poignée de misérables: L'épuration de la société française après la Seconde Guerre Mondiale*, ed. Marc Olivier Baruch (Paris: Fayard, 2003), 37–61; Benjamin

Frommer, *National Cleansing: Retribution against Nazi Collaborators in Postwar Czechoslovakia* (Cambridge, UK: Cambridge University Press, 2005), 192–206.

11. István Deák, Jan T. Gross, and Tony Judt, eds., *The Politics of Retribution in Europe: World War II and its Aftermath* (Princeton, NJ: Princeton University Press, 2000). Klaus-Dietmar Henke and Hans Voller, eds., *Politische Säuberung in Europa: Die Abrechnung mit Faschismus und Kollaboration nach dem Zweiten Weltkrieg* (Munich: Deutscher Taschenbuch Verlag, 1991).

12. Anna D. Jaroszyńska-Kirchmann, *The Exile Mission: The Polish Political Diaspora and Polish Americans, 1939–1956* (Athens, OH: Ohio University Press, 2004), 64.

13. *IRO Executive Council, 1951*, IRO Records, 43AJ–166.

14. Winifred N. Hadsel, "Can Europe's Refugees Find New Homes?" *Foreign Policy Reports* 19, no. 10 (August 1943): 110–19.

15. Woodbridge, *UNRRA*, 3:142 and 2:486.

16. René Ristelhueber, *Au secours des réfugiés: L'œuvre de l'Organisation Internationale des Réfugiés* (Paris: Plon, 1951), 139.

17. A. L. Gould, "A Report on the Political Situation in the DP camps and its Relation to the DP Law of 1948," undated, Robert F. Wagner Labor Archives, Tamiment Library, New York University, Jacob Pat Papers, Box 1, Folder 53.

18. Ira A. Hirschmann, *The Embers Still Burn: An Eye-Witness View of the Postwar Ferment in Europe and the Middle East and Our Disastrous Get-Soft-with-Germany Policy* (New York: Simon & Schuster, 1949), 84.

19. IRO Records, 43AJ–166.

20. Jacobmeyer, *Vom Zwangsarbeiter*, 106.

21. Cited by Mark Wyman, *DPs: Europe's Displaced Persons, 1945–1951* (Ithaca, NY: Cornell University Press, 1998), 58.

22. Marta Dyczok, *The Grand Alliance and Ukrainian Refugees* (New York: St Martin's, 2000), 139–40; Ben Shephard, *The Long Road Home: The Aftermath of the Second World War* (London: Bodley Head, 2010), 213–18.

23. *Lithuanian Bulletin*, January-February 1947, in IRO Records, 43AJ–155.

24. Léon Richard, "Le problème peut-il être résolu?" in Berge, *Personnes déplacées*, 338.

25. Walter Dushnyck and William J. Gibbons, *Refugees Are People: The Plight of Europe's Displaced Persons* (New York: American Press, 1947), 56.

26. M. F. Potter, "Le filtrage des réfugiés" in Berge, *Personnes déplacées*, 134.

27. Jacobmeyer, *Vom Zwangsarbeiter*, 104–14.

28. Ristelhueber, *Au secours des réfugiés*, 139.

29. Eileen Egan, *For Whom There Is No Room: Scenes from the Refugee World* (New York: Paulist Press 1995), 140.

30. United Nations, Economic and Social Council E/816, *Report on the Progress and Prospect of Repatriation, Resettlement and Repatriation of Refugees*, June 1948.

31. "Is it Nothing to You?" Refugee Defence Committee, London, January 1949.

32. IRO Records, *Manual for Eligibility Officers* (1950), 43AJ–1251.

33. Ibid, Case 1243.

34. Ristelhueber, *Au secours des réfugiés*, 145.

35. Arieh J. Kochavi, *Prelude to Nuremberg: Allied War Crimes Policy and the Question of Punishment* (Chapel Hill: University of North Carolina Press, 1998), 94.

36. Eduard Reut-Nicolussi, "Displaced Persons and International Law," *Recueil de Cours* 73 (1948), 64.

37. Holborn, *International Refugee Organization*, 207.

38. *Manual for Eligibility Officers*, 6.

39. *Review Board: Semestrial Report, Second Semester 1948*, IRO Records, 43AJ–574.

40. Léon Richard, "Réfugiés et personnes déplacées" in Berge, *Personnes déplacées*, 33.

41. *Histoire du Conseil du Recours* (1951), IRO Records, 43AJ–140.

42. Proudfoot, *European Refugees*, 242.

43. *Review Board: Semestrial Report to the Director General, First Semester 1949*, IRO Records, 43AJ–574.

44. IRO Records, 43AJ–166.

45. *Review Board: Semi Annual Report: Half-Year Ending on July 1, 1948*, IRO Records, 43AJ–574.

46. Holborn, *International Refugee Organization*, 210.

47. IRO Records, 43AJ–140.

48. Although the vast majority of confidential files were destroyed in the early 1950s, a significant number of refugee petitions survived in the IRO archives deposited at the Archives Nationales in Paris.

49. Holborn, *International Refugee Organization*, 186.

50. Ristelhueber, *Au secours des réfugiés*, 143.

51. *Manual for Eligibility Officers*, case 353.

52. IRO Records, 43AJ–477.

53. Now the city of Lviv in Ukraine, it was in Poland in the interwar period and was then known as Lwów.

54. IRO Records, 43AJ–574.

55. IRO Records, 43AJ–141

56. IRO Records, 43AJ–141

57. IRO Records, 43AJ–574. The "Beneš Decree" of August 2, 1945 (Decree 33) revoked the Czechoslovak citizenship of persons of "German and Magyar ethnicity."

58. IRO Records, 43AJ–142.

59. IRO Records, 43AJ–490.

60. IRO Records, 43AJ–141.

61. IRO Records, 43AJ–142.

62. Holborn, *International Refugee Organization*, 376.

63. IRO Records, 43AJ–166.

64. IRO Records, 43AJ–140.

65. Holborn, *International Refugee Organization*, 211.

66. *The Case of Admiral Horthy, Ex-Regent of Hungary, December 1, 1948*, IRO Records, 43AJ–574.

67. IRO Records, 43AJ–471.

68. IRO Records, 43AJ–469.

69. Ristelhueber, *Au secours des réfugiés*, 145.

70. Humanity Calls, *Stop Crimes Against Humanity Perpetrated by the International Refugee Organization*, July 1950 (in IRO Records, 43AJ–574).

71. Simon Wiesenthal to Dr Bedo, Chief Eligibility Officer in Salzburg, October 28, 1948, IRO Records, 43AJ–457.

72. Tom Segev, *Simon Wiesenthal: The Life and Legends* (New York: Doubleday, 2010), 69; Guy Walters, *Hunting Evil: The Nazi War Criminals Who Escaped and the Quest to Bring Them To Justice* (New York: Broadway Books, 2009), 98; Michael John, "Upper Austria, Intermediate Stop: Reception Camps and Housing Schemes for Jewish DPs and Refugees in Transit," *Journal of Israeli History* 19 (October 1998), 21–47.

73. IRO Records, 43AJ–475.

74. Kim Salomon, *Refugees in the Cold War Era: Toward a New International Refugee Regime in the Early Postwar Era* (Lund, Sweden: Lund University Press, 1991), 243.

75. IRO Records, 43AJ–469.

76. DP Act of June 16, 1950, Public Law No. 81–555, Section 13.

77. IRO Records, 43AJ–477.

78. IRO Records, 43AJ–166.

79. IRO Records, 43AJ– 148.

80. IRO Records, 43AJ–471.

81. William I. Hitchcock, *The Bitter Road To Freedom: A New History of the Liberation of Europe* (New York: Free Press, 2008), 241.

82. Ruth Feder, "Displaced Persons Go Home: How They Are Received in Yugoslavia," in *Churchman* 161 (November 1947): 15–16.

83. IRO Constitution, Part I, Paragraph 2, Section A.

84. *Manual for Eligibility Officers*, 5–8.

85. Robert F. Barsky, *Constructing a Productive Other: Discourse Theory and the Convention Refugee Hearing* (Amsterdam: Benjamins, 1994).

86. Prokop Tomek, "The Highs and Lows of Czech and Slovak Émigré Activism," in *Anti-Communist Minorities in the U.S. Political Activism of Ethnic Refugees*, ed. Ieva Zake (New York: Palgrave Macmillan, 2009), 109–26.

87. Kathleen McLaughlin, "Czechs in Bavaria Protest on Care; Refugees Object to Being Put With Sudeten Germans in Camp For Exiles," *New York Times*, March 7, 1948; Roland J Hoffman, "Zur Aufnahme der Flüchtlinge aus der ČSR in der US-Zone Deutschlands nach der kommunistischen Machtergreifung vom Februar 1948," in *Bohemia* 36 (January 1995): 69–112.

88. Göran Rystad, "Victims of Oppression or Ideological Weapons? Aspects of US Refugee Policy in the Post-War Era," in *The Uprooted: Forced Migration as an International Problem in the Post-War Era*, ed. Göran Rystad (Lund, Sweden: Lund University Press, 1990), 195–227.

89. Genêt [Janet Flanner], "Letter from Wurzburg," *New Yorker*, November 6, 1948.

90. Ristelhueber, *Au secours des réfugiés*, 141.

91. Genêt, "Letter from Wurzburg."

92. Ivor C. Jackson, *The Refugee Concept in Group Situations* (The Hague: Nijhoff, 1999), 23–24.

93. John Hope Simpson, *The Refugee Problem: Report of a Survey* (London: Oxford University Press, 1939), 4.

94. Marvin Klemme, *The Inside Story of UNRRA: An Experience in Internationalism; A First Hand Report on the Displaced Persons of Europe* (New York: Lifetime, 1949), 149.

95. Hirschmann, *Embers Still Burn*, 140.

96. Salomon, *Refugees in the Cold War*, 147.

97. *Review Board: Semetrial Report to the Director General, First Semester 1949*, IRO Records, 43AJ–574.

98. IRO Records, 43AJ–141.

99. Ibid.

100. Ibid.

101. Ibid.

102. IRO Records, 43AJ–166.

103. IRO Records, 43AJ–570. To stem emigration, the Czechoslovak government installed electric fences along the western borders with Austria and Germany. Tomek, "Highs and Lows," 113.

104. IRO Records, 43AJ–142.

105. IRO Records, 43AJ–457.

106. Ibid.

107. Ibid.

108. David Wingeate Pike, "L'immigration espagnole en France (1945–1952)," *Revue d'Histoire Moderne et Contemporaine* 24 (April 1977): 286–300.

109. IRO Records, 43AJ–306.

110. *Manual for Eligibility Officers*, 68.

111. Jacques Vernant, *The Refugee in the Post-War World* (New Haven, CT: Yale University Press), 280.

112. IRO Records, 43AJ–306.

113. Ibid.

114. Ibid.

115. Volker Ackermann, *Der "echte" Flüchtling: Deutsche Vertriebene und Flüchtlinge aus der DDR, 1945–1961* (Osnabrück, Germany: Universitätsverlag Rasch, 1995);

Ackermann, "Discerner le vrai du faux: un débat sur les réfugiés en Allemagne de l'Ouest (1945–1961)," *Migrance* 17–18, (2001): 38–46.

116. Susan L. Carruthers, "Between Camps: Eastern Bloc 'Escapees' and Cold War Borderlands," *American Quarterly* 57, no. 3 (2005): 911–42.

117. Florence Guilhem, *L'obsession du retour: les républicains espagnols 1939–1975* (Toulouse, Presses Universitaires du Mirail, 2005), 57–60. Geneviève Dreyfus-Armand, *L'exil des Républicains espagnols en France. De la Guerre civile à la mort de Franco* (Paris: Albin Michel, 1999), 202–205.

118. Rieko Karatani, "How History Separated Refugee and Migrant Regimes: In Search of their Institutional Origins," *International Journal of Refugee Law* 17 (September 2005): 517–41.

119. Jerzy Sztucki, "Who Is a Refugee? The Convention Definition: Universal or Obsolete?" in *Refugee Rights and Realities: Evolving International Concepts and Regimes*, ed. Frances Nicholson and Patrick Twomey (Cambridge, UK: Cambridge University Press, 1999), 55–81.

CHAPTER 3

1. John F. Hutchinson, *Champions of Charity: War and the Rise of the Red Cross* (Boulder, CO: Westview, 1996); Annette Becker, *Oubliés de la Grande Guerre: Humanitaire et culture de guerre, 1914–1918; Populations occupées, déportés civils, prisonniers de guerre* (Paris: Noêsis, 1998).

2. Keith David Watenpaugh, "The League of Nations' Rescue of Armenian Genocide Survivors and the Making of Modern Humanitarianism, 1920–1927," *American Historical Review* 115 (December 2010): 1315–39; Clare Mulley, *The Woman Who Saved the Children: A Biography of Eglantyne Jebb, Founder of Save the Children* (Oxford: Oneworld, 2009).

3. Francesca M. Wilson, *In the Margins of Chaos: Recollections of Relief Work in and between Three Wars* (New York: Macmillan, 1945), 293; David Stafford, *Endgame 1945: Victory, Retribution, Liberation* (London: Little, Brown, 2007), 19–21; Ben Shephard, "'Becoming Planning Minded': The Theory and Practice of Relief 1940–1945," *Journal of Contemporary History* 43 (July 2008): 405–19.

4. James T. Shotwell, *The Great Decision* (New York: Macmillan, 1944), 171.

5. H. J. Laski, "The Machinery of International Relief," in *When Hostilities Cease: Papers on Relief and Reconstruction Prepared for the Fabian Society* (London: Gollancz, 1943), 30–42.

6. Cited in George Woodbridge, *UNRRA: The History of the United Nations Relief and Rehabilitation Administration* (New York: Columbia University Press, 1950), Volume I, 114.

7. Grace Fox, "The Origins of UNRRA," *Political Science Quarterly* 65 (December 1950): 561–84; Philip C. Jessup, "UNRRA, Sample of World Organization," *Foreign Affairs* 22 (April 1944: 362–73).

8. Elizabeth Borgwardt, *A New Deal for the World: America's Vision for Human Rights* (Cambridge, MA: Belknap Press of Harvard University Press, 2005), 119.

9. "The Members of the League agree to encourage the establishment and co-operation of duly authorized voluntary national Red Cross organizations having as purposes the improvement of health, the prevention of disease and the mitigation of suffering throughout the world" (Covenant of the League of Nations, Article 25).

10. Sol Bloom, *Our Heritage: George Washington and the Establishment of the American Union* (New York: Putnam, 1944), 52.

11. Wilson, *Margins of Chaos*, 292.

12. Merle Curti, *American Philanthropy Abroad: A History* (New Brunswick, NJ: Rutgers University Press, 1963), 506–7.

13. J. Bruce Nichols, *The Uneasy Alliance: Religion, Refugee Work, and U.S. Foreign Policy* (New York: Oxford University Press, 1988), 5.

14. United Nations, Department of Public Information, *What The United Nations Is Doing for Refugees and Displaced Persons* (Lake Success, NY: United Nations, 1948), 12.

15. Jay Howard Geller, *Jews in Post-Holocaust Germany, 1945–1953* (Cambridge, UK: Cambridge University Press, 2005), 55.

16. UNESCO, International Conference on Social Work, Paris, February 1947 (in IRO Records, 43AJ–20).

17. Fred K. Hoehler, "Displaced Persons," in *Persistent International Issues*, ed. George B. de Huszar (New York: Harper, 1947), 41–69.

18. The United Nations Relief and Works Agency, created in 1949, is specifically dedicated to the humanitarian care of Palestinian refugees in the Middle East. The Office of the United Nations High Commissioner for Refugees, established in 1951, is in charge of most internally displaced persons and refugees in the world.

19. Woodbridge, *UNRRA*, 2:469.

20. Woodbridge, *UNRRA*, 3:416.

21. Kathryn Hulme, *The Wild Place* (Boston: Little, Brown, 1953), x–xi.

22. Susan T. Pettiss, with Lynne Taylor, *After the Shooting Stopped: The Story of an UNRRA Welfare Worker in Germany, 1945–1947* (Victoria, BC: Trafford, 2004), 7.

23. William I. Hitchcock, *The Bitter Road to Freedom: A New History of the Liberation of Europe* (New York: Free Press, 2008), 224; Tara Zahra, "Lost Children: Displacement, Family, and Nation in Postwar Europe," *Journal of Modern History* 81 (March 2009): 45–86. On Gene Delano's relief work in Germany see Harry Truman Library, Official File 127, Box 674; on Iris Murdoch see Ben Shephard, *The Long Road Home: The Aftermath of the Second World War* (London: Bodley Head, 2010), 57.

24. Marvin Klemme, *The Inside Story of UNRRA: An Experience in Internationalism; A First Hand Report on the Displaced Persons of Europe* (New York: Lifetime, 1949), 12.

25. W. B. Courtney, "Unwanted," *Collier's*, July 1948, 28.

26. Mary Hornaday, "Private Groups Carry Torch for Continued Charity Relief," *The Christian Science Monitor*, August 3, 1946.

27. Wilson, *Margins of Chaos*, 306.

28. Francesca M. Wilson, *Aftermath: France, Germany, Austria, Yugoslavia 1945 and 1946* (New York: Penguin Books, 1947), 79.

29. René Ristelhueber, *Au secours des réfugiés: L'œuvre de l'Organisation Internationale des Réfugiés* (Paris: Plon, 1951), 67.

30. John George Stoessinger, *The Refugee and the World Community* (Minneapolis: University of Minnesota Press, 1956), 148.

31. Hulme, *Wild Place*, 190.

32. Johannes-Dieter Steinert, "British Humanitarian Assistance: Wartime Planning and Postwar Realities," *Journal of Contemporary History* 43 (July 2008): 421–35.

33. Louise W. Holborn, *The International Refugee Organization: A Specialized Agency of the United Nations; Its History and Work, 1946–1952* (London: Oxford University Press, 1956), 152.

34. Ristelhueber, *Au service des réfugiés*, 66.

35. Maurice Grimaud, *Quatre années avec les réfugiés*, unpublished autobiographical manuscript kindly given to me by the author. See also Maurice Grimaud, *Je ne suis pas né en mai 1968: Souvenirs et carnets 1934–1992* (Paris: Tallandier, 2007), 60–67.

36. Kathleen Woodroofe, *From Charity to Social Work in England and the United States* (London: Routledge & Kegan Paul, 1962), 167–68; James Leiby, *A History of Social Welfare and Social Work in the United States* (New York: Columbia University Press, 1978), 217–44.

37. "New Type of World Pictured at Social Work Conference," *The Christian Science Monitor*, May 20, 1946.

38. Mary Kinnear, *Woman of the World: Mary McGeachy and International Cooperation* (Toronto: University of Toronto Press, 2004), 160–63.

39. Wilson, *Aftermath*, 253.

40. Woodbridge, *UNRRA*, 2:522.

41. Dean Acheson, *Present at the Creation: My Years in the State Department* (New York: Norton, 1969), 69.

42. Speech before the Women's Division of the United Jewish Appeal of Greater New York (February 20th, 1946) in *The Eleanor Roosevelt Papers*, vol. 1, *The Human Rights Years, 1945–1948*, ed. Allida Black (Detroit: Thompson Gale, 2007), 258.

43. Woodbridge, *UNRRA*, 2:523.

44. Margaret McNeill, *By the Rivers of Babylon: A Story of Relief Work among the Displaced Persons of Europe* (London: Bannisdale, 1950), 212.

45. H. H. Fisher, *The American Relief Administration in Russia, 1921–1923* (New York: Russell Sage Foundation, 1943).

46. Curti, *American Philanthropy*, 478; Laura Hilton, "Prisoners of Peace: Rebuilding Community, Identity and Nationality in Displaced Persons Camps in Germany 1945–1952" (Ph.D. diss., Ohio State University, 2001), 173–79.

47. Ristelhueber, *Au secours des réfugiés*, 185.

48. United Nations, Economic and Social Council, *Report on the Progress and Prospect of Repatriation, Resettlement and Immigration of Refugees and Displaced Persons*, June 10, 1948.

49. Malcolm J. Proudfoot, *European Refugees: 1939–1952; A Study in Forced Population Movement* (Evanston, IL: Northwestern University Press, 1956), 409.

50. Hulme, *Wild Place*, xii.

51. Roosevelt, *Eleanor Roosevelt Papers*, 1:255.

52. T. F. Johnson, *International Tramps: From Chaos to Permanent World Peace* (London: Hutchinson, 1938), 232.

53. Claudena M. Skran, *Refugees in Inter-war Europe: The Emergence of a Regime* (Oxford: Clarendon, 1995), 179.

54. Henry Morgenthau, with French Strother, *I Was Sent to Athens* (Garden City, NY: Doubleday, Doran, 1929), 50–51.

55. Wilson, *Margins of Chaos*, 298.

56. Denis Peschansky, *La France des camps: L'internement, 1938–1946* (Paris: Gallimard, 2002), 36–94; Anne Grynberg, *Les camps de la honte: Les internés juifs des camps français, 1939–1944* (Paris: Découverte, 1991), 40–86; Nicolas Fisher, "L'internement républicain," *Plein Droit* 58 (December 2003): 18–21.

57. Curt Bondy, "Problems of Internment Camps," *Journal of Abnormal and Social Psychology* 38 (October 1943): 453–75.

58. Wilson, *Margins of Chaos*, 305.

59. Lawrence Frenkel, *Displaced Persons Camps: Typescript Memorandum (1947)*, Hoover Institution, Stanford, CA (4086947.1).

60. McNeill, *Rivers of Babylon*, 85.

61. Malcolm J. Proudfoot, "The Anglo-American Displaced Persons Program for Germany and Austria," *American Journal of Economics and Sociology* 6 (October 1946): 33–54.

62. Cited in Mark Wyman, *DPs: Europe's Displaced Persons, 1945–1951* (Ithaca, NY: Cornell University Press, 1998), 52.

63. Malcolm Proudfoot, "The Anglo-American Displaced Persons Program for Germany and Austria," *American Journal of Economics and Sociology* 6 (1946): 33–54, here p. 51.

64. Kenneth G. Brooks, "The Re-establishment of Displaced Peoples," in *When Hostilities Cease*, 99–124.

65. Hannah Arendt, "The Stateless People," in *Contemporary Jewish Record* 8 (April 1945): 137–53.

66. Hannah Arendt, "'The Rights of Man': What Are They?" in *Modern Review* 3 (June 1949): 24–39.

67. Hannah Arendt, *The Origins of Totalitarianism* (New York: Schocken Books, 2004), 361.

68. Holborn, *International Refugee Organization*, 218.

69. McNeill, *Rivers of Babylon*, 38.

70. Genêt [Janet Flanner], "Letter from Aschaffenburg," *New Yorker*, October 30, 1948.

71. Proudfoot, "Anglo-American Displaced Persons Program," 52.

72. United Nations, *The Question of Refugees: Documents for the Special Committee on Refugees and Displaced Persons*, E/REF/1, February 12, 1946.

73. The full text of the Harrison Report is available at United States Holocaust Memorial Museum Web site, http://www.ushmm.org/museum/exhibit/online/dp/resourc1.htm.

74. Proudfoot, "The Anglo-American Displaced Persons Program," 44.

75. Hulme, *Wild Place*, 192.

76. Ristelhueber, *Au secours des réfugiés*, 151.

77. Thomas Lane, *Victims of Stalin and Hitler: The Exodus of Poles and Balts to Britain* (New York: Palgrave Macmillan, 2004), 166.

78. Hulme, *Wild Place*, 125.

79. Anna Holian, "Between National Socialism and Soviet Communism: The Politics of Self-Representation among Displaced Persons in Munich, 1945–1951" (Ph.D. diss., University of Chicago, 2005), 53.

80. Docteur Robineau, "Démographie et problèmes sanitaires dans la zone française d'occupation en Allemagne," in *Personnes déplacées*, ed. François Berge (Paris: Clermont, 1948), 217–21.

81. Atina Grossmann, *Jews, Germans, and Allies: Close Encounters in Occupied Germany* (Princeton, NJ: Princeton University Press, 2007).

82. H. B. M. Murphy, "The Camps," in *Flight and Resettlement* (Paris: UNESCO, 1955), 58–64.

83. Eileen Egan, *For Whom There Is No Room: Scenes from the Refugee World* (New York: Paulist Press, 1995), 143.

84. David Rousset, *L'univers concentrationnaire* (Paris: Editions du Pavois, 1946).

85. Claude Bourdet, "Le grand scandale," in Berge, *Personnes déplacées*, 15–18.

86. François Nourissier, "Le monde des réfugiés," *Esprit*, January 1951, 19–40.

87. Murphy, "The Camps," 58.

88. Zeev W. Mankowitz, *Life between Memory and Hope: The Survivors of the Holocaust in Occupied Germany* (Cambridge, UK: Cambridge University Press, 2002).

89. Quoted in Wyman, *DPs*, 135.

90. Anna D. Jaroszyńska-Kirchmann, *The Exile Mission: The Polish Political Diaspora and Polish Americans, 1939–1956* (Athens, OH: Ohio University Press, 2004).

91. Giorgio Agamben, *Homo Sacer: Sovereign Power and Bare Life*, trans. Daniel Heller-Roazen (Stanford, CA: Stanford University Press, 1998).

92. Agamben, *Homo Sacer*, 132.

93. Giorgio Agamben, "Beyond Human Rights," in *Means without End: Notes on Politics* (Minneapolis: University of Minnesota Press, 2000), 14–25.

94. Quotation from Jenny Edkins, *Trauma and the Memory of Politics* (Cambridge, UK: Cambridge University Press, 2003), 195–97; see also Peter Nyers, *Rethinking Refugees: Beyond States of Emergency* (New York: Routledge, 2006), 25–43; Prem Kumar Rajaram and Carl Grundy-Warr, "The Irregular Migrant as Homo Sacer: Migration and Detention in Australia, Malaysia, and Thailand," *International Migration* 42 (January 2004): 33–64.

95. Michel Foucault, "Governmentality," in *The Foucault Effect: Studies in Governmentality*, ed. Graham Burchell, Colin Gordon, and Peter Miller (Chicago: University of Chicago Press, 1991), 102.

96. Guglielmo Verdirame and Barbara Harrell-Bond, eds., *Rights in Exile: Janus-Faced Humanitarianism* (New York: Berghahn Books, 2005), 328; Randy Lippert, "Governing Refugees: The Relevance of Governmentality to Understanding the International Refugee Regime," *Alternatives* 24 (July 1999): 295–329.

97. Liisa H. Malkki, "Refugees and Exile: From 'Refugee Studies' to the National Order of Things," *Annual Review of Anthropology* 24 (1995): 495–523.

98. Ilana Feldman, "Difficult Distinctions: Refugee Law, Humanitarian Practice, and Political Identification in Gaza," *Cultural Anthropology* 22 (February 2007): 129–69; Jennifer Hyndman, *Managing Displacement: Refugees and the Politics of Humanitarianism* (Minneapolis: University of Minnesota Press, 2000); Michel Agier, *Gérer les indésirables: Des camps de réfugiés au gouvernement humanitaire* (Paris: Flammarion, 2008); Didier Fassin, *La raison humanitaire. Une histoire morale du temps présent* (Paris: Seuil/Gallimard, 2010), 7–27.

99. Jacques Vernant, *The Refugee in the Post-War World* (New Haven, CT: Yale University Press, 1953), 163.

100. Wolfgang Jacobmeyer, "The Displaced Persons Problem: Repatriation and Resettlement," in *European Immigrants in Britain, 1933–1950*, ed. Johannes-Dieter Steinert and Inge Weber-Newth (Munich: Saur, 2003), 137–49.

101. IRO, *S.O.S. 100,000 êtres humains en détresse appellent à l'aide*, Geneva, July 1950.

102. Suzanne Langlois, "La contribution du cinéma documentaire en faveur de l'Administration des Nations Unies pour les Secours et la Reconstruction (UNRRA) 1943–1947," in *Lendemains de guerre*, ed. Roch Legault and Magali Deleuze (Montreal: Lux Editeur, 2006), 129–47.

103. IRO Records, 43AJ/668.

104. Holborn, *International Refugee Organization*, 543.

105. Donald Lanz, "Films about Displaced Persons," *International Journal of Religious Education* 36 (July 1949): 36.

106. Edward A. Shils, "Social and Psychological Aspects of Displacement and Repatriation," *Journal of Social Issues* 2 (August 1946): 3–18.

107. Genêt, "Letter from Aschaffenburg."

108. IRO Records, 43AJ–1135.

109. IRO Records, 43AJ–980.

110. IRO Records, 43AJ–406.

111. Nick Cullather, "The Foreign Policy of the Calorie," *American Historical Review* 112 (April 2007): 337–65.

112. Grimaud, *Quatre années avec les réfugiés*; Genêt, "Letter from Wurzburg."

113. Welfare Officer, Ansbach, US Zone of Germany, March 28, 1950, cited in Holborn, *The International Refugee Organization*, 82; Ristelhueber, *Au secours des réfugiés*, 62.

114. Robert Kee, *Refugee World* (London: Oxford University Press, 1961), 3.

115. Eduard Bakis, "DP Apathy," in Murphy, *Flight and Resettlement*, 87.

116. H. G. Adler, "Aufzeichnungen einer Displaced Person," *Merkur* 6, 1952, 1040–49.

117. IRO Records, 43AJ–666.

CHAPTER 4

1. Paul Gordon Lauren, *The Evolution of International Human Rights: Visions Seen* (Philadelphia: University of Pennsylvania Press, 1998), 130–205.

2. Michael Ignatieff, *Human Rights as Politics and Idolatry* (Princeton, NJ: Princeton University Press, 2001), 5.

3. Louis Henkin, *The Age of Rights* (New York: Columbia University Press, 1990), 193.

4. Ignatieff, *Human Rights*, 4.

5. See Samantha Power's introduction to Hannah Arendt, *The Origins of Totalitarianism* (New York: Schocken Books, 2004), xix.

6. Cited by Clinton Timothy Curle, *Humanité: John Humphrey's Alternative Account of Human Rights* (Toronto: University of Toronto Press, 2007), 161.

7. Samuel Moyn, *The Last Utopia: Human Rights in History* (Cambridge, MA: Belknap Press of Harvard University Press, 2010), 6.

8. A. W. Brian Simpson, *Human Rights and the End of Empire: Britain and the Genesis of the European Convention* (Oxford University Press, 2001), vii.

9. Mark Mazower, "The Strange Triumph of Human Rights, 1933–1950," *Historical Journal* 47, no. 2 (2004), 379–98.

10. Hans Kelsen, "The Preamble of the Charter—A Critical Analysis," *Journal of Politics* 8 (1946): 134–59. See also Kelsen, *The Law of the United Nations: A Critical Analysis of its Fundamental Problems* (1950; repr., Union, NJ: Lawbook Exchange, 2000), 30.

11. Cited by Martti Koskenniemi, *The Gentle Civilizer of Nations: The Rise and Fall of International Law, 1870–1960* (Cambridge, UK: Cambridge University Press, 2002), 394–95.

12. René Cassin, "La declaration universelle et la mise en œuvre des droits de l'homme," *Recueil des Cours* 79 (1951): 241–367.

13. Josef L. Kunz, "The United Nations Universal Declaration of Human Rights," *American Journal of International Law* 43(April 1949): 316–23.

14. United Nations, Department of Social Affairs, *The Impact of the Universal Declaration of Human Rights*, New York, 1951.

15. William Korey, *NGOs and the Universal Declaration of Human Rights: A Curious Grapevine* (New York: St. Martin's, 1998), 3.

16. United Nations, General Assembly, Official Records (First Part of First Session), Report of Third Committee A/45, Thirtieth Plenary Meeting, February 12, 1946.

17. Louise W. Holborn, *The International Refugee Organization: A Specialized Agency of the United Nations: Its History and Work 1946–1952* (London, New York: Oxford University Press, 1956), 348–52.

18. United Nations Department of Public Information, *Magna Carta for Refugees* (New York: 1953), 2.

19. Eduard Reut-Nicolussi, "Displaced Persons and International Law," *Recueil des Cours* 73 (1948), 19–64.

20. Rudolf Laun, *Das Recht auf die Heimat* (Hanover, West Germany: Schroedel, 1951); Lora Wildenthal, "Human Rights Activism in Occupied and Early West Germany: The Case of the German League for Human Rights," *Journal of Modern History* 80 (September 2008), 515–56.

21. Roger Nathan-Chapotot, *Les Nations Unies et les réfugiés: Le maintien de la paix et le conflit de qualifications entre l'Ouest et l'Est* (Paris: Pedone, 1949), 126. Reut-Nicolussi, *Displaced Persons*, 64.

22. See in particular: "Die Entrechten und Entwürdigten" (The rightless and worthless), published in the New York Jewish émigré publication *Aufbau* on December 15, 1944; "The Stateless People," *Contemporary Jewish Record* 8 (April 1945): 137–53; "'The Rights of Man': What Are They?" *Modern Review* 3 (June 1949): 24–37.

23. Marie Claire Caloz-Tschopp, *Les Sans-Etat dans la philosophie d'Hannah Arendt: Les humains superflus, le droit d'avoir des droits et la citoyenneté* (Lausanne, Switzerland: Payot, 2000); Bridget Cotter, "Hannah Arendt and 'The Right to Have Rights,'" in *Hannah Arendt and International Relations: Readings Across the Lines*, ed. Anthony F. Lang, Jr., and John Williams, 95–112 (New York: Palgrave Macmillan, 2005).

24. Arendt, "Stateless People," 151.

25. Arendt, "Rights of Man," 25.

26. Arendt, *The Origins of Totalitarianism* (1951; repr., New York: Harcourt, Brace & World, 1966), 292.

27. Arendt, "Rights of Man," 25.

28. Arendt, *Origins of Totalitarianism*, 293.

29. T. F. Johnson, *International Tramps: From Chaos to Permanent World Peace* (London: Hutchinson, 1938); Claudena M. Skran, *Refugees in Inter-war Europe: The Emergence of a Regime* (Oxford: Clarendon, 1995). Michael R. Marrus, *The Unwanted: European Refugees in the Twentieth Century* (New York: Oxford University Press, 1985), 51–121.

30. Carole Fink, *Defending the Rights of Others: The Great Powers, the Jews and International Minority Protection, 1878–1938* (Cambridge, UK: Cambridge University Press, 2004).

31. Michael Hansson, *The Refugee Problem: Two Speeches Made at the Invitation of the League of Nations Union*, Annemasse, France, 1936, 18.

32. Mark Vishniak, *The Legal Status of Stateless Persons* (New York: American Jewish Committee, 1945), 7. The only interwar study of statelessness in the United States is Catheryn Seckler-Hudson, *Statelessness: With Special Reference to the United States; A Study in Nationality and Conflict of Laws* (Washington, DC: Digest, 1934).

33. See among others: Antoine Pillet, *Traité pratique de droit international privé* (Paris: Sirey, 1923–24); André Colaneri, *De la condition des "sans-patrie": Etude critique de l'heimatlosat* (Paris: Sirey, 1932); Jacques Scheftel, "L'apatridie des réfugiés russes," *Journal de Droit International* 61 (1934): 36–69. I. G. Lipovano, *L'apatridie* (Paris: Les Editions Internationales, 1935).

34. Cited in Colaneri, *Condition des sans-patrie*, 19.

35. Dzovinar Kévonian, "Les juristes juifs russes en France et l'action internationale dans les années vingt," *Archives Juives* 2 (2001): 72–94

36. James C. Hathaway, "The Evolution of Refugee Status in International Law: 1920–1950," *International and Comparative Law Quarterly* 33 (1984): 348–80.

37. "Resolution Concerning Stateless Persons and Refugees," *Annuaire de l'Institut de Droit International* 2 (1936): 298.

38. J. L. Rubinstein, "The Refugee Problem," *International Affairs* 15 (September–October 1936): 716–34.

39. John Hope Simpson, *The Refugee Problem: Report of a Survey* (London: Oxford University Press, 1939), 4.

40. Louise W. Holborn, "The Legal Status of Political Refugees, 1920–1938," *American Journal of International Law* 32 (October 1938): 680–703.

41. A. N. Lequeux, "L'état de réfugié," *Esprit* 94 (November 1940): 84–89.

42. Joseph Chamberlain, "Without a Country," *Survey Graphic* 34 (March 1945): 85.

43. Jane Perry Clark Carey, "Some Aspects of Statelessness since World War I," *American Political Science Review* 40 (February 1946): 113–23.

44. United Nations General Assembly, resolution 8 (I) of February 12, 1946.

45. *A Study of Statelessness* (Lake Success, NY: Department of Social Affairs, 1949).

46. Vishniak, *Legal Status of Stateless Persons*, 24.

47. *Study of Statelessness*, 11–15.

48. "Statement by Albert Cohen, Legal Adviser's Office, on immediate task of field protection," October 6, 1947, IRO Records, 43AJ–459; Jacques Lecarme, "Images de la S.D.N chez Céline et chez Cohen," in *Albert Cohen dans son siècle*, ed. Alain Schaffner and Philippe Zard (Paris: Editions Le Manuscrit, 2005), 223–36.

49. *Study of Statelessness*, 8–9.

50. Cited in Vishniak, *Legal Status of Stateless Person*, 4.

51. Cited in Albert Verdoodt, *Naissance et signification de la Déclaration Universelle des Droits de l'Homme* (Louvain, Belgium: Warny, 1964), 156.

52. Arendt, "Rights of Man," 29.

53. Seyla Benhabib, *The Reluctant Modernism of Hannah Arendt*, rev. ed. (Lanham, MD: Rowman & Littlefield, 2003), 193; Serena Parekh, *Hannah Arendt and the Challenge of Modernity: A Phenomenology of Human Rights* (New York: Routledge, 2008), 36–41.

54. IRO Records, 43AJ–232.

55. Paul Weis to O. E. Stone, April 28, 1948, IRO Records, 43AJ–202.

56. The replies to the UNESCO questionnaire were later published in *Human Rights: Comments and Interpretations* (London: Wingate, 1949).

57. Mary Ann Glendon, *A World Made New: Eleanor Roosevelt and the Universal Declaration of Human Rights* (New York: Random House, 2001), 187–88.

58. Lynn Hunt, *Inventing Human Rights: A History* (New York: Norton, 2007), 202–11.

59. Mazower, "Strange Triumph," 389; *No Enchanted Palace: The End of Empires and the Ideological Origins of the United Nations* (Princeton, NJ: Princeton University Press, 2009), 104–149.

60. A. W. Brian Simpson, *Human Rights*, 245–48.

61. Max Gottschalk and Abraham G. Duker, *Jews in the Post-war World* (New York: Dryden, 1945), 167; Lev Salmanovits, "Political Status of the Jews in Post-war Europe," in *The Future of the Jews: A Symposium*, ed. J. J. Lynx (London: Drummond, 1945), 120–34. Joseph Tenenbaum, *Peace for the Jews* (New York: American Federation for Polish Jews, 1945).

62. Jay Winter, *Dreams of Peace and Freedom: Utopian Moments in the Twentieth Century* (New Haven, CT: Yale University Press, 2006), 108–10.

63. Dzovinar Kévonian, "Question des réfugiés, droits de l'homme: Eléments d'une convergence pendant l'entre-deux-guerres," *Matériaux pour l'histoire de notre temps* 72 (2003): 40–49.

64. Arendt, *Origins of Totalitarianism*, 281.

65. René Cassin, "Vers l'organisation de la vie international—de la Société des Nations aux Nations Unies d'aujourd'hui," in *La pensée et l'action* (Boulogne sur-Seine, France: Lalou, 1972), 124.

66. Cassin describes the Universal Declaration as the result of a long "path towards universality." See Cassin, "Historique de la Déclaration universelle des droits de l'homme de 1948," in Cassin, *La pensée et l'action*, 114. Glenda Sluga, "René Cassin: *Les droits de l'homme* and the Universality of Human Rights," in *Human Rights in the Twentieth Century*, ed. Stefan-Ludwig Hoffmann (Cambridge, UK: Cambridge University Press, 2010), 107–24.

67. Jan Herman Burgers, "The Road to San Francisco: The Revival of the Human Rights Idea in the Twentieth Century," *Human Rights Quarterly* 14 (1992): 447–77.

68. René Cassin, "L'état Leviathan contre l'homme et la communauté humaine," in Cassin, *La pensée et l'action*, 63–71.

69. Quincy Wright, "Human Rights and the World Order," *International Conciliation* 389 (April 1943): 239–62.

70. Karl R. Popper, *The Open Society and Its Enemies*, rev. ed. (Princeton, NJ: Princeton University Press, 1950), 576.

71. Hathaway, "Evolution of Refugee Status," 370–76; Ivor C. Jackson, *The Refugee Concept in Group Situations* (The Hague: Nijhoff, 1999), 26–37.

72. Nathan-Chapotot, *Les Nations Unies et les réfugiés*, 151.

73. Nevzat Soguk, *States and Strangers: Refugees and Displacements of Statecraft* (Minneapolis: University of Minnesota Press, 1999), 160.

74. Emma Haddad, *The Refugee in International Society: Between Sovereigns* (Cambridge, UK: Cambridge University Press, 2008), 140.

75. United Nations Department of Public Information, *Magna Carta for Refugees* (New York: United Nations, 1953).

76. Niraj Nathwani, *Rethinking Refugee Law* (The Hague: Nijhoff, 2003), 18.

77. Philip C. Jessup, *A Modern Law of Nations: An Introduction* (New York: Macmillan, 1948), 27.

78. Georges Scelle, *Manuel de droit international public* (Paris: Domat-Montchrestien, 1948), 511.

79. Hersch Lauterpacht, *International Law and Human Rights* (New York: Praeger, 1950), 4.

80. Marek St. Korowicz, "The Problem of the International Personality of Individuals," *American Journal of International Law* 50 (July 1956): 533–62.

81. Paul Weis to O. E. Stone, Instructions to Drafting Committee, April 28, 1948; IRO Records, 43AJ–202. The head of the Protection Division at the IRO headquarters in Geneva, Paul Weis later became a leading expert in refugee and nationality law.

82. Korey, *NGOs and the Universal Declaration*, 52.

83. Daniel Roger Maul, "The International Labor Organization and the Globalization of Human Rights," in Hoffmann, *Human Rights in the Twentieth Century*, 301–20.

84. Paul Weis, "Future of Elan's Freedom: How IRO Will Enforce a New Standard of International Conduct," *Wiener Library Bulletin* 6 (September 1948): 6–8.

85. Johannes Morsink, *The Universal Declaration of Human Rights: Origins, Drafting and Intent* (Philadelphia: University of Pennsylvania Press, 1999).

86. "Statement by Albert Cohen, Legal Adviser's Office, on immediate task of field protection," October 6, 1947, IRO Records, 43AJ–459.

87. "IRO Memorandum to Economic and Social Council," December 13, 1948, IRO Records 43AJ–459.

88. Mazower, *No Enchanted Palace*, 130.

89. Paul Weis to O. E Stone, Instructions to drafting committee, April 28, 1948, IRO Records, 43AJ–202.

90. Morsink, *Universal Declaration*, 82.

91. "U.N. Body Rejects Plan for Stateless," *New York Times*, June 5, 1948.

92. A. W. Brian Simpson, *Human Rights*, 451.

93. The "Cassin Draft" is reproduced as in appendix in Glendon, *World Made New*, 275–80.

94. "Statement of the Position of the United States on Petitions by Individuals in Relation to a Covenant on Human Rights," April 30, 1948. Harry S. Truman Library, Truman Papers, Official File 85Q, Box 533.

95. "Report on the UN Commission of Human Rights," June 9, 1948, IRO Records, 43AJ–202.

96. Gil Loescher and John A. Scanlan, *Calculated Kindness: Refugees and America's Half Open Door, 1945 to the Present* (New York: Free Press, 1986).

97. The genesis of Articles 14 and 15 is described in Verdoodt, *Naissance et signification*, 150–56; Morsink, *Universal Declaration*, 75–83; and Glendon, *World Made New*, 153.

98. René Cassin, "Déclaration universelle," 288.

99. "WJC memorandum regarding the right of asylum," August 3, 1948, IRO Records, 43AJ–202; Nehemiah Robinson, *The United Nations and the World Jewish Congress* (New York: Institute of Jewish Affairs, 1955), 74.

100. Holborn, *International Refugee Organization*, 327; Paul Weis, "The International Protection of Refugees," *American Journal of International Law* 48 (April 1954): 193–221. The previous Geneva Conventions (of 1864, 1906, and 1929) only mentioned the rights of belligerents or contracting parties. The Hague Conventions of 1899 and 1907 proclaimed the right of captured soldiers to be treated as prisoners of war.

101. G. Kuhlman to John Humphrey, February 7, 1950, IRO Records, 43AJ–459.

102. Louis K. Hyde, *The United States and the United Nations, Promoting the Public Welfare: Examples of American Co-operation, 1945–1955* (New York: Manhattan, 1960), 79.

103. United Nations Department of Public Information, *Magna Carta for Refugees*, 3.

CHAPTER 5

1. "IRO Press Release 233, October 22, 1951," IRO Records, 43AJ–894; "Immigration: The 1,000,000th DP," *Time*, November 26, 1951.

2. Akira Iriye, *Global Community: The Role of International Organizations in the Making of the Contemporary World* (Berkeley: University of California Press, 2002).

3. Elizabeth Borgwardt, *A New Deal for the World: America's Vision for Human Rights* (Cambridge, MA: Belknap Press of Harvard University Press, 2005).

4. Eugene Kulischer, *Europe on the Move: War and Population Changes, 1917–47* (New York: Columbia University Press, 1948), 325.

5. International Refugee Organization, *Migration from Europe: A Report* (Geneva, Switzerland: IRO, 1951), vi.

6. Louise W. Holborn, *The International Refugee Organization: A Specialized Agency of the United Nations; Its History and Work, 1946–1952* (London: Oxford University Press, 1956), 365.

7. Margaret Sanger, ed., *Proceedings of the World Population Conference* (London: Arnold, 1927), 256–65.

8. Albert Thomas, "Albert Thomas on the International Control of Migration," *Population and Development Review* 9 (December 1983): 703–11.

9. Matthew Connelly, *Fatal Misconception: The Struggle to Control World Population* (Cambridge, MA: Belknap Press of Harvard University Press, 2008), 70–73; Alison Bashford, "Nation, Empire, Globe: The Spaces of Population Debate in the Interwar Years," *Comparative Studies in Society and History* 49 (January 2007), 170–201.

10. Henry Field, *"M" Project for FDR: Studies on Migration and Settlement* (Ann Arbor, MI: Edwards Brothers, 1962). A curator in physical anthropology at the Field Museum of Natural Sciences in Chicago, Henry Field supervised research for M-Project alongside anthropologist Isaiah Bowman (Johns Hopkins University) and the State Department official John Franklin Carter.

11. Greg Robinson, "Le Projet M de Franklin D. Roosevelt: Construire un monde grâce à la science...des races," *Critique Internationale* 27 (2005), 65–82.

12. Ladislas Farago, "Refugees: The Solution as FDR Saw It," *United Nations World* 1 (June-July 1947): 14–15, reprinted in Field, *M Project*, 374–77.

13. Diana Kay, "The Resettlement of Displaced Persons in Europe, 1946–1951" in *The Cambridge Survey of World Migration*, ed. Robin Cohen (Cambridge, UK: Cambridge University Press, 1995), 154–58.

14. Francis Blanchard, "Le problème des réfugiés devant l'opinion," *Politique Etrangère* 14 (March 1949): 167–172.

15. IRO Records, 43AJ–1171.

16. Silvia Salvatici, "From Displaced Persons to Laborers: Allied Employment Policies towards DPs in Post-war Germany," in Jessica Reinisch and Elizabeth White, eds, *The Disentanglement of Populations: Migration, Expulsion and Displacement in postwar Europe, 1944–49* (New York: Palgrave Macmillan, 2011), 210–228.

17. "The Displaced Persons Problem in Germany and Austria," *Intelligence Review* 43 (December 5, 1946): 32–38.

18. Robert Prigent, "La France doit-elle recueillir les Personnes Déplacées?" *Monde*, December 29, 1945.

19. Several historians have argued that British efforts to bring DP workers into the United Kingdom were motivated by racial motivations. See among others Kathleen Paul, *Whitewashing Britain: Race and Citizenship in the Postwar Era* (Ithaca, NY: Cornell University Press, 1997); Diana Kay and Robert Miles, eds., *Refugees or Migrant Workers? European Volunteer Workers in Britain, 1946–1951* (London:

Routledge, 1992); Johannes-Dieter Steinert, "British Post-War Migration Policies and Displaced Persons in Europe," in Reinisch and White, eds, *The Disentanglement of Populations*, 229–250. Randall Hansen challenges this racial intepretation in *Citizenship and Immigration in Post-war Britain* (New York, Oxford University Press, 2000).

20. International Labour Office, "Post-war Manpower Problems in Europe," *International Labor Review* 55, no. 6 (June 1947): 485–511.

21. Jane Perry Clark Carey, *The Role of Uprooted People in European Recovery* (Washington, DC: National Planning Association, 1948), 60.

22. Prigent, "La France doit-elle recueillir les Personnes Déplacées?"

23. Kathryn Hulme, *The Wild Place* (Boston: Little, Brown, 1953), 178.

24. Eileen Egan, *For Whom There Is No Room: Scenes from the Refugee World* (New York: Paulist Press, 1995), 143.

25. IRO Records, 43AJ–79 and 43AJ–238.

26. IRO Records, 43AJ–411.

27. "More DPs Admitted to Britain in Year Than Any Other Land," *New York Herald Tribune*, August 25, 1948; Inge Weber-Newth, "Displaced Persons als 'European Volunteer Workers' in Grossbritannien: Anwerbung, Aufnahme, Verbleib," *Zeitschrift für Geschitswissenshaft* 55 (April 2007): 937–54.

28. Marvin Klemme, *The Inside Story of UNRRA. An Experience in Internationalism; A First Hand Report on the Displaced Persons of Europe* (New York: Lifetime, 1949), 279.

29. IRO Records, 43AJ–628.

30. *Times* (London), "Work for the Homeless," May 21, 1951; IRO Records, 43AJ–628 and 43AJ–630.

31. John George Stoessinger, *The Refugee and the World Community* (Minneapolis: University of Minnesota Press, 1956), 117.

32. Vincent Viet, *La France immigrée: Construction d'une politique, 1914–1997* (Paris: Fayard, 1998), 146–7; "Pas de foyer d'infection fasciste en France!" *L'Humanité*, August 20, 1947.

33. House Committee on Foreign Affairs, *Displaced Persons and the International Refugee Organization: Report of a Special Subcommittee on Foreign Affairs* ["Fulton Report"], 80th Cong., 1st sess., 1947, 71.

34. *New York Herald Tribune*, November 16, 1947.

35. *Le Monde*, February 15, 1948.

36. Archives du Quai d'Orsay, *Unions Internationales, Troisième Versement, Article 1123*, April 22, 1947.

37. IRO Records, 43AJ–702.

38. "Compte rendu de Mr Demonrosty en Allemagne," February 26, 1947, Centre des Archives Contemporaines (Fontainebleau, France), CAC 770623, article 172.

39. "Outgoing Secret Cipher Message, conference with the French Mission," February 14, 1947, IRO Records, 43AJ–80.

40. "Réunion du comité consultatif de la sidérurgie," November 20, 1948, French National Archives, Série F12 10946.

41. IRO Records, 43AJ–80.

42. "Commandement en Chef Français en Allemagne à Quai d'Orsay," October 20, 1947, CAC 770623, article 172.

43. IRO Records, 43AJ–628.

44. Louis Chevalier, "Bilan d'une immigration," *Population* 5 (January-March 1950): 129–40.

45. "Rapport commun établi par les membres de la mission d'information envoyée dans les trois zones d'occupation," February 9–23, 1947, CAC 770623, article 172.

46. Ibid.

47. Kay and Miles, *Refugees or Migrant Workers?* 50.

48. "Notes sur les personnes déplacées baltes dans les camps de l'UNRRA," February 12, 1947, CAC 770623, article 173.

49. Frank Chelf, cited by Leonard Dinnerstein, *America and the Survivors of the Holocaust* (New York: Columbia University Press, 1982), 21.

50. The first fifteen member countries of the IRO were the United States, the United Kingdom, France, Canada, Australia, New Zealand, Belgium, the Netherlands, Luxembourg, Norway, Denmark, Iceland, Guatemala, the Dominican Republic, and China.

51. United Nations, Department of Public Information, *What The United Nations is Doing For Refugees and Displaced Persons* (Lake Success, NY: United Nations, 1948), 3. The IRO only repatriated 54,687 DPs, most of them to Poland. See Holborn, *International Refugee Organization*, 355.

52. Arthur Rucker, "The Work of the International Refugee Organization," *International Affairs* 25 (January 1949): 66–73.

53. Kathryn Hulme, *The Wild Place*, 210.

54. George S. Marshall, "Concern Expressed on Resettlement of DPs; Statement by Secretary of State," *Department of State Bulletin*, July 27, 1947, 194–97.

55. Ibid.

56. Holborn, *International Refugee Organization*, 415.

57. "Statement by the President, June 25, 1948," Truman Library, Official File 127, Box 674.

58. Haim Genizi, *America's Fair Share: The Admission and Resettlement of Displaced Persons, 1945–1952* (Detroit: Wayne State University Press, 1993).

59. Henriette von Holleuffer, "Seeking New Horizons in Latin America: The Resettlement of 100,000 European Displaced Persons between the Gulf of Mexico and Patagonia (1947–1951)," *Jahrbüch für Geschichte Lateinamerikas* 39 (2002): 125–61.

60. Malcolm Proudfoot, *European Refugees 1939–1952: A Study in Forced Population Movement* (Evanston, Ill.; Northwestern University Press, 1956), 424.

61. IRO, "Conference on Displaced Persons Publicity," Bad Kissingen, US Zone, Germany, November 15 and 16, 1948.

62. Ibid.

63. IRO, *Migration from Europe*, 37.

64. IRO, *Occupational Skills of Refugees*, Geneva, Switzerland: Office of Statistics and Operational Reports, September 1948.

65. House Committee, *Displaced Persons*, 67.

66. IRO Press Release, "IRO's Head Criticizes Lack of World Support for Refugees," May 4, 1948.

67. Ibid.

68. United Nations, Department of Public Information, "Statement of J. Donald Kingsley, Director-General of IRO, before the Third Committee of the General Assembly," November 10, 1949, IRO Records, 43AJ–398.

69. Grigor McClelland, *Embers of War: Letters from a Quaker Relief Worker in War-Torn Germany* (London: British Academic Press, 1997), 196.

70. Francesca Wilson, "Emigration: New Style," transcript of a BBC World Service broadcast, January 15, 1952, IRO Records, 43AJ–717.

71. G. Mikhailov, "Who Needs the IRO, and For What?" *New Times*, January 18, 1950, 11–15.

72. *Monde*, "Un nouveau marché d'esclaves au coeur de l'Europe," July 4, 1948.

73. Pierre Scize, "Cette malédiction, l'intelligence," *Figaro*, January 16, 1949.

74. Claude Bourdet, "Le grand scandale," in François Berge, ed., *Personnes déplacées* (Paris: Clermont, 1948), 18.

75. W. B. Courtney, "Unwanted," *Collier's*, July 17, 1948, 27–28.

76. Jack Bell, *Chicago Daily News*, October 27, 1948 in IRO Records 43AJ–1135.

77. United Nations, Economic and Social Council, "Report on the Progress and Prospect of Repatriation, Resettlement and Repatriation of Refugees," June 1948, UN Doc. E/816 (hereafter "Hambro-Williams Report"); Paul H. Griffith, National Commander of the American Legion, "Report of the European Tour," September 1947, HSTL, Official File 127, Box 674.

78. United Nations, *What the United Nations Is Doing*, 15.

79. Angelika Eder, "Displaced Persons/'Heimatlose Ausländer' als Arbeitskräfte in Westdeutschland," *Archiv für Sozialgeschichte* 42 (2002): 1–17.

80. Scize, "Cette malédiction, l'intelligence."

81. Genêt [Janet Flanner], "Letter from Würzburg," *New Yorker*, November 6, 1948.

82. IRO, *Occupational Skills of Refugees*.

83. *Resettlement of Specialists*, April 1948, IRO Records, 43AJ–646.

84. Jacques Vernant, *The Refugee in the Post-war World* (New Haven, CT: Yale University Press, 1953), 589.

85. International Refugee Organization, *The Forgotten Elite: The Story of Refugee Specialists* (Geneva, Switzerland: International Refugee Organization, 1950); IRO News Report, "26,000 of IRO's remaining refugees are some of the best trained Europeans," June 1949.

86. International Refugee Organization, *Forgotten Elite*, 4.

87. IRO Records, 43AJ–57 and 43AJ–1253.

88. Stephen Duggan and Betty Drury, *The Rescue of Science and Learning: The Story of the Emergency Committee in Aid of Displaced Foreign Scholars* (New York: Macmillan, 1948).

89. Avinoam J. Patt, *Finding Home and Homeland: Jewish Youth and Zionism in the Aftermath of the Holocaust* (Detroit, MI: Wayne University Press, 2009), 155–197.

90. "Hambro-Williams Report."

91. Carey, *Role of Uprooted People*, 59; Philip S. Bernstein, "Strength, Not Idealism," *Christian Century* 66 (July 20, 1949): 864–66.

92. "Hambro-Williams Report."

93. David Cesarani, *Justice Delayed: How Britain Became a Refuge for Nazi War Criminals* (London: Phoenix, 2001), 78–81.

94. Archives du Quai d'Orsay, Unions Internationales, Troisième Versement, Article 1123, "Point de vue exprimé par les autorités américaines à l'occasion de pourparlers franco-américains sur le recrutement des travailleurs pour la France parmi les personnes déplacées," February 19, 1947.

95. CAC 770623, article 172.

96. IRO Records, 43AJ–596, June 17, 1947.

97. Sydney Liskofsky, "Jewish Postwar Immigration Prospects," *ORT Economic Review* 7 (December 1947): 39–55.

98. Ibid.

99. Holleuffer, "Seeking New Horizons," 161.

100. Holborn, *International Refugee Organization*, 440.

101. "Proposed Home for Jews," *Ladies Home Journal*, September 1948.

102. "Hambro-Williams Report."

103. See in particular Idith Zertal, *From Catastrophe to Power: Holocaust Survivors and the Emergence of Israel* (Berkeley: University of California Press, 1998); Yosef Grodzinsky, *In the Shadow of the Holocaust: The Struggle between Jews and Zionists in the Aftermath of World War II* (Monroe, ME: Common Courage, 2004).

104. Pierre Jacobsen, "L'œuvre de l'Organisation Internationale des Réfugiés," *Population* 6 (January-March 1951): 27–40.

105. Benny Morris, *1948: A History of the First Arab Israeli War* (New Haven, CT: Yale University Press, 2008), 304–5; Yoav Gelber, *Palestine 1948: War, Escape and the Emergence of the Palestinian Refugee Problem* (Brighton, UK: Sussex Academic Press, 2001), 282–85.

106. H. B. M. Murphy, "The Resettlement of Jewish Refugees in Israel, with Special Reference to Those Known as Displaced Persons," *Population Studies* 5, no. 2 (Nov.1951): 153–74; Julius Isaac, "Israel—A New Melting Pot?" in *The Cultural Integration of Immigrants*, ed. W. D. Borrie (Paris: UNESCO, 1959), 234–66.

107. United States Displaced Persons Commission, *Memo to America: The DP Story: The Final Report of the U.S. Displaced Persons Commission* (Washington, DC: Government Print Office, 1952), 6.

108. Kulischer, *Europe on the Move*, 321.

109. International Refugee Organization, *Migration from Europe*, 14.

110. Harry Truman, cited by Cheryl Shanks, *Immigration and the Politics of American Sovereignty, 1890–1990* (Ann Arbor: University of Michigan Press, 2001), 126.

111. Henry Carter, *The Refugee Problem in Europe and the Middle East*, Beckly Occasional Papers 1 (London: Epworth, 1949), 29; "Refugees and Migrations: The Transfer of Surplus Populations," *Times* (London), June 11, 1951.

112. Joseph Velikonja, "Postwar Population Movements in Europe," *Annals of the Association of American Geographers* 48 (December 1958): 458–72.

113. World Council of Churches, *The Plight of Refugees: Europe's Homeless; An International Problem* (Geneva, Switzerland: World Council of Churches 1951), 4.

114. Tara Zahra, "Prisoners of the Postwar": Expellees, Displaced Persons, and Jews in Austria after World War II, " *Austrian History Yearbook* 41 (2010): 191–215.

115. Council of Europe, *No Room for Them: Commentary on the Problem of Refugees and Surplus Elements of Population in Europe* (Strasbourg, France: Council of Europe, 1953), 14.

116. G. J van Heuven Goedhart, "People Adrift," *Journal of International Affairs* 7, no. 1 (1953): 7–49.

117. Edward Marks, "Internationally Assisted Migration: ICEM Rounds Out Five Years of Resettlement," *International Organization* 11, no. 3 (Summer 1957): 481–94.

118. Frank W. Notestein, Irene B. Taeuber, and Dudley Kirk, eds., *The Future Population of Europe and the Soviet Union: Population Projections, 1940–1970* (Geneva, Switzerland: League of Nations, 1944); E. W Hofstee, "Population Pressure and the Future of Western Civilization in Europe," *American Journal of Sociology* 15, no. 6 (May 1950): 523–32.

119. Warren S. Thompson, *Plenty of People: The World's Population Pressures, Problems and Policies and How They Concern Us*, rev. ed. (New York: Press, 1948), 109.

120. *Foreign Relations of the United States 1950*, vol. 3, *Western Europe* (Washington, DC: Government Printing Office, 1977), 1043.

121. United States Displaced Persons Commission, *Memo to America*, 351.

122. Ernest R. May, ed., *American Cold War Strategy: Interpreting NSC 68* (Boston: Bedford Books of St. Martin's, 1993).

123. "Schuman to French President of Republic," July 17, 1951, IRO Records, 43AJ–1258.

124. Proceedings of the Migration Conference organized by the International Labor Organization, Brussels, November 26 to December 8, 1951, Documents and Summary Records, IRO Records, 43 AJ–1259.

125. House Committee, *Displaced Persons*, 71.

126. Georges Pernot, "L'Europe face aux problèmes de population," *Revue Politique des Idées et des Institutions* (January 1952): 17–23.

127. Council of Europe, *No Room for Them*, 13.

128. See Eugene Kulischer's report on behalf of the International Labor Organization: *The Displacement of Population in Europe* (Montreal: International Labour Office, 1943).

129. Cited by Richard Symonds and Michael Carder, *The United Nations and the Population Question, 1945–1970* (New York: McGraw-Hill, 1973), 48.

130. "Nations Begin Study of Migration," *New York Times*, October 3, 1951.

131. IRO Records, 43AJ–1259.

132. This agency was initially called the Provisional Intergovernmental Committee for the Movement of Migrants from Europe. See "International Committee for European Migration," *International Organization* 7 (February 1953): 169–70; Hugh Gibson, "Migration From Western Europe Under the International Committee for European Migration," *Department of State Bulletin*, July 27, 1953.

133. Marks, "Internationally Assisted Migration," 484.

134. International Committee for European Migration, *The Naples Conference, 1960, and the Millionth Migrant* (Geneva, Switzerland: International Committee for European Migration, 1960).

135. Susan L. Carruthers, "Between Camps: Eastern Bloc 'Escapees' and Cold War Borderland," *American Quarterly* 57, no. 3 (2005): 911–42; "West Bitter Haven for Red Refugees," *New York Times*, September 19, 1951.

136. H. A Citroen, *European Emigration Overseas Past and Future* (The Hague: Nijhoff, 1951), 38–39.

137. Symonds and Carder, *United Nations and the Population Question*, 48.

138. United Nations, *Proceedings of the World Population Conference 1954* (New York: United Nations, 1955), 2:103.

139. Marianne Ducasse-Rogier, *The International Organization for Migration, 1951–2001* (Geneva, Switzerland: IOM, 2001), 47.

140. Louise W. Holborn, "International Organizations for Migration of European Nationals and Refugees," *International Journal* 20, no. 3 (Summer 1965): 331–40.

CHAPTER 6

1. The "surviving remnant" or "she'erit hapletah" is a label for survivors of the Holocaust referring to a biblical passage (2 Kings 19:30) narrating the story of Jews who survived the Assyrian conquest of ancient Israel in the eighth century BCE.

2. Avinoam J. Patt and Michael Berkowitz, eds., *"We Are Here": New Approaches to Jewish Displaced Persons in Postwar Germany* (Detroit: Wayne State University Press, 2010), 3.

3. Dalia Ofer, "Holocaust Survivors as Immigrants: The Case of Israel and the Cyprus Detainees," *Modern Judaism* 16 (January 1996): 1–3.

4. Amir Weiner, *Making Sense of War: The Second World War and the Fate of the Bolshevik Revolution* (Princeton, NJ: Princeton University Press, 2001); Maria Ferreti, "The Shoah and the Gulag in Russian Memory," in *Clashes in European Memory. The Case of Communist Repression and the Holocaust*, eds. Muriel Blaive, Christian Gerbel and Thomas Lindenberger (Innsbruck: StudienVerlag, 2011), 23–36; Joanna Michlic, "The Holocaust and its Aftermath as Perceived in Poland: Voices of Polish Intellectuals, 1945–1947," in *The Jews Are Coming Back: The Return of the Jews to their Countries of Origin after WW II*, ed. David Bankier (New York: Berghan Books, 2005), 206–31; Annette Wieviorka, *Déportation et génocide: Entre la mémoire et l'oubli* (Paris: Plon, 1992); Pieter Lagrou, *The Legacy of Nazi Occupation: Patriotic Memory and National Recovery in Western Europe, 1945–1965* (Cambridge, UK: Cambridge University Press, 2000.)

5. Zeev W. Mankowitz, *Life between Memory and Hope and Hope: The Survivors of the Holocaust in Occupied Germany* (Cambridge, UK: Cambridge University Press, 2002). On the Jewish DP musical band named the Happy Boys see Ruth Gay, *Safe among the Germans: Liberated Jews after World War II* (New Haven, CT: Yale University Press, 2002), 57.

6. Atina Grossmann, *Jews, Germans, and Allies: Close Encounters in Occupied Germany* (Princeton, NJ: Princeton University Press, 2007).

7. Foreign Office, FO 1049/416.

8. Mankowitz, *Life between Memory and Hope*, 286.

9. Michael Brenner, *After the Holocaust: Rebuilding Jewish Lives in Postwar Germany* (Princeton, NJ: Princeton University Press, 1997); Jay Howard Geller, *Jews in Post-Holocaust Germany, 1945–1953* (Cambridge, UK: Cambridge University Press, 2002).

10. Zorach Warhaftig, *Uprooted: Jewish Refugees and Displaced Persons after Liberation* (New York: Institute of Jewish Affairs of the American Jewish Congress and World Jewish Congress, 1946), 121; Anglo-Jewish Association, *The Future of European Jewry and Other Papers* (London: Anglo-Jewish Association, 1946).

11. Alexander S. Kohanski, ed., *The American Jewish Conference: Its Organization and Proceedings of the First Session* (New York: American Jewish Conference, 1944), 189.

12. Paul Mendes-Flohr and Jehuda Reinharz, eds., *The Jew In the Modern World: A Documentary History*, 2nd ed. (New York: Oxford University Press, 1995), 522.

13. Jacob Robinson, "Postwar Jewish Problems," *Congress Weekly*, June 25, 1943.

14. Kohanski, *Proceedings of the First Session*, 186.

15. Naomi W. Cohen, *The Americanization of Zionism, 1897–1948* (Hanover, NH: University Press of New England for Brandeis University Press, 2003).

16. Jacob Robinson, "Uprooted Jews in the Immediate Postwar World," *International Conciliation* 389 (April 1943), 291–310.

17. Alexander S. Kohanski, ed., *The American Jewish Conference: Proceedings of the Second Session* (New York: American Jewish Conference, 1945), 315.

18. World Jewish Congress, *Memorandum on Jewish Status*, February 17, 1944, IRO Records, 43AJ–48.

19. Kohanski, *Proceedings of the First Session*, 187.

20. Ibid.

21. Kohanski, *Proceedings of the Second Session*, 237.

22. Hannah Arendt, "Die jüdischen Chancen: Geringe Aussichten—gespaltene Vertretung," *Aufbau*, April 20, 1945, reprinted in *Vor Antisemitismus ist man nur noch auf dem Monde sicher: Beiträge für die deutsch-jüdische Emigrantenzeitung "Aufbau" 1941–1945*, ed. Marie Luise Knott (Munich: Piper Verlag, 2000): 181.

23. Kohanski, *Proceedings of the Second Session*, 238.

24. Ibid, 315.

25. Ibid, 239. Shalom Reichman, Yossi Katz, and Yair Paz, "The Absorptive Capacity of Palestine, 1882–1948," *Middle Eastern Studies* 33 (April 1997): 338–61.

26. Kohanski, *Proceedings of the First Session*, 316; Zorach Warhaftig, *Relief and Rehabilitation: Implications of the UNRRA Program for Jewish Needs* (New York: Institute of Jewish Affairs of the American Jewish Congress and World Jewish Congress, 1944), 168.

27. American Jewish Conference, *The Jewish Position at the United Nations Conference on International Organization: A Report to the Delegates of the American Jewish Conference* (New York: Parish, 1945). Lipsky nonetheless competed with Joseph Proskauer, the representative of the American Jewish Committee who had consultative status at the San Francisco conference. See Michael Galchinsky, *Jews and Human Rights: Dancing at Three Weddings* (Lanham, MD: Rowman & Littlefield, 2007), 3–35.

28. American Jewish Conference, *Statement Submitted to the United Nations Special Committee on Palestine* (New York: American Jewish Conference, 1947).

29. Max Gottschalk and Abraham G. Duker, *Jews in the Post-war World* (New York: Dryden, 1945), 167.

30. George Woodbridge, *UNRRA: The History of the United Nations Relief and Rehabilitation Administration* (New York: Columbia University Press, 1950), 3:137.

31. Hannah Arendt, "The Stateless People," *Contemporary Jewish Record* 8 (April 1945): 137–53.

32. Malcolm J. Proudfoot, *European Refugees: 1939–1952; A Study in Forced Population Movement* (Evanston, IL: Northwestern University Press, 1956), 330. Postwar estimates on the number of surviving Jews found by the Western Allies in Germany and Austria varied greatly. Contrary to Proudfoot, Kurt R. Grossmann calculated that between 90,000 and 100,000 Jews were encountered by the Allied in liberated concentration and labor camps, out of which 70,000 survived the first weeks of freedom. See Kurt R. Grossmann, *Refugees, DP's, and Migrants* (New York: Institute of Jewish Affairs and World Jewish Congress, 1962), 4–8

33. Leonard Dinnerstein, *America and the Survivors of the Holocaust* (New York: Columbia University Press, 1982), 13.

34. SHAEF Administrative Memorandum 39 of April 16, 1945, appendix to Proudfoot, *European Refugees*, 445–69.

35. Leonard Dinnerstein, "Does Anyone Want the Displaced Persons?" *Diplomatic History* 27 (January 2003): 167–170.

36. Allis Radosh and Ronald Radosh, *A Safe Haven: Harry S. Truman and the Founding of Israel* (New York: HarperCollins, 2009), 92–12; Dinnerstein, *America and the Survivors*, 39–41.

37. Patrick Weil, "Races at the Gate: Racial Distinctions in Immigration Policy; A Comparison between France and the United States," in *Migration Control in the North Atlantic World: The Evolution of State Practices in Europe and the United States from the French Revolution to the Inter-war Period*, ed. Andreas Fahrmeir, Olivier Faron, and Patrick Weil (New York: Berghahn Books, 2003), 271–97.

38. Proudfoot, *European Refugees*, 327.

39. Dan Diner, "Elemente der Subjektwerdung: Jüdische DPs in historischem Kontext," in *Überlebt und unterwegs: Jüdische Displaced Persons in Nachkriegsdeutschland*, ed. Fritz Bauer Institut (Frankfurt: Campus, 1997), 229–48.

40. Woodbridge, *UNRRA*, 2:510.

41. FO 1049/416.

42. Proudfoot, *European Refugees*, 341.

43. Ibid, 350.

44. Eugene M. Kulischer, "The IRO and the Jewish Refugees," *Rescue* 4 (April 1947), 4.

45. Michael Marrus, comp., *The Nuremberg War Crimes Trial, 1945–46: A Documentary History*. (Boston: Bedford Books, 1997), 254.

46. John George Stoessinger, *The Refugee and the World Community* (Minneapolis: University of Minnesota Press, 1956), 82.

47. Hyperbolic estimates of the population of Jewish DPs were not just a Soviet specialty. In a speech delivered in February 1946, Harry Truman declared that "there are left in Europe 1,500,000 Jews, men, women and children, whom the ordeal has left homeless, hungry, sick and without assistance." "Statement by the President to a Delegation from the United Jewish Appeal," HSTL, Official File 127, Box 673.

48. United Nations, *The Question of Refugees: Documents for the Special Committee on Refugees and Displaced Persons*, E/REF/1, 1946.

49. Ernest F. Penrose, "Negotiating on Refugees and Displaced Persons, 1946," in *Negotiating with the Russians*, ed. Raymond Dennett and Joseph E. Johnson (Boston: World Peace Foundation, 1951), 139–71.

50. Yuri Slezkine, *The Jewish Century* (Princeton, NJ: Princeton University Press, 2004), 289.

51. Jan T. Gross, *Fear: Anti-Semitism in Poland after Auschwitz; An Essay in Historical Interpretation* (New York: Random House, 2006).

52. Woodbridge, *UNRRA*, 2: 423.

53. "U.N. Refugee Group to Swift Jewish Data," *The New York Times*, May 4, 1946.

54. United Nations, *Official Records of the Second Part of the First Session of the General Assembly, Third Committee, Social, Humanitarian and Cultural Questions, Summary Record of Meetings, 24 October-December 12, 1946.*

55. Poland's population was only 68 percent Polish in 1938 but overwhelmingly ethnically Polish by 1947. See Tony Judt, *Postwar: A History of Europe since 1945* (New York: Penguin, 2005), 28; Anita J. Prażmowska, *Civil War in Poland, 1942–1948* (New York: Palgrave Macmillan, 2004), 168–90.

56. IRO Records, 43AJ–1074.

57. Ignacy Walczewski, *Destin tragique des polonais déportés en Allemagne: La crise de la famille polonaise dans les camps de personnes déplacées* (Rome: Editions Hosanium, 1951).

58. Gross, *Fear*, 259.

59. "Polish plenipotentiary for Repatriation Questions to Mr. Manningham-Buller, M.P, February 9, 1946," FO 1049/416.

60. IRO Records, 43AJ–1074.

61. IRO Records, 43AJ–893.

62. Lauterpacht's legal opinion on Law No. 1 (March 1946) is in IRO Records, 43AJ–48.

63. UN Economic and Social Council, Second Session, Special Supplement 1, *Report of Special Committee on Refugees and Displaced Persons*, June 7, 1946, E/REF/75.

64. Dienke Hondius, "Bitter Homecoming: The Return and Reception of Dutch and Stateless Jews in the Netherlands," in Bankier, *The Jews Are Coming Back*, 108–35.

65. *Report of Special Committee on Refugees and Displaced Persons*, June 7, 1946, E/REF/75.

66. Cited in Kulischer, *IRO and the Jews*, 4.

67. "Arab League Asks U.N. Palestine Bans," *New York Times*, June 20, 1946.

68. Constitution of the International Refugee Organization, Part I, Section A, Paragraph 4.

69. Arieh J. Kochavi, *Post-Holocaust Politics: Britain, the United States, and Jewish Refugees, 1945–1948* (Chapel Hill: University of North Carolina Press, 2001); Idith Zertal, *From Catastrophe to Power: Holocaust Survivors and the Emergence of Israel* (Berkeley: University of California Press, 1998); Leonard Dinnerstein, "Britische und amerikanishe DP-Politik," in Fritz Bauer Institut, *Überlebt und unterwegs*, 109–19.

70. *Report of the Director-General on Immigration into the Countries of the Middle East, December 22, 1948*, IRO Records, 43AJ–687.

71. Following the first truce of June 11–July 8, 1948, Folke Bernadotte proposed the return of a limited number of refugees to their homes. This demand was reiterated in his report to the Security Council (August 1, 1948) and in his last progress report of September 16, 1948. See Lex Takkenberg, *The Status of Palestinian Refugees in International Law* (Oxford: Clarendon, 1998), 22.

72. Ibid.

73. The IRO Executive Committee was composed of nine nations: Australia, Belgium, Canada, China, France, Norway, the United Kingdom, the United States, and Venezuela.

74. IRO Executive Committee, *Summary Record of Fourteenth Meeting*, January 26, 1949 in IRO Records, 43AJ-687.

75. Benny Morris, *1948: A History of the First Arab-Israeli War* (New Haven, CT: Yale University Press, 2008), 308–9.

76. *Summary Record of Fourteenth Meeting.*

77. IRO Public Information Office, Monthly Digest 6, February 1949, in IRO Records, 43AJ–1074.

78. United Nations General Assembly, May 12, 1949.

79. IRO Executive Committee, Tenth Meeting, December 10, 1948 in IRO Records, 43AJ-687.

80. The United Nations Relief for Palestinian Refugees (UNRPR) was established by the General Assembly "to relieve the desperate plight of Palestinian refugees of all communities." See United Nations, General Assembly, Third Session, 163rd Plenary Meeting, November 19, 1948 (Doc A/731).

81. Department of State, *United States Participation in the United Nations: Report by the President to the Congress for the Year 1949 on the Activities of the United Nations and the Participation of the United States Therein* (Washington, DC: Government Printing Office, 1950), 40–41.

82. "The problem of the Palestine Arab refugees and its relation to the proposed international service," October 28, 1949, IRO Records, 43AJ–687.

83. Ilan Pappe, *The Ethnic Cleansing of Palestine* (Oxford, UK: Oneworld, 2006), 236.

84. Ibid.

85. UN Security Council, August 18, 1948. In his iconoclastic novel *Khirbet Khizeh* published in 1949, the Israeli novelist S. Yizhar (an intelligence officer during the 1948 war) vividly described this qualitative superiority: "Everything, everything was for the refugees, their welfare, their rescue. Our refugees, naturally. Those we were driving out—that was a totally different matter. Wait. Two thousand years of exile. The whole story. Jews being killed. Europe. We were the masters now." S. Yizhar, *Khirbet Khizeh*, translated by Nicholas de Lange and Yaacob Dweck (Jerusalem: Ibis, 2008).

86. Randa Farah, "The Marginalization of Palestinian Refugees," in *Problems of Protection: The UNHCR, Refugees, and Human Rights*, ed. Niklaus Steiner, Mark Gibney, and Gil Loescher, (New York: Routledge, 2003), 155–74; Susan Akram, "Reinterpreting Palestinian Refugee Rights under International Law," in *Palestinian Refugees: The Right of Return*, ed. Naseer Aruri (London: Pluto, 2001), 165–94.

87. *Interim Report of UNRWA Director*, October 19, 1950, IRO Records, 43AJ–1255.

88. Benjamin N. Schiff, *Refugees unto the Third Generation: UN Aid to Palestinians* (Syracuse NY: Syracuse University Press, 1995), 10.

89. Ilana Feldman, "Difficult Distinctions: Refugee Law, Humanitarian Practice, and Political Identification in Gaza," *Cultural Anthropology* 22 (February 2007): 129–69.

90. *Manual for Eligibility Officers*, IRO Records, 43AJ–1251.

91. Jacques Vernant, *The Refugee in the Post-war World* (New Haven, CT: Yale University Press, 1953), 64.

92. Susan L. Carruthers, "Between Camps: Eastern Bloc 'Escapees' and Cold War Borderlands," *American Quarterly* 57, no. 3 (2005): 911–42.

93. IRO Records, 43AJ–1251.

94. IRO Records, 43AJ-574.

95. Nathan Feinberg, "The Recognition of the Jewish People in International Law," in *The Jewish Yearbook of International Law*, ed. N. Feinberg and J. Stoyanovsky (Jerusalem, 1949), reprinted in Feinberg, *Studies in International Law: With Special Reference to the Arab-Israeli Conflict* (Jerusalem: Magnes, 1979), 229–62.

96. Uri Ram, "Zionist Historiography and the Invention of Modern Jewish Nationhood: The Case of Ben Zion Dinur," *History and Memory* 7, no. 1 (1995): 91–124.

97. Cited in Gulie Ne'eman Arad, "Israel and the Shoah: A Tale of Multifarious Taboos," *New German Critique* 90 (Autumn 2003): 526.

98. Feinberg, "Recognition of the Jewish People," 262.

EPILOGUE

1. G. J. van Heuven Goedhart, preface to James Morgan Read, *Magna Carta for Refugees* (New York: United Nations Department of Public Information, 1953).

2. Jacques Vernant, *The Refugee in the Post-war World* (New Haven, CT: Yale University Press, 1953), 170; Michael Brenner, *After the Holocaust: Rebuilding Jewish Lives in Postwar Germany* (Princeton, NJ: Princeton University Press, 1997), 41–42.

3. Michael L. Hoffman, "10,000,000 Appeal for World Refuge," *New York Times*, March 16, 1951.

4. Michael L. Hoffman, "Cut in UN Budget Hits Refugee Aid," *New York Times*, October 7, 1951.

5. Joseph P. Chamberlain to Philip Ryan, IRO Chief Operations, US Zone of Germany, February 3, 1949, IRO Records, 43AJ–893.

6. Gene M. Lyons, "American Policy and the United Nation's Program for Korean Reconstruction," *International Organization* 12 (1958): 180–92.

7. George L. Warren, "The United States and Refugee Relief," unpublished manuscript, 1972, Harry S Truman Library (HSTL), George L. Warren Papers, Box 1, 5.

8. Paul Weis, *The Refugee Convention, 1951: The Travaux Préparatoires Analysed, with a Commentary*, Cambridge International Documents 7 (Cambridge, UK: Cambridge University Press, 1995).

9. Michael L. Hoffman, "UN Refugee Code Near Completion," *New York Times*, July 21, 1951.

10. Paul Weis, cited by Ivor C. Jackson, *The Refugee Concept in Group Situations* (The Hague: Nijhoff, 1999), 79.

11. United Nations, Economic and Social Council, *Report on the Progress and Prospect of Repatriation, Resettlement and Repatriation of Refugees*, June 1948, E/Ref/816.

12. Nehemiah Robinson, *Convention Relating to the Status of Refugees: Its History, Contents, and Interpretation; A Commentary* (New York: Institute for Jewish Affairs, World Jewish Congress, 1953), 4; Gilbert Jaeger, "On the History of the International Protection of Refugees," *International Review of the Red Cross* 83 (September 2001): 727–37.

13. An ad hoc drafting committee comprising thirteen states was appointed by the General Assembly in January 1950. The collected *Travaux Préparatoires* of the 1951 Geneva Convention are now available online at http://www.unhcr.org/cgi-bin/texis/vtx/search%5C?page=&comid=3c07a8642&cid=49aea9390&scid=49aea9398. See also Alex Takkenberg and Christopher C. Tahbaz, comps., *The Collected Travaux Préparatoires of the 1951 Geneva Convention Relating to the Status of Refugees* (Amsterdam: Dutch Refugee Council under the auspices of the European Legal Network on Asylum, 1989); Jackson, *Refugee Concept*, 47–81; Kazimierz Bem, "The Coming of a 'Blank Cheque': Europe, the 1951 Convention, and the 1967 Protocol," *International Journal of Refugee Law* 16, no. 4 (2004), 609–27.

14. Takkenberg and Tahbaz, *Collected Travaux Préparatoires*, 1:165.

15. "United States Position on the Convention Relating to the Status of Refugees," HSTL, Papers of George L. Warren, Box 1. The United States only ratified the 1951 convention and its 1967 protocol in March 1980.

16. George L. Warren, "The Escapee Program," *Journal of International Affairs* 7, no. 1 (March 1953), 83–86.

17. Conference of Plenipotentiaries on the Status of Refugees, *Summary Records of the Nineteenth Meeting*, http://www.unhcr.org/3ae68cda4.html.

18. Bernard Toussaint to Robert Schuman, August 31, 1950, Centre des Archives Diplomatiques de Nantes (France), Unions Internationales, Troisième Versement, Article 1147. Nehemiah Robinson, a Lithuanian-born international jurist representing Israel at the conference, played a prominent role in the drafting process.

19. *Summary Records of the Nineteenth Meeting*.

20. Memorandum by Mr. Rochefort, June 25, 1951, IRO Records, 43AJ–1261. The draft of the Geneva Convention provided colonial powers with specific guarantees against this type of situations. A "colonial application clause," prudently renamed "territorial application clause" at the urging of France, allowed signatories to inde-

pendently decide whether the convention should come into force in their overseas territories (Article 40).

21. Takkenberg and Tahbaz, *Collected Travaux Préparatoires*, 3:382.

22. *Summary Records of the Nineteenth Meeting.*

23. For the international jurist James C. Hathaway, "the definition adopted was intended to share out the European refugee problem without any binding obligation...to the provision of assistance to non-European refugees." See Hathaway, "A Reconsideration of the Underlying Premise of Refugee Law," *Harvard International Law Journal* 31 (Winter 1990), 129–83.

24. *Summary Records of the Nineteenth Meeting.*

25. "Geneva Convention, Petition and Press Releases," IRO Records, 43AJ–1261.

26. Hoffman, "UN Refugee Code."

27. H. B. M Murphy, ed., *Flight and Resettlement* (Paris: UNESCO, 1955), 22.

28. Liisa H. Malkki, "Refugees and Exile: From Refugees to the National Order of Things," *Annual Review of Anthropology* 24 (1995): 495–523. The birth of "refugee studies" also resulted from the new expertise garnered from contact with displaced persons. See Richard Black, "Fifty Years of Refugee Studies: From Theory to Policy," in "UNHCR at 50: Past, Present, and Future of Refugee Assistance," special issue, *International Migration Review* 35, no. 1 (Spring 2001): 57–78.

29. Barbara Harrell-Bond, "Refugees' Experience as Aid Recipients" in *Refugees: Perspectives on the Experience of Forced Migration*, ed. Alastair Ager (London: Continuum, 1999), 136–68.

30. Edward A. Shils, "Social and Psychological Aspects of Displacement and Repatriation," *Journal of Social Issues* 2 (August 1946): 3–18.

31. Edward Bakis, "The So-Called DP-Apathy of Germany's DP camps," *Transactions of the Kansas Academy of Sciences* 55 (1952): 62–86, reprinted as "DP Apathy" in Murphy, *Flight and Resettlement*, 76–91; M. Brzezinski, "Kompleksy D.P.," *Kultura* 14 (1948): 88–94; K. C. Cirtautas, *Porträt des Heimatlosen: Heimatlosigkeit als Weltschicksal; Ein Essay* (Coburg, West Germany: Veste Verlag, 1950); English translation: as *The Refugee: A Psychological Study* (Boston: Meador, 1957).

32. Vernant, *Refugee in the Post-war World*, 17.

33. Henry Carter, *The Refugee Problem in Europe and the Middle East*, Beckly Occasional Papers 1 (London: Epworth, 1949), 35.

34. Dominique Pire, *Souvenirs et entretiens* (Paris: Julliard, 1959), 78.

35. Jan Cep, "Réflexions d'un immigré," in *Le Monde*, October 28, 1948.

36. François Nourrissier, "Le monde des réfugiés," *Esprit*, January 1951, 19–40.

37. Georges Duhamel, "Le temps des résidus humains," *Figaro*, December 12, 1953. Other prominent intellectuals such as François Mauriac, Gabriel Marcel, Paul Claudel, and Etienne Gilson endorsed the Acceuil Catholique Français, a Catholic welfare organization for refugees and DPs.

38. Pire, *Souvenirs et Entretiens*, 88.

39. Roger Braun, *Le problème des réfugiés: Ses conséquences morales et religieuses*, Cahiers de la Nouvelle Revue Théologique 7 (Paris: Casterman, 1951): 54.

40. Oscar Handlin, *The Uprooted*, 2nd ed. (Boston: Little, Brown, 1973), 56.

41. John Bodnar, *The Transplanted: A History of Immigrants in Urban America* (Bloomington: Indiana University Press, 1985).

42. Liisa H. Malkki, "National Geographic: The Rooting of Peoples and the Territorialization of National Identity among Scholars and Refugees," *Cultural Anthropology* 7, no. 1 (1992): 24–44.

43. Pire, *Souvenirs et Entretiens*, 89.

44. Elfan Rees, *Century of the Homeless Man*, International Conciliation 515 (New York: Carnegie Endowment for International Peace, 1957): 193.

45. Robert Kee, *Refugee World* (London: Oxford University Press, 1961), 8; Edgard S. H Chandler, *The High Tower of Refuge* (New York: Frederick A. Praeger, 1959), 224.

46. Susan L. Carruthers, *Cold War Captives: Imprisonment, Escape, and Brainwashing* (Berkeley: University of California Press, 2009).

47. Quoted by George L. Warren, "The US Government and Refugee Relief: A Study" (1972), HSTL, Papers of George L. Warren, Box 1.

48. Ibid.

49. Rees, *Century of the Homeless Man*; Michael Marrus, *The Unwanted: European Refugees in the Twentieth Century* (New York: Oxford University Press, 1985), 358–61.

50. Georges L. Warren, "The Development of United States Participation in Intergovernmental Efforts to Resolve Refugee Problems," HSTL, Papers of George L. Warren, Box 1.

51. Chandler, *High Tower of Refuge*.

52. Archives of the World Council of Churches (Geneva), *A Program of Inter-Church Aid and Service to Palestine Refugees in the Near East* (dated 1952), Box 425.1.047.

53. Michael Christopher King, *The Palestinians and the Churches*, vol. 1, *1948–1956* (Geneva, Switzerland: World Council of Churches, 1981), 14.

54. Ibid, 60.

55. Ibid, 15.

56. Kee, *Refugee World*, vii.

57. Aaron Levenstein, *Escape to Freedom: The Story of the International Rescue Committee* (Westport, CT: Greenwood, 1983), 64.

58. United Nations, The International Committee for World Refugee Year 1959–1961 (Geneva, Switzerland: United Nations, 1961); United Nations, *List of Documents Issued by the Office of the Special Representative of the Secretary General for World Refugee Year as of February 29, 1960* (Geneva, Switzerland: United Nations, 1961).

59. Yul Brynner, *Bring Forth the Children: A Journey to the Forgotten People of Europe and the Middle East* (London: Barker, 1960); "Yul Brynner to be Special Consultant to UN High Commissioner," UNHCR Press release, September 11, 1959 at http://www.flickr.com/photos/unhcr/4115212672/#/

60. "Life Begins at Ten", Catalogue of United Nations Audio Library at http://www.unmultimedia.org/radio/library/classics/alpha.html.

61. Department of State, Office of Public Services, *World Refugee Year July 1959–June 1960: Report on the Participation of the United States Government* (Washington, DC: Government Printing Office, 1960), 5.

62. *A Time of Compassion: A Report on the Churches' Contribution to World Refugee Year* (Geneva, Switzerland: World Refugee Council, 1961).

63. Peter Gatrell, *Free World? The Campaign to Save the World's Refugees 1956–1963* (Cambridge, UK: Cambridge University Press), 2011, 77–210.

64. United Nations Staff Fund for Refugees, *The World Refugee Year Postage Stamps* (Geneva, Switzerland: United Nations, 1961); Gatrell, *Free World?*, 180–193.

65. David P. Gaines, *The World Council of Churches. A Study of Its Background and History* (Peterborough, NH: Richard R. Smith, 1966), 874.

66. United Nations, *International Committee for World Refugee Year*, 15–21.

67. Gatrell, *Free World?*, 201.

68. Department of State, *World Refugee Year*.

69. Harold Karan Jacobson, *The USSR and the UN's Economic and Social Activities* (Notre Dame, IN: University of Notre Dame Press, 1963), 82.

70. Gil Loescher, *The UNHCR and World Politics: A Perilous Path* (Oxford: Oxford University Press, 2001), 105–34.

71. Gil Loescher, "The UNHCR at Fifty," in *Problems of Protection: The UNHCR, Refugees, and Human Rights*, ed. Niklaus Steiner, Mark Gibney, and Gil Loescher (New York: Routledge, 2003), 7.

72. Luc Legoux, *La crise de l'asile politique en France* (Paris: Ceped, 1995).

73. Matthew J. Gibney, *The Ethics and Politics of Asylum: Liberal Democracy and the Response to Refugees* (Cambridge, UK: Cambridge University Press, 2004), 7.

74. Matthew E. Price, *Rethinking Asylum: History, Purpose, and Limits* (Cambridge, UK: Cambridge University Press, 2009), 5–6.

Select Bibliography

ARCHIVES

Archives du Quai D'Orsay, Séries Unions Internationales, Paris and Nantes.
Harry S. Truman Presidential Library, Independence, MO.
National Archives of the United Kingdom and the Wiener Library London; available in the database *Post-war Europe: Refugees: Exile and Resettlement 1945–1950.* Farmington Hills, MI: Gale Cengage Learning, 2007.
Records of the International Refugee Organization (1946–1952), Archives Nationales, Paris.
Robert F. Wagner Labor Archives, Tamiment Library, New York University.

PUBLISHED PRIMARY SOURCES

United Nations Documents

Economic and Social Council. *Report of the Special Committee on Refugees and Displaced Persons,* 1946, E/REF/75.
——. *Report on the progress and prospect of repatriation, resettlement and immigration of refugees and DPs,* June 1948, E/REF/816.
Official Records of the General Assembly, Third Committee, Summary Records of Meetings (1946).
Official Records of the General Assembly, Plenary Meetings (1946).
The Question of Refugees: Documents for the Special Committee for Refugees and Displaced Persons, E/REF/1.
Read, James Morgan. *Magna Carta for Refugees.* Rev. ed. New York: United Nations, Department of Public Information, 1953.
United Nations, Department of Public Information. *Protecting the Refugee: The Story of UN Effort on Behalf of the Refugee.* New York: United Nations, 1953.
United Nations, Department of Social Affairs, *The Impact of the Universal Declaration of Human Rights.* New York: United Nations, 1951.

———. *A Study of Statelessness.* Lake Success, NY: United Nations, 1949.

United Nations, Office of Public Information. *What the United Nations is Doing for Refugees and Displaced Persons.* Lake Success, NY: United Nations, 1949. United Nations Weekly Bulletin, 1946–1950.

United States Government Documents

US Congress. House. *Displaced Persons and the International Refugee Organization: Report of a Special Subcommittee of the Committee on Foreign Affairs.* 80th Congress, 1st sess., 1947.

US Congress. Senate. Committee on the Judiciary. *Displaced Persons in Europe: Report Pursuant to S. Res. 137, a Resolution to Make an Investigation of the Immigration System.* Washington, DC: Government Printing Office, 1948.

US Department of State. *The Displaced Persons Problem: A Collection of Recent Official Statements.* Washington, DC: Government Printing Office, 1947.

———. *Foreign Affairs Background Summary.* Washington, DC: Government Printing Office, 1948.

———. *Some Aspects of the Displaced Persons Problem.* Washington, DC: Government Printing Office, 1947.

US Displaced Persons Commission. *Memo to America: The DP Story; The Final Report of the US Displaced Persons Commission.* Washington, DC: Government Printing Office, 1952.

WORKS CITED

Acheson, Dean. *Present at the Creation: My Years in the State Department.* New York: Norton, 1969.

Ackermann, Volker. *Der "echte" Flüchtling: Deutsche Vertriebene und Flüchtlinge aus der DDR, 1945–1961.* Osnabrück, Germany: Universitätsverlag Rasch, 1995.

———. "Discerner le vrai du faux: Un débat sur les réfugiés en Allemagne de l'Ouest (1945–1961)." *Migrance* 17–18 (2001): 38–46.

Adler, H.G. "Aufzeichnungen einer Displaced Person." *Merkur* 6 (1952): 1040–49.

Agamben, Giorgio. *Homo Sacer: Sovereign Power and Bare Life.* Translated by Daniel Heller-Roazen. Stanford, CA: Stanford University Press, 1998.

———. *Means without End: Notes on Politics.* Minneapolis: University of Minnesota Press, 2000.

Ager, Alastair, ed. *Refugees: Perspectives on the Experience of Forced Migration.* London: Continuum, 1999.

Agier, Michel. *Gérer les indésirables: Des camps de réfugiés au gouvernement humanitaire.* Paris: Flammarion, 2008.

Arad, Gulie Ne'eman. "Israel and the Shoah: A Tale of Multifarious Taboos." *New German Critique* 90 (Autumn 2003): 5–26.

Arendt, Hannah. *The Origins of Totalitarianism.* New York: Schocken Books, 2004. First published 1951.

———. "'The Rights of Man': What Are They? *Modern Review* 3 (June 1949), 24–37.

———. "The Stateless People." *Contemporary Jewish Record* 8 (April 1945): 137–53.

———. *Vor Antisemitismus ist man nur noch auf dem Monde sicher: Beiträge für die deutsch-jüdische Emigrantenzeitung "Aufbau" 1941–1945.* Edited by Marie Luise Knott. Munich: Piper Verlag, 2000.

Aruri, Naseer, ed. *Palestinian Refugees: The Right of Return.* London: Pluto, 2001.

Bankier, David, ed. *The Jews Are Coming Back: The Return of the Jews to their Countries of Origin after WW II.* New York: Berghan Books, 2005.

Bashford, Alison. "Nation, Empire, Globe: The Spaces of Population Debate in the Interwar Years." *Comparative Studies in Society and History* 49 (January 2007): 170–201.

Barsky, Robert F. *Constructing a Productive Other: Discourse Theory and the Convention Refugee Hearing.* Amsterdam: John Benjamins Publishing Company, 1994.

Becker, Annette. *Oubliés de la Grande Guerre: Humanitaire et culture de guerre, 1914–1918; Populations occupies, déportés civils, prisonniers de guerre.* Paris: Noêsis, 1998.

Bem, Kazimierz. "The Coming of a 'Blank Cheque': Europe, the 1951 Convention, and the 1967 Protocol." *International Journal of Refugee Law* 16, no. 4 (2004): 609–27.

Benhabib, Seyla. *The Reluctant Modernism of Hannah Arendt.* Rev. ed. Lanham, MD: Rowman & Littlefield, 2003.

Bentwich, Norman. *The Rescue and Achievement of Refugee Scholars.* The Hague: Nijhoff 1953.

Berge, François, ed. *Personnes déplacées.* Paris: Clermont, 1948.

Black, Richard. "Fifty Years of Refugee Studies: From Theory to Policy." In "UNHCR at 50: Past, Present, and Future of Refugee Assistance," Special issue, *International Migration Review* 35, no. 1 (Spring 2001): 57–78.

Blanchard, Francis. "Le problème des réfugiés devant l'opinion." *Politique Etrangère* 14 (March 1949): 167–72.

Bodnar, John. *The Transplanted: A History of Immigrants in Urban America.* Bloomington: Indiana University Press, 1985.

Bondy, Curt. "Problems of Internment Camps." *Journal of Abnormal and Social Psychology* 38 (October 1943): 453–75.

Borgwardt, Elizabeth. *A New Deal for the World: America's Vision for Human Rights.* Cambridge, MA: Belknap Press of Harvard University Press, 2005.

Borrie, W.D., ed. *The Cultural Integration of Immigrants.* Paris: UNESCO, 1959.

Brenner, Michael. *After the Holocaust: Rebuilding Jewish Lives in Postwar Germany.* Translated by Barbara Harshav. Princeton, NJ: Princeton University Press, 1997.

Brooks, Kenneth G. "The Re-establishment of Displaced Peoples." In *When Hostilities Cease: Papers on Relief and Reconstruction Prepared for the Fabian Society,* 99–12. London: Gollancz, 1943.

Burgers, Jan Herman. "The Road to San Francisco: The Revival of the Human Rights Idea in the Twentieth Century." *Human Rights Quarterly* 14 (1992): 447–77.

Caloz-Tschopp, Marie Claire. *Les Sans-Etat dans la philosophie d'Hannah Arendt: Les humains superflus, le droit d'avoir des droits et la citoyenneté.* Lausanne, Switzerland: Payot, 2000.

Carey, Jane Perry Clark. *The Role of Uprooted People in European Recovery.* Washington, DC: National Planning Association, 1948.

———. "Some Aspects of Statelessness since World War I." *American Political Science Review* 40 (February 1946): 113–23.

Carruthers, Susan L. "Between Blocs: 'Escapees' and Cold War Borderlands." *American Quarterly* 57, no. 3 (2005): 911–42.

———. *Cold War Captives: Imprisonment, Escape, and Brainwashing.* Berkeley: University of California Press, 2009.

Carter, Henry. *The Refugee Problem in Europe and the Middle East.* Beckly Occasional Papers 1. London: Epworth, 1949.

Cassin, René. "La declaration universelle et la mise en œuvre des droits de l'homme." *Recueil des Cours* 79 (1951): 241–367.

———. *La pensée et l'action.* Boulogne-sur-Seine, France: Lalou, 1972.

Cesarani, David. *Justice Delayed: How Britain Became a Refuge for Nazi War Criminals.* London: Phoenix, 2001.

Chandler, Edgar H.S. *The High Tower of Refuge: The Inspiring Story of Refugee Relief throughout the World.* New York: Praeger, 1959.

Chevalier, Louis. "Bilan d'une immigration." *Population* 5 (January-March 1950): 129–40.

Cirtautas, K.C. *Porträt des Heimatlosen: Heimatlosigkeit als Weltschicksal; Ein Essay* (Coburg, West Germany: Veste Verlag, 1950). English translation: *The Refugee: A Psychological Study* (Boston: Meador, 1957).

Citroen, H.A. *European Emigration Overseas Past and Future.* The Hague: Nijhoff, 1951.

Cohen, Gerard Daniel. "Between Relief and Politics: Refugee Humanitarianism in Occupied Germany, 1945–1946." *Journal of Contemporary History* 43 (July 2008): 437–49.

———. "The Politics of Recognition: Jewish Refugees in Relief Policies and Human Rights Debates, 1945–1950." *Immigrants and Minorities* 24 (July 2006): 125–43.

———. "Remembering Post-war Displaced Persons: From Omission to Resurrection." In *Enlarging European Memory: Migration Movements in Historical Perspective,* edited by Mareike König and Rainer Ohliger, 87–97. Ostfildern, Germany: Thorbecke Verlag, 2006.

Cohen, Naomi W. *The Americanization of Zionism, 1897–1948.* Hanover, NH: University Press of New England for Brandeis University Press, 2003.

Colaneri, André. *De la condition des "sans-patrie": Etude critique de l'heimatlosat.* Paris: Sirey, 1932.

Connelly, Matthew. *Fatal Misconception: The Struggle to Control World Population.* Cambridge, MA: Belknap Press of Harvard University Press, 2008.

Corni, Gustavo, and Tamas Stark, eds. *People on the Move: Forced Population Movements in Europe in the Second World War and its Aftermath.* Oxford: Berg, 2008.

Coudry, Georges. *Les camps soviétiques en France: Les "Russes" livrés à Staline en 1945.* Paris: Michel, 1997.

Cronin, Bruce. *Institutions for the Common Good: International Protection Regimes in International Society.* Cambridge, UK: Cambridge University Press, 2003.

Cullather, Nick. "The Foreign Policy of the Calorie." *American Historical Review* 112 (April 2007): 337–65.

Curle, Clinton Timothy. *Humanité: John Humphrey's Alternative Account of Human Rights.* Toronto: University of Toronto Press, 2007.

Curti, Merle. *American Philanthropy Abroad: A History.* New Brunswick, NJ: Rutgers University Press, 1963.

Dallin, David J., and Boris I. Nicolaevsky. *Forced Labor in Soviet Russia.* New Haven, CT: Yale University Press, 1947.

Deák, István, Jan T. Gross, and Tony Judt, eds. *The Politics of Retribution in Europe: World War II and its Aftermath.* Princeton, NJ: Princeton University Press, 2000.

Diner, Dan. *Cataclysms: A History of the Twentieth Century from Europe's Edge.* Translated by William Templer and Joel Golb. Madison: University of Wisconsin Press, 2008.

Dinnerstein, Leonard. *America and the Survivors of the Holocaust.* New York: Columbia University Press, 1982.

———."Does Anyone Want the Displaced Persons?," *Diplomatic History* 27 (January 2003): 167–170.

Dreyfus-Armand, Geneviève, *L'exil des Républicains espagnols en France. De la Guerre civile à la mort de Franco.* Paris: Albin Michel, 1999.

Ducasse-Rogier, Marianne. *The International Organization for Migration, 1951–2001.* Geneva, Switzerland: IOM, 2001.

Duggan, Stephen, and Betty Drury. *The Rescue of Science and Learning: The Story of the Emergency Committee in Aid of Displaced Foreign Scholars.* New York: Macmillan, 1948.

Dushnyck, Walter, and William J. Gibbons. *Refugees Are People: The Plight of Europe's Displaced Persons.* New York: American Press, 1947.

Dyczok, Marta. *The Grand Alliance and Ukrainian Refugees.* New York: St. Martin's Press, 2000.

Eder, Angelika. "Displaced Persons/'Heimatlose Ausländer' als Arbeitskräfte in Westdeutschland." *Archiv für Sozialgeschichte* 42 (2002): 1–17.

Edkins, Jenny. *Trauma and the Memory of Politics.* Cambridge, UK: Cambridge University Press, 2003.

Egan, Eileen. *For Whom There Is No Room: Scenes from the Refugee World.* New York: Paulist Press, 1995.

Elliott, Mark R. *Pawns of Yalta: Soviet Refugees and America's Role in their Repatriation.* Urbana: University of Illinois Press, 1982.

Emerson, Herbert. "Post-war Problems of Refugees." *Foreign Affairs,* January 1943, 211–20.

Fassin, Didier. *La raison humanitaire. Une histoire morale du temps present.* Paris, Seuil/ Gallimard, 2010.

Feder, Ruth. "Displaced Persons Go Home: How They Are Received in Yugoslavia." *Churchman* 161 (November 1947): 15–16.

Feinberg, Nathan. "The Recognition of the Jewish People in International Law." In *The Jewish Yearbook of International Law,* edited by N. Feinberg and J. Stoyanovsky. Jerusalem: Mass, 1949. Reprinted in *Studies in International Law: With Special Reference to the Arab-Israeli Conflict,* 229–62. Jerusalem: Magnes, 1979.

Feldman, Ilana. "Difficult Distinctions: Refugee Law, Humanitarian Practice, and Political Identification in Gaza. *Cultural Anthropology* 22 (February 2007), 129–69.

Ferreti, Maria. "The Shoah and the Gulag in Russian Memory," in *Clashes in European Memory. The Case of Communist Repression and the Holocaust,* eds. Muriel Blaive, Christian Gerbel and Thomas Lindenberger (Innsbruck: StudienVerlag, 2011), 23–36.

Field, Henry. *"M" Project for FDR: Studies on Migration and Settlement.* Ann Arbor, MI: Edwards Brothers, 1962.

Fink, Carole. *Defending the Rights of Others: The Great Powers, the Jews and International Minority Protection, 1878–1938.* Cambridge, UK: Cambridge University Press, 2004.

Fisher, H.H. *The American Relief Administration in Russia, 1921–1923.* New York: Russell Sage Foundation, 1943.

Fisher, Nicolas. "L'internement républicain." *Plein Droit* 58 (December 2003): 18–21.

Foucault, Michel. *The Foucault Effect: Studies in Governmentality.* Edited by Graham Burchell, Colin Gordon, and Peter Miller. Chicago: University of Chicago Press, 1991.

Fox, Grace. The Origins of UNRRA. *Political Science Quarterly* 65 (December 1950): 561–84.

Fritz Bauer Institut. *Überlebt und unterwegs: Jüdische Displaced Persons in nachtkriegs-deutschland.* Frankfurt: Campus, 1997.

Frommer, Benjamin. *National Cleansing: Retribution against Nazi Collaborators in Postwar Czechoslovakia.* Cambridge, UK: Cambridge University Press, 2005.

Gaines, David P. *The World Council of Churches. A Study of Its Background and History.* Peterborough, NH: Richard R. Smith, 1996.

Galchinsky, Michael. *Jews and Human Rights: Dancing at Three Weddings.* Lanham, MD: Rowman & Littlefield, 2007.

Gatrell, Peter. *Free World? The Campaign to Save the World's Refugees 1956–1963.* Cambridge, UK: Cambridge University Press, 2011.

———. "Introduction: World Wars and Population Displacement in Europe in the Twentieth Century." *Contemporary European History* 16, no. 4 (2007): 415–26.

Gay, Ruth. *Safe among the Germans: Liberated Jews after World War II.* New Haven, CT: Yale University Press, 2002.

Gelber, Yoav. *Palestine 1948: War, Escape and the Emergence of the Palestinian Refugee Problem.* Brighton, UK: Sussex Academic Press, 2001.

Geller, Jay Howard. *Jews in Post-Holocaust Germany, 1945–1953.* Cambridge, UK: Cambridge University Press, 2005.

Genêt [Janet Flanner]. "Letter from Aschaffenburg." *New Yorker,* October 30, 1948.

———. "Letter from Wurzburg." *New Yorker,* November 6, 1948.

Genizi, Haim. *America's Fair Share: The Admission and Resettlement of Displaced Persons, 1945–1952.* Detroit: Wayne State University Press, 1993.

Gibney, Matthew J. *The Ethics and Politics of Asylum: Liberal Democracy and the Response to Refugees.* Cambridge, UK: Cambridge University Press, 2004.

Ginsburgs, George. "The Soviet Union and the Problem of Refugees and Displaced Persons, 1917–1956." *American Journal of International Law* 51 (April 1957): 325–61.

Glendon, Mary Ann. *A World Made New: Eleanor Roosevelt and the Universal Declaration of Human Rights.* New York: Random House, 2001.

Gottlieb, Amy Zahl. "Refugee Immigration: The Truman Directive." *Prologue* 13 (Spring 1981): 5–17.

Gottschalk, Max, and Abraham G. Duker. *Jews in the Post-war World.* New York: Dryden, 1945.

Grimaud, Maurice. *Je ne suis pas né en mai 1968: Souvenirs et carnets (1934–1992).* Paris: Tallandier, 2007.

Grodzinsky, Yosef. *In the Shadow of the Holocaust: The Struggle between Jews and Zionists in the Aftermath of World War II.* Monroe, ME: Common Courage, 2004.

Gross, Jan T. *Fear: Anti-Semitism in Poland after Auschwitz; An Essay in Historical Interpretation.* New York: Random House, 2006.

Grossmann, Atina. *Jews, Germans, and Allies: Close Encounters in Occupied Germany.* Princeton, NJ: Princeton University Press, 2007.

Grossmann, Kurt R. *Refugees, DP's, and Migrants.* New York: Institute of Jewish Affairs and World Jewish Congress, 1962.

Grynberg, Anne. *Les camps de la honte: Les internés juifs des camps français, 1939–1944.* Paris: Découverte, 1991.

Guilhem, Florence. *L'obsession du retour: les républicains espagnols 1939–1975.* Toulouse, Presses Universitaires du Mirail, 2005.

Haddad, Emma. *The Refugee in International Society: Between Sovereigns.* Cambridge, UK: Cambridge University Press, 2008.

Hadsel, Winifred N. "Can Europe's Refugees Find New Homes?" *Foreign Policy Reports* 19, no. 10 (August 1943): 110–19.

Handlin, Oscar. *The Uprooted.* 2nd ed. Boston: Little, Brown, 1973.

Hansen, Randall. *Citizenship and Immigration in Post-war Britain.* New York: Oxford University Press, 2000.

Hathaway, James C. "The Evolution of Refugee Status in International Law: 1920–1950." *International and Comparative Law Quarterly* 33 (1984): 348–80.

——. "A Reconsideration of the Underlying Premise of Refugee Law." *Harvard International Law Journal* 31 (Winter 1990): 129–83.

——. *The Rights of Refugees under International Law*. Cambridge, UK: Cambridge University Press, 2005.

Henke, Klaus-Dietmar, and Hans Voller, eds. *Politische Säuberung in Europa: Die Abrechnung mit Faschismus und Kollaboration nach dem Zweiten Weltkrieg*. Munich: Deutscher Taschenbuch Verlag, 1991.

Henkin, Louis. *The Age of Rights*. New York: Columbia University Press, 1990.

Herzfeld, Michael. *The Social Production of Indifference: Exploring the Symbolic Roots of Western Bureaucracy*. New York: Berg, 1992.

Heuven Goedhart, G.J. van. "People Adrift." *Journal of International Affairs* 7, no. 1 (1953): 7–49.

Hilton, Laura. "Prisoners of Peace: Rebuilding Community, Identity and Nationality in Displaced Persons Camps in Germany, 1945–1952." Ph.D. diss., Ohio State University, 2001.

Hirschmann, Ira A. *The Embers Still Burn: An Eye-Witness View of the Postwar Ferment in Europe and the Middle East and Our Disastrous Get-Soft-with-Germany Policy*. New York: Simon & Schuster, 1949.

Hitchcock, William I. *The Bitter Road to Freedom: A New History of the Liberation of Europe*. New York: Free Press, 2008.

Hoffman, Roland J. "Zur Aufnahme der Flüchtlinge aus der ČSR in der US-Zone Deutschlands nach der kommunistischen Machtergreifung vom Februar 1948." *Bohemia* 36 (January 1995): 69–112.

Hoffmann, Stefan-Ludwig, ed. *Human Rights in the Twentieth Century*. Cambridge, UK: Cambridge University Press, 2010.

Hofstee, E.W. "Population Pressure and the Future of Western Civilization in Europe." *American Journal of Sociology* 15, no. 6 (May 1950): 523–32.

Holborn, Louise W. *The International Refugee Organization: A Specialized Agency of the United Nations; Its History and Work, 1946–1952*. London: Oxford University Press, 1956.

——. "The Legal Status of Political Refugees, 1920–1938." *American Journal of International Law* 32 (October 1938): 680–703.

——. "International Organizations for Migration of European Nationals and Refugees," *International Journal* 20, no. 3 (Summer 1965): 331–40.

Holian, Anna. "Anticommunism in the Streets: Refugee Politics in Cold War Germany." *Journal of Contemporary History* 45 (January 2010): 134–61.

——. "Between National Socialism and Soviet Communism: The Politics of Self-Representation among Displaced Persons in Munich, 1945–1951." Ph.D. diss., University of Chicago, 2005.

Holleuffer, Henriette von. "Seeking New Horizons in Latin America: The Resettlement of 100,000 European Displaced Persons between the Gulf of Mexico and Patagonia (1947–1951)." *Jahrbüch für Geschichte Lateinamerikas* 39 (2002): 125–61.

———. *Zwischen Fremde und Fremde: Displaced Persons in Australien, den USA und Kanada, 1946–1952.* Osnabrück, Germany: Universitätsverlag Rasch, 2001.

Hulme, Kathryn. *The Wild Place.* Boston: Little, Brown, 1953.

Hunt, Lynn. *Inventing Human Rights: A History.* New York: Norton, 2007.

Huszar, George B. de, ed. *Persistent International Issues.* New York: Harper, 1947.

Hutchinson, John F. *Champions of Charity: War and the Rise of the Red Cross.* Boulder, CO: Westview, 1996.

Hyde, Louis K. *The United States and the United Nations, Promoting the Public Welfare: Examples of American Co-operation, 1945–1955.* New York: Manhattan, 1960.

Hyndman, Jennifer. *Managing Displacement: Refugees and the Politics of Humanitarianism.* Minneapolis: University of Minnesota Press, 2000.

Ignatieff, Michael. *Human Rights as Politics and Idolatry.* Princeton, NJ: Princeton University Press, 2001.

Iriye, Akira. *Global Community: The Role of International Organizations in the Making of the Contemporary World.* Berkeley: University of California Press, 2002.

Jackson, Ivor C. *The Refugee Concept in Group Situations.* The Hague: Nijhoff, 1999.

Jacobmeyer, Wolfgang. *Vom Zwangsarbeiter zum heimatlosen Ausländer: Die Displaced Persons in Westdeutschland, 1945–1951.* Göttingen, West Germany: Vandenhoeck & Ruprecht, 1985.

Jacobsen, Pierre. "L'œuvre de l'Organisation Internationale des Réfugiés." *Population* 6 (January-March 1951): 27–40.

Jacobson, Harold Karan. *The USSR and the UN's Economic and Social Activities.* Notre Dame, IN: University of Notre Dame Press, 1963.

Jaeger, Gilbert. "On the History of the International Protection of Refugees." *International Review of the Red Cross* 83 (September 2001): 727–37.

Jaroszyńska-Kirchmann, Anna D. *The Exile Mission: The Polish Political Diaspora and Polish Americans, 1939–1956.* Athens, OH: Ohio University Press, 2004.

Jessup, Philip C. *A Modern Law of Nations: An Introduction.* New York: Macmillan, 1948.

———. "UNRRA, Sample of World Organization." *Foreign Affairs* 22 (April 1944): 362–73

John, Michael. "Upper Austria, Intermediate Stop: Reception Camps and Housing Schemes for Jewish DPs and Refugees in Transit." *Journal of Israeli History* 19 (October 1998): 21–47.

Johnson, T.F. *International Tramps: From Chaos to Permanent World Peace.* London: Hutchinson, 1938.

Judt, Tony. *Postwar: A History of Europe since 1945.* New York: Penguin, 2005.

Kanstroom, Daniel. *Deportation Nation: Outsiders in American History*. Cambridge, MA: Harvard University Press, 2007.

Karatani, Rieko. "How History Separated Refugee and Migrant Regimes: In Search of Their Institutional Origins." *International Journal of Refugee Law* 17 (September 2005): 517–41.

Kay, Diana. "The Resettlement of Displaced Persons in Europe, 1946–1951." In *The Cambridge Survey of World Migration*, edited by Robin Cohen, 154–58. Cambridge, UK: Cambridge University Press, 1995.

Kay, Diana, and Robert Miles. *Refugees or Migrant Workers? European Volunteer Workers in Britain, 1946–1951*. London: Routledge, 1992.

Kee, Robert. *Refugee World*. London: Oxford University Press, 1961.

Kelsen, Hans. *The Law of the United Nations*. 1950. Reprint, Union, NJ: Lawbook Exchange, 2000.

———. "The Preamble of the Charter—A Critical Analysis." *Journal of Politics* 8 (1946): 134–59.

Kévonian, Dzovinar. Les juristes juifs russes en France et l'action internationale dans les années vingt. *Archives Juives* 2 (2001): 72–94.

———. Question des réfugiés, droits de l'homme: Eléments d'une convergence pendant l'entre-deux-guerres. *Matériaux pour l'histoire de notre temps* 72 (2003): 40–49.

———. *Réfugiés et diplomatie humanitaire: Les acteurs européens et la scène proche-orientale pendant l'entre-deux-guerres*. Paris: Publications de la Sorbonne, 2004.

King, Michael Christopher. *The Palestinians and the Churches*. Vol. 1, *1948–1956*. Geneva, Switzerland: World Council of Churches, 1981.

Kinnear, Mary. *Woman of the World: Mary McGeachy and International Cooperation*. Toronto: University of Toronto Press, 2004.

Klemme, Marvin. *The Inside Story of UNRRA: An Experience in Internationalism; A First Hand Report on the Displaced Persons of Europe*. New York: Lifetime, 1949.

Kochavi, Arieh J. *Post-Holocaust Politics: Britain, the United States, and Jewish Refugees, 1945–1948*. Chapel Hill: University of North Carolina Press, 2001.

———. *Prelude to Nuremberg: Allied War Crimes Policy and the Question of Punishment*. Chapel Hill: University of North Carolina Press, 1998.

Kohanski, Alexander S., ed. *The American Jewish Conference: Its Organization and Proceedings of the First Session*. New York: American Jewish Conference, 1944.

———. *The American Jewish Conference: Proceedings of the Second Session*. New York: American Jewish Conference, 1945.

Korey, William. *NGOs and the Universal Declaration of Human Rights: A Curious Grapevine*. New York: St. Martin's, 1998.

Korowicz, Marek St. The Problem of the International Personality of Individuals. *American Journal of International Law* 50 (July 1956): 533–62.

Koskenniemi, Martti. *The Gentle Civilizer of Nations: The Rise and Fall of International Law, 1870–1960*. Cambridge, UK: Cambridge University Press, 2002.

Kulischer, Eugene M. *The Displacement of Population in Europe.* Montreal: International Labour Office, 1943.

———. *Europe on the Move: War and Population Changes, 1917–47.* New York: Columbia University Press, 1948.

Kunz, Josef L. "The United Nations Universal Declaration of Human Rights." *American Journal of International Law* 43 (April 1949): 316–23.

Lagrou, Pieter. *The Legacy of Nazi Occupation: Patriotic Memory and National Recovery in Western Europe, 1945–1965.* Cambridge, UK: Cambridge University Press, 2000.

Lane, Thomas. *Victims of Stalin and Hitler: The Exodus of Poles and Balts to Britain.* New York: Palgrave Macmillan, 2004.

Lang, Anthony F., Jr., and John Williams, eds. *Hannah Arendt and International Relations: Readings Across the Lines.* New York: Palgrave Macmillan, 2005.

Langlois, Suzanne. La contribution du cinéma documentaire en faveur de l'Administration des Nations Unies pour les Secours et la Reconstruction (UNRRA) 1943–1947." In *Lendemains de guerre,* edited by Roch Legault and Magali Deleuze, 129–47. Montreal: Lux Editeur, 2006.

Lary, Diana, and Stephen MacKinnon, eds. *Scars of War: the Impact of Warfare on Modern China.* Vancouver: University of British Columbia Press, 2001.

Laski, H.J. "The Machinery of International Relief." In *When Hostilities Cease: Papers on Relief and Reconstruction Prepared for the Fabian Society,* 30–42. London: Gollancz, 1943.

Lauren, Paul Gordon. *The Evolution of International Human Rights: Visions Seen.* Philadelphia: University of Pennsylvania Press, 1998.

Lauterpacht, Hersch. *International Law and Human Rights.* New York: Praeger, 1950.

Leiby, James. *A History of Social Welfare and Social Work in the United States.* New York: Columbia University Press, 1978.

Levantrosser, William F., ed. *Harry S. Truman: The Man from Independence.* New York: Greenwood, 1986.

Levenstein, Aaron. *Escape to Freedom: The Story of the International Rescue Committee.* Westport, CT: Greenwood, 1983.

Lippert, Randy. "Governing Refugees: The Relevance of Governmentality to Understanding the International Refugee Regime." *Alternatives* 24 (July 1999): 295–329.

Liskofsky, Sydney. "Jewish Postwar Immigration Prospects." *ORT Economic Review* 7 (December 1947): 39–55.

Loescher, Gil. *Beyond Charity: International Cooperation and the Global Refugee Crisis.* New York: Oxford University Press, 1993.

———. *The UNHCR and World Politics: A Perilous Path.* Oxford: Oxford University Press, 2001.

Loescher, Gil, and John A. Scanlan. *Calculated Kindness: Refugees and America's Half-Open Door, 1945 to the Present.* New York: Free Press, 1986.

Luciuk, Lubomyr Y. *Searching for Place: Ukrainian Displaced Persons, Canada, and the Migration of Memory.* Toronto: University of Toronto Press, 2000.

Lynx, J. J., ed. *The Future of the Jews: A Symposium.* London: Drummond, 1945.

Lyons, Gene M. "American policy and the United Nation's Program for Korean Reconstruction." *International Organization* 12 (1958): 180–92.

Malin, Patrick Murphy. "The Refugee: A Problem for International Organization." *International Organization* 1 (September 1947): 443–59.

Malkki, Liisa H. "National Geographic: The Rooting of Peoples and the Territorialization of National Identity among Scholars and Refugees." *Cultural Anthropology* 7, no. 1 (1992): 24–44.

———. "Refugees and Exile: From 'Refugee Studies' to the National Order of Things." *Annual Review of Anthropology* 24 (1995): 495–523.

Mankowitz, Zeev W. *Life between Memory and Hope: The Survivors of the Holocaust in Occupied Germany.* Cambridge, UK: Cambridge University Press, 2002.

Marks, Edward. "Internationally Assisted Migration: ICEM Rounds Out Five Years of Resettlement." *International Organization* 11, no. 3 (Summer 1957): 481–94.

Marrus, Michael R. *The Unwanted: European Refugees in the Twentieth Century.* New York: Oxford University Press, 1985.

———. *The Nuremberg War Crimes Trial, 1945–46: A Documentary History.* Boston: Bedford Books, 1997.

Mather, Carol. *Aftermath of War: Everyone Must Go Home.* London: Brassey's, 1992.

May, Ernest R., ed. *American Cold War Strategy: Interpreting NSC 68.* Boston: Bedford Press of St. Martin's, 1993.

Mazower, Mark. *No Enchanted Palace: The End of Empire and the Ideological Origins of the United Nations.* Princeton, NJ: Princeton University Press, 2009.

———. "The Strange Triumph of Human Rights, 1933–1950." *Historical Journal* 47, no. 2 (2004): 379–98.

McClelland, Grigor. *Embers of War: Letters from a Quaker Relief Worker in War-Torn Germany.* London, British Academic Press, 1997.

McDowell, Linda. *Hard Labour: The Forgotten Voices of Latvian Migrant "Volunteer" Workers.* London: University College of London Press, 2005.

McNeill, Margaret. *By the Rivers of Babylon: A Story of Relief Work among the Displaced Persons of Europe.* London: Bannisdale, 1950.

Merridale, Catherine. *Ivan's War: The Red Army 1939–45.* London: Faber & Faber, 2005.

Morgenthau, Henry, with French Strother. *I Was Sent to Athens.* Garden City, NY: Doubleday, Doran, 1929.

Morris, Benny. *1948: A History of the First Arab-Israeli War.* New Haven, CT: Yale University Press, 2008.

Morsink, Johannes. *The Universal Declaration of Human Rights: Origins, Drafting, and Intent.* Philadelphia: University of Pennsylvania Press, 1999.

Mounier, Emmanuel. "Les nouveaux réprouvés." In *Œuvres,* vol. 4, *Recueils Posthumes; Correspondance.* Paris: Seuil, 1963.

Moyn, Samuel. *The Last Utopia: Human Rights in History.* Cambridge, MA: Belknap Press of Harvard University Press, 2010.

Mulley, Clare. *The Woman Who Saved the Children: A Biography of Eglantyne Jebb, Founder of Save the Children.* Oxford: Oneworld, 2009.

Murphy, H. B. M. *Flight and Resettlement.* Paris: UNESCO, 1955.

Murphy, H. B. M. "The Resettlement of Jewish Refugees in Israel, with Special Reference to Those Known as Displaced Persons," *Population Studies* 5, no. 2 (Nov.1951): 153–74.

Nachmani, Amikam. *Great Power Discord in Palestine: The Anglo-American Committee of Inquiry into the Problems of European Jewry and Palestine 1945–1946.* London: Cass, 1987.

Nathan-Chapotot, Roger. *Les Nations Unies et les réfugiés: Le maintien de la paix et le conflit des qualifications entre l'Ouest et l'Est.* Paris: Pedone, 1949.

Nathwani, Niraj. *Rethinking Refugee Law.* The Hague: Nijhoff, 2003.

Neal, Steve, ed. *HST: Memories of the Truman Years.* Carbondale: Southern Illinois University Press, 2003.

Nichols, J. Bruce. *The Uneasy Alliance: Religion, Refugee Work, and U.S. Foreign Policy.* New York: Oxford University Press, 1988.

Nicholson, Frances, and Patrick Twomey, eds. *Refugee Rights and Realities: Evolving International Concepts and Regimes.* Cambridge, UK: Cambridge University Press, 1999.

Notestein, Frank W., Irene B. Taeuber, and Dudley Kirk, eds. *The Future Population of Europe and the Soviet Union: Population Projections, 1940–1970.* Geneva, Switzerland: League of Nations, 1944.

Nourissier, François. "Le monde des réfugiés." *Esprit,* January 1951, 19–40.

Nyers, Peter. *Rethinking Refugees: Beyond States of Emergency.* New York: Routledge, 2006.

Ofer, Dalia. "Holocaust Survivors as Immigrants: The Case of Israel and the Cyprus Detainees." *Modern Judaism* 16 (January 1996): 1–23.

Pappe, Ilan. *The Ethnic Cleansing of Palestine.* Oxford: Oneworld, 2006.

Parekh, Serena. *Hannah Arendt and the Challenge of Modernity: A Phenomenology of Human Rights.* New York: Routledge, 2008.

Patrick, Stewart. *Best Laid Plans: The Origins of American Multilateralism and the Dawn of the Cold War.* Lanham, MD: Rowman &Littlefield, 2009.

Patt, Avinoam J. *Finding Home and Homeland: Jewish Youth and Zionism in the Aftermath of the Holocaust.* Detroit: Wayne University Press, 2009.

Patt, Avinoam J, and Michael Berkowitz, eds. *"We Are Here": New Approaches to Jewish Displaced Persons in Postwar Germany.* Detroit: Wayne State University Press, 2010.

Paul, Kathleen. *Whitewashing Britain: Race and Citizenship in the Postwar Era.* Ithaca, NY: Cornell University Press, 1997.

Penrose, Ernest F. "Negotiating on Refugees and Displaced Persons, 1946." In *Negotiating with the Russians,* edited by Raymond Dennett and Joseph E. Johnson, 139–71. Boston: World Peace Foundation, 1951.

Pernot, Georges. "L'Europe face aux problèmes de population." *Revue Politique des Idées et des Institutions* (January 1952): 17–23.

Peschansky, Denis. *La France des camps: L'internement, 1938–1946.* Paris: Gallimard, 2002.

Pettiss, Susan T., with Lynne Taylor. *After the Shooting Stopped: The Story of an UNRRA Welfare Worker in Germany, 1945–1947.* Victoria, BC: Trafford, 2004.

Pike, David Wingeate. "L'immigration espagnole en France (1945–1952)." *Revue d'Histoire Moderne et Contemporaine* 24 (April 1977): 286–300.

Pire, Dominique. *Souvenirs et entretiens.* Paris: Julliard, 1959.

Polian, Pavel. *Deportiert nach Hause: Sowjetische Kriegsgefangene im Dritten Reich und ihre Repatriierung.* Munich: Oldenbourg, 2001.

———. "The Internment of Returning Soviet Prisoners of War after 1945." In *Prisoners of War, Prisoners of Peace: Captivity, Homecoming and Memory in World War II,* edited by Bob Moore and Barbara Hately-Broad, 123–39. Oxford: Berg, 2005.

Popper, Karl R. *The Open Society and Its Enemies.* Rev. ed. Princeton, NJ: Princeton University Press, 1950.

Prażmowska, Anita J. *Civil War in Poland, 1942–1948.* New York: Palgrave Macmillan, 2004.

Price, Matthew E. *Rethinking Asylum: History, Purpose, and Limits.* Cambridge, UK: Cambridge University Press, 2009.

Proudfoot, Malcolm J. "The Anglo-American Displaced Persons Program for Germany and Austria." *American Journal of Economics and Sociology* 6 (October 1946): 33–54.

———. *European Refugees: 1939–1952; A Study in Forced Population Movement.* Evanston, IL: Northwestern University Press, 1956.

Radosh, Allis, and Ronald Radosh. *A Safe Haven: Harry S. Truman and the Founding of Israel.* New York: HarperCollins, 2009.

Ram, Uri. "Zionist Historiography and the Invention of Modern Jewish Nationhood: The Case of Ben Zion Dinur." *History and Memory* 7, no. 1 (1995): 91–124.

Rees, Elfan. *The Refugee and the United Nations.* International Conciliation 492. New York: Carnegie Endowment for International Peace, 1953.

———. *Century of the Homeless Man.* International Conciliation 515. New York: Carnegie Endowment for International Peace, 1957.

Reichman, Shalom, Yossi Katz, and Yair Paz. "The Absorptive Capacity of Palestine, 1882–1948." *Middle Eastern Studies* 33 (April 1997): 338–61.

Reinisch Jessica, and Elizabeth White, eds. *The Disentanglement of Populations. Migration, Expulsion and Displacement in Post-War Europe, 1944–9.* New York, Palgrave Macmillan, 2011.

Rendel, George. *The Sword and the Olive: Recollections of Diplomacy and the Foreign Service, 1913–1954.* London: Murray, 1957.

Reston, James. "Negotiating with the Russians." *Harper's,* August 1947.

Reut-Nicolussi, Eduard. "Displaced Persons and International Law." *Recueil des Cours* 73 (1948): 1–68.

Ristelhueber, René. *Au secours des réfugiés: L'œuvre de l'Organisation Internationale des Réfugiés*. Paris: Plon, 1951.

Robinson, Greg. "Le Projet M de Franklin D. Roosevelt: Construire un monde grâce à la science . . . des races." *Critique Internationale* 27 (2005): 65–82.

Robinson, Jacob. "Uprooted Jews in the Immediate Postwar World." *International Conciliation* 389 (April 1943): 291–310.

Robinson, Nehemiah. *Convention Relating to the Status of Refugees: Its History, Contents, and Interpretation; A Commentary*. New York: Institute of Jewish Affairs, World Jewish Congress, 1953.

———. *The United Nations and the World Jewish Congress*. New York: Institute of Jewish Affairs, 1955.

Roman, Agnes. "UNRRA in China." *Far Eastern Survey*, November 7, 1945, 61–74.

Roosevelt, Eleanor. *The Eleanor Roosevelt Papers*. Vol. 1, *The Human Rights Years, 1945–1948*. Edited by Allida Black. Detroit: Thomson Gale, 2007.

———. *On My Own*. New York: Harper, 1958.

Rothwell, Charles Easton. "International Organization and World Politics." *International Organization* 3 (November 1949): 605–19.

Rousset, David. *L'univers concentrationnaire*. Paris: Editions du Pavois, 1946.

Rubinstein, J. L. "The Refugee Problem." *International Affairs* 15 (September-October 1936): 716–34.

Rucker, Arthur. "The Work of the International Refugee Organization." *International Affairs* 25 (January 1949): 66–73.

Rystad, Göran, ed. *The Uprooted: Forced Migration as an International Problem in the Post-war Era*. Lund, Sweden: Lund University Press, 1990.

Salomon, Kim. *Refugees in the Cold War: Toward a New International Refugee Regime in the Early Postwar Era*. Lund, Sweden: Lund University Press, 1991.

Salvatici, Silvia. *Senza casa e senza paese: Profughi europei nel secondo dopoguerra* Bologna, Italy: Mulino, 2008.

Sanger, Margaret, ed. *Proceedings of the World Population Conference*. London, Arnold, 1927.

Sanua, Marianne R. *Let Us Prove Strong: The American Jewish Committee, 1946–2006*. Waltham, MA: Brandeis University Press, 2007.

Scelle, Georges. *Manuel de droit international public*. Paris: Domat-Montchrestien, 1948.

Schaffner, Alain, and Philippe Zard, eds. *Albert Cohen dans son siècle*. Paris: Editions Le Manuscrit, 2005.

Schiessl, Christoph. "Nazi Collaborators from Eastern Europe as US Immigrants and the Displaced Persons Act." *Michigan Academician* 35 (2003): 295–320.

Schiff, Benjamin N. *Refugees unto the Third Generation: UN Aid to Palestinians*. Syracuse NY: Syracuse University Press, 1995.

Segev, Tom. *Simon Wiesenthal: The Life and Legends*. New York: Doubleday, 2010.

Sereny, Gitta. *The German Trauma: Experiences and Reflections, 1938–2000*. London: Penguin, 2001.

Shanks, Cheryl. *Immigration and the Politics of American Sovereignty, 1890–1990.* Ann Arbor: University of Michigan Press, 2001.

Shephard, Ben. "'Becoming Planning Minded': The Theory and Practice of Relief 1940–1945." *Journal of Contemporary History* 43 (July 2008): 405–19.

———. *The Long Road Home: The Aftermath of the Second World War.* London: Bodley Head, 2010.

Shils, Edward A. "Social and Psychological Aspects of Displacement and Repatriation." *Journal of Social Issues* 2 (August 1946): 3–18.

Shotwell, James T. *The Great Decision.* New York: Macmillan, 1944.

Simpson, A.W. Brian. *Human Rights and the End of Empire: Britain and the Genesis of the European Convention.* Oxford: Oxford University Press, 2001.

Simpson, John Hope. *The Refugee Problem: Report of a Survey.* London: Oxford University Press, 1939.

Sjöberg, Tommie. *The Powers and the Persecuted: The Refugee Problem and the Intergovernmental Committee on Refugees (IGCR), 1938–1947.* Lund, Sweden: Lund University Press, 1991.

Skran, Claudena M. *Refugees in Inter-war Europe: The Emergence of a Regime.* Oxford: Clarendon, 1995.

Slezkine, Yuri. *The Jewish Century.* Princeton, NJ: Princeton University Press, 2004.

Soguk, Nevzat. *States and Strangers: Refugees and Displacements of Statecraft.* Minneapolis: University of Minnesota Press, 1999.

Stadulis, Elizabeth. "The Resettlement of Displaced Persons in the United Kingdom." *Population Studies* 5 (1952): 207–37.

Stafford, David. *Endgame 1945: Victory, Retribution, Liberation.* London: Little, Brown, 2007.

Steiner, Niklaus, Mark Gibney, and Gil Loescher, eds. *Problems of Protection: The UNHCR, Refugees, and Human Rights.* New York: Routledge, 2003.

Steinert, Johannes-Dieter. "British Humanitarian Assistance: Wartime Planning and Postwar Realities." *Journal of Contemporary History* 43 (July 2008): 421–35.

Steinert, Johannes-Dieter, and Inge Weber-Newth, eds. *European Immigrants in Britain, 1933–1950.* Munich: Saur, 2003.

Stoessinger, John George. *The Refugee and the World Community.* Minneapolis: University of Minnesota Press, 1956.

Symonds, Richard, and Michael Carder. *The United Nations and the Population Question, 1945–1970.* New York: McGraw-Hill, 1973.

Taeuber, Irene B. "Population Displacement in Europe." *Annals of the American Academy of Political and Social Science* 234 (July 1944): 1–12.

Takkenberg, Alex, and Christopher C. Tahbaz, comps. *The Collected Travaux Préparatoires of the 1951 Geneva Convention Relating to the Status of Refugees.* 3 volumes. Amsterdam: Dutch Refugee Council under the auspices of the European Legal Network on Asylum, 1989.

Takkenberg, Lex. *The Status of Palestinian Refugees in International Law.* Oxford, Clarendon, 1998.

Tenenbaum, Joseph. *Peace for the Jews*. New York: American Federation for Polish Jews, 1945.

Ther, Philipp, and Siljak Ana, eds. *Redrawing Nations: Ethnic Cleansing in East Central Europe, 1944–1948*, Lanham, Rowman, 2001.

Thomas, Albert, "Albert Thomas on the International Control of Migration," *Population and Development Review* 9 (December 1983): 703–11.

Thompson, Warren S. *Plenty of People: The World's Population Pressures, Problems and Policies and How They Concern Us*. Rev. ed. New York: Press, 1948.

Velikonja, Joseph. "Postwar Population Movements in Europe." *Annals of the Association of American Geographers* 48 (December 1958): 458–72.

Verdirame, Guglielmo, and Barbara Harrell-Bond, eds. *Rights in Exile: Janus-Faced Humanitarianism*. New York: Berghahn Books, 2005.

Verdoodt, Albert. *Naissance et signification de la Déclaration Universelle des Droits de l'Homme*. Louvain, Belgium: Warny, 1964.

Vernant, Jacques. *The Refugee in the Post-war World*. New Haven, CT: Yale University Press, 1953.

Viet, Vincent. *La France immigrée: Construction d'une politique, 1914–1997*. Paris: Fayard, 1998.

Vishniak, Mark. *The Legal Status of Stateless Persons*. New York: American Jewish Committee, 1945.

Voisin, Vanessa. "Le retour et la réintégration des rapatriés soviétiques dans la région russe de Kalinine en 1945–1956." In *Les réfugiés en Europe du XVIe au XXe siècles*, edited by Olivier Forcade and Philippe Nivet, 253–72. Paris: Nouveau Monde, 2008.

Walczewski, Ignacy. *Destin tragique des polonais déportés en Allemagne: La crise de la famille polonaise dans les camps de personnes déplacées*. Rome: Editions Hosanium, 1951.

Walters, Guy. *Hunting Evil: The Nazi War Criminals Who Escaped and the Quest to Bring them to Justice*. New York: Broadway Books, 2009.

Warhaftig, Zorach. *Relief and Rehabilitation: Implications of the UNRRA Program for Jewish Needs*. New York: Institute of Jewish Affairs of the American Jewish Congress and World Jewish Congress, 1944.

———. *Uprooted: Jewish Refugees and Displaced Persons after Liberation*. New York: Institute of Jewish Affairs of the American Jewish Congress and World Jewish Congress, 1946.

Warren, George L. "The Escapee Program." *Journal of International Affairs* 7, no. 1 (March 1953): 83–86.

Watenpaugh, Keith David. "The League of Nations' Rescue of Armenian Genocide Survivors and the Making of Modern Humanitarianism, 1920–1927." *American Historical Review* 115 (December 2010): 1315–39.

Weber-Newth, Inge. "Displaced Persons als 'European Volunteer Workers' in Grossbritannien: Anwerbung, Aufnahme, Verbleib." *Zeitschrift für Geschitswissenshaft* 55 (April 2007): 937–54.

Weil, Patrick. "Races at the Gate: Racial Distinctions in Immigration Policy; A Comparison between France and the United States." In *Migration Control in the North Atlantic World: The Evolution of State Practices in Europe and the United States from the French Revolution to the Inter-war Period,* edited by Andreas Fahrmeir, Olivier Faron, and Patrick Weil, 271–97. New York: Berghahn Books, 2003.

Weiner, Amir. *Making Sense of War: The Second World War and the Fate of the Bolshevik Revolution.* Princeton NJ: Princeton University Press, 2001.

Weis, Paul. "The International Protection of Refugees." *American Journal of International Law* 48 (April 1954): 193–221.

Wieviorka, Annette. *Déportation et génocide: Entre la mémoire et l'oubli.* Paris: Plon, 1992.

Wildenthal, Lora. "Human Rights Activism in Occupied and Early West Germany: The Case of the German League for Human Rights." *Journal of Modern History* 80 (September 2008): 515–56.

Williams, Pierce. *Preliminary Summary of a Report on Refugees and Displaced Persons: An Urgent United Nations Problem.* New York: Russell Sage Foundation, 1946.

Wilson, Francesca M. *Aftermath: France, Germany, Austria, Yugoslavia, 1945 and 1946.* New York: Penguin Books, 1947.

———. *In the Margins of Chaos: Recollections of Relief Work in and between Three Wars.* New York: Macmillan, 1945.

Winter, Jay. *Dreams of Peace and Freedom: Utopian Moments in the Twentieth Century.* New Haven, CT: Yale University Press, 2006.

Woodbridge, George. *UNRRA: The History of the United Nations Relief and Rehabilitation Administration.* 3 vols. New York: Columbia University Press, 1950.

Woodroofe, Kathleen. *From Charity to Social Work in England and the United States.* London: Routledge & Kegan Paul, 1962.

Wright, Quincy. "Human Rights and the World Order." *International Conciliation* 389 (April 1943): 239–62.

Wyman, Mark. *DPs: Europe's Displaced Persons, 1945–1951.* Ithaca, NY: Cornell University Press, 1998.

Zahra, Tara. "Lost Children: Displacement, Family, and Nation in Postwar Europe." *Journal of Modern History* 81 (March 2009): 45–86.

———. "Prisoners of the Postwar": Expellees, Displaced Persons, and Jews in Austria after World War II." *Austrian History Yearbook* 41 (2010): 191–215.

Zake, Ieva, ed. *Anti-Communist Minorities in the U.S: Political Activism of Ethnic Refugees.* New York: Palgrave Macmillan, 2009.

Zertal, Idith. *From Catastrophe to Power: Holocaust Survivors and the Emergence of Israel.* Berkeley: University of California Press, 1998.

Zolberg, Aristide R., Astri Suhrke, and Sergio Aguayo, eds. *Escape from Violence: Conflict and the Refugee Crisis in the Developing World.* New York: Oxford University Press, 1989.

Index

CPSIA information can be obtained
at www.ICGtesting.com
Printed in the USA
BVOW04s2248040617

485947BV00003B/10/P

9 780190 840808